TO HOPE AND BEYOND:

Tales and Poems of British Columbia

Written and compiled by
Penny Smith
And
Yasmin John-Thorpe
Co-founders of
Penticton Writers and Publishers
(PWAP)

Dedicated to all the writers for their stories and poems on people, places and events in British Columbia.

Thanks to Protocol and Events office of the Government of British Columbia, for the use of the flag for our cover.

Copyright © 2004 Penticton Writers and Publishers
Published by Penticton Writers and Publishers (PWAP). June 2004.

Compiled and written by Penny Smith and Yasmin John-Thorpe.

Text editor Darcy Nybo.

Typesetter Dawn Renaud

Cover Design by Stuart Bish of Stuart Bish Photography and Design.

ISBN 0-9698449-6-4

    1.   Canadian literature (English) – British Columbia. 2. Canadian literature (English) – 21st Century. I. Smith, Penny, 1952 - II. John-Thorpe, Yasmin, 1950 - III. Penticton Writers and Publishers.

PS8255.B7T6 2004-03-18   C810.8'09711   C2004-901071-9

Printed and Bound in Canada by Friesens.

Contents

FOREWORD

BRITISH COLUMBIA

We live in a great province, with exceptional people. It's the spirit of British Columbians that makes this the best place in the world to live, work and build a future.

Through their stories, poems and prose, the writers represented in this collection are helping showcase our history, culture and this remarkable land we share – not just to ourselves, but to the rest of Canada and to readers around the globe.

I want to congratulate the Penticton Writers and Publishers on their 10th anniversary, and thank them for working to foster a strong writing community in the Southern Interior and throughout our province. They have done an exceptional job in compiling this wonderful collection of works that reflect the true diversity of British Columbia's colourful history, characters and cultures.

I encourage you to share this book with others in your life, especially your children. There is no better way to open up a young person's mind to the world, and all that it offers, than by sharing reading with them, and no greater gift we can give our children than the gift of literacy and the love of reading and writing.

I hope the talented contributors to this book inspire you to seek out and enjoy more works by the countless gifted writers across our province so willing to share their passion with all of us.

Sincerely,

Gordon Campbell
Premier

VANCOUVER 2010

Province of British Columbia
Office of the Premier
www.gov.bc.ca

INTRODUCTION

We've come a long way! And Oh! How we've grown!

These are our thoughts as co-founders of Penticton Writers and Publishers. In 1994, PWAP was started as a group of writers helping other writers. To celebrate this 10th anniversary, we, with the assistance of our associated group members, undertook to publish this anthology, featuring work from emerging writers and poets of British Columbia.

To Hope And Beyond joins past publications from PWAP, which also toasted established and emerging writers. The list includes *Penticton And Area Secrets & Surprises; The Novel Approach to Self-Publishing; Supernatural Stories Around British Columbia; Penticton, British Columbia Silhouette Of Four Seasons;* and *Lovescape: The Romantic Novella Magazine.*

As a group we continue to help writers of all genres by hosting writers' workshops and annual conferences. For us, the most rewarding work has been assisting and mentoring writers, both young and old.

Within these pages are tales from and about pioneers and special people, to poems of natural disasters: from hopes and dreams of young and old to the natural and supernatural of the province.

Thanks to all, who took the time to submit their work. Without the submissions of these emerging and established writers this anthology would not have been published.

Enjoy,

Penny Smith & Yasmin John-Thorpe

PWAP Co-Founders

The Actor, the Cannery and the Catalyst

Kyle Anderson

Catalyst. ('ka-t al-ist) n . An agent that provokes or speeds significant change or action.

That's the Merriam-Webster Dictionary definition of a force that can change lives. Bare Bones Theatre in Penticton's Cannery Trade Centre is such a force. It helped to reinvigorate an outdated industrial building and it helped to reinvigorate me.

First, some history.

I was born in Penticton. I went to schools, which don't even exist anymore. Through elementary school, I could have been the poster child for class clowns. Eventually, my grade seven teacher harnessed my considerable energy in the classroom and steered it toward more productive avenues such as music and theatre. All through my teenage years, I worked and played in both genres regularly, but, as is the way with so many talents learned in school, when I graduated, I never pursued acting again.

When I was young, the Aylmer Cannery started its life as the biggest business on Fairview Road, processing fruits and vegetables for public consumption. I remember the tall smokestack, proclaiming its owner with the company name written proudly down its face.

Changing markets affected our old cannery and it eventually was closed down.

Then a metamorphosis occurred. With the vision of its new owners, The Cannery reopened, filled with shops and services for a variety of blue-collar needs. No glitz, no glamour, just a place to get your keys cut or television fixed. Today, The Cannery has also become host to a center for artists, a gymnastics club, the largest dance studio in town, and the smallest theatre company.

Bare Bones Theatre became a reality in the summer of 2000 from the dream of Tom Cowles. He, and original partner Harold Courchene, thought Penticton had a large enough theatre-going audience to warrant a year-round facility. They invested time, money and a lot of black paint into the creation of the 90-seat theatre in The Cannery.

I met Tom in 2001, during a local production of Joseph and the Amazing Technicolor Dreamcoat. He impressed me with his considerable talent and warm demeanor. I had no idea how serendipitous this meeting would become.

When he called me the following winter, he asked me to participate in the Christian musical *Cotton Patch Gospel*. At first I wasn't interested in his offer. It was for all the usual reasons: I was too busy or I had previous commitments or... well, practically any excuse would have helped. In fact, acting was a forgotten territory to me and I was terrified. The last time I acted in a play, the Cannery was a cannery. Sure, I had been performing in a singing group for years, but the ad-lib shtick I used in my band wasn't the same as this.

This was acting.

Tom finally convinced me to climb back onstage after so many years. He asked me to track down musicians, who could play and sing bluegrass music. I recruited my close friend and band mate, Ric Johnston, and Jeff Queen, another local musician, to join the cast.

Rehearsal time was 40 hours. That's it - 40 hours.

Learning the music and blocking the play worked out to be a pretty intense three-week schedule. It was tough. We, as musicians, were made painfully aware of how cushy our regular four-rehearsals-a-month routines were.

Photo courtesy of Bare Bones Theatre Company. From left to right: Jeff Queen, Ric Johnston, Tom Cowles and Kyle Anderson star in Bare Bones Theatre's production of Cotton Patch Gospel.

But we got the job done and the experience was wonderful! The play ran for four weeks initially and was held over for another. We revived it at a number of venues: at Bare Bones Theatre, Penticton's Cleland Community Theatre, in Summerland, and in Victoria. To this day, Cotton Patch Gospel continues to be a crowd pleaser.

That was two years ago. Bare Bones Theatre Company, now under the sole direction of Tom Cowles, has become a success and produces half a dozen or so productions every year. This little corner of the Cannery has nurtured an ever-growing family of actors, directors, stage managers, sound and lighting technicians, set builders, costume designers, props people and, of course, me.

The considerable energy that continues to burn inside me has once again been channelled through my involvement with Bare Bones as an actor, publicity manager and graphics designer. I look back fondly on *Cotton Patch Gospel*. It literally changed my life. The play gave me the desire to perform as an actor again. And most importantly, the play touched me. Its message was delivered with light-hearted humour and sensitivity, and the joy I received from performing it with the cast and the Bare Bones family made me feel good to my soul.

Acting as the catalyst, Bare Bones Theatre awakened a new spirit in the Cannery; it also awakened a new spirit in me.

I believe we're both better for it.

AUTUMN GALES
Violet Smith

Fall rushes in, on Autumn gale;
And with careless ease,
Bows the trees, in supplication,
And strips the dying leaves.

The leaves as they fall,
In a last frantic dance,
Pirouette, on their way down,
And lie in wondrous colours,
Carpeting the ground.

Even Firs of sturdy growth,
Bend at the winds onslaught,
And scudding clouds of sullen hue
Fly though the heavens,
As the gale sweeps through.

Now peace descends on the stricken vale
Softly, the moon peeps through,
Shedding soft light on the bare spreading boughs,
Where once green foliage grew.

ALL ABOARD!
Yasmin John-Thorpe

LESS THAN FIFTY YEARS AGO travel by plane, ship or train was one of those special events in a person's life. You'd dress up, wearing your 'Sunday best', while family and friends came to the airport, the pier or the train station to send you off on your journey. Last minute hugs, kisses, tears and confetti were the order of the day.

Today travel is no longer considered a special event. It has become an everyday occurrence. Family and friends no longer drop everything to come and send you off. Recently though, we discovered there is still a send off of sorts at the Vancouver Terminal, when my husband and I took one of the Rocky Mountaineer Railtours.

From the moment we arrived to check in at Vancouver station to the moment we stepped off in Calgary, the well-trained staff made us feel we were back fifty years and that this was one special event we would re-member for the rest of our lives.

With smiling faces and lots of waves, members of staff lined the length of the train platform and gave us a 'Grand Send-Off'. Looking out our glass-domed train carriage we waved back as the train snaked slowly out of the station. We were close to the rear of the train, travelling aboard the Gold Leaf carriage, which held 70 passengers, each with a 180-degree view of the surroundings. Below us, we had a 35 seat dining car with Kyle and Meredith, our young host and hostess. In the adjoining galley were two chefs and several assistants.

Filled with anticipation, we settled into posh recliner seats for the two-day trip. Our journey began with introductions to our Onboard At-tendants, Ted, Dawn and Shauna, who quietly ushered the first 35 passengers, seated to the front of the carriage down to the dining car for breakfast. We, at the rear of the carriage, were served coffee, tea, juice and warm rolls while we waited our turn in the dining car. We met our fellow travelers across the aisle, June and Mirto Sappe from Jersey Is-land, UK. We chatted about our homes and when it was our turn to have breakfast, we shared a table with the friendly couple. June and Mirto became our partners for all our meals, which turned out to be a gourmet delight and surprise in our onboard dining carriage.

On our way to Kamloops we travelled pass many cities and towns of the lower mainland. Photo opportunities slipped by our windows. Ted and Shauna regaled us with tales of pioneers and historical facts. Each marker, whether we rode on CN or CP track, brought a snippet of information we had not known before and like the visitors onboard from different countries, we too learned more about our own province.

We even had an opportunity to shop while onboard from the Rocky Mountaineer Store Catalogue. For those buying jackets we were encouraged to choose two sizes just in case one did not fit. The items awaited us the following morning as we returned aboard after a fabulous night in Kamloops, attending the Two River Junction Dinner and Musical Revue. The Musical Revue told the story of Billy Miner, train robber, who stole $15 and was caught shortly after by the RCMP.

On route to Calgary the historical storytelling continued and the meals were as tasty and gourmet as the day before. Each hour was not complete without an osprey sighting or a breathtaking photo opportunity of the surrounding scenery. We enjoyed the darkness of Mount Macdonald Tunnel. At

June and Mirto Sappe.

14.4 km long, it is the largest in North America. The Lower and Upper Spiral Tunnels have to be experienced to understand the feat of construction, each climbing and turning 250 degrees, doubling back twice, crossing the river twice and tunneling under mountains to cut down the grade. We also witnessed the smoke from fires, devastating several areas that summer.

As we arrived at the station in Calgary, like us many of our fellow passengers showed signs of regret that our two-day adventure was over. We took our good-byes still in awe of all that we'd seen and enjoyed, wishing we were making the return trip back to Vancouver the following day.

We had to agree rail travel was alive and well and that it had been one very special way to be a tourist in our own province.

ANOTHER DAY, ANOTHER DOLLAR
Vicki Bissillion

I'VE JUST RETURNED from her funeral, so it seems like a good time to write the final chapter about an amazing lady. The well-attended service was basic and colourless, which surprised me, but then I really didn't know the woman, except as a customer.

I met her on a quiet Monday at the Credit Union, the last day of winter. My co-workers and I were competing over the few customers that straggled in. It looked to be a long, uneventful day when suddenly, a young man threw open the door and yelled, "Somebody help! A lady's fainted, out here!"

Through the glass doors at the front, I saw a white-haired lady, lying on the sidewalk. An empty aluminium walker stood nearby. Running, I hollered over my shoulder, "Call 911 right away!"

Outside, a man was answering questions on his cell phone to 911. I recognized the lady as a charming old customer I had served in the past, though I had forgotten her name. Pushing through the crowd, I announced I had CPR training and knelt to try to rouse her.

No luck.

The cell phone man was also on his knees, reporting, "She's breathing."

Relief washed over me as I rolled her into "recovery position" and put a striped, grey car blanket, produced from the growing curious throng around us, under her curly white head.

Somehow, 'Mr. Fate' had orchestrated this drama with some irony. I had just completed the CPR course two weeks earlier so the procedure was still fresh in my mind.

Assess the scene, secure the area, et cetera, I rehearsed mutely. Suddenly, my helper announced that the woman's pulse had stopped! She wasn't breathing!

Rolling the limp lady onto her back, I pinched her nose and blew two quick puffs into her mouth. I hollered to my co-worker Debby, "Get the mask from the First Aid Kit, quick!"

Next, I loosened her soft pink coat, fumbling around to locate the right spot on her chest, *a hand span above the solar plexus* and, counting out loud, gave 15 pumps of CPR "1001, 1002, 1003..." Back now, to her mouth, listening and watching - nothing! – two more puffs – she gasped faintly, so we again rolled her into *recovery position*, just as Debby arrived with a broken CPR mask. In the distance we heard the heavenly sound of approaching sirens.

It was a relief to turn her over to the professionals. Admonishing the crowd to, "Move back. Give us room!" they laid her flat and began checking vital signs. Immediately, one of the attendants began the CPR compressions on her chest. Then they strapped on oxygen as they loaded her onto a stretcher. The medical team sounded subdued, sort of grave – like … it didn't look very hopeful.

I spoke up. "There's an inhaler in her purse, but I don't know what it's for."

"Purse? Where's her purse? We'll need that," the attendant demanded.

"Here it is, and while you're watching me I'll just look to get her account number so we can notify her family," I said, quickly slipping the familiar turquoise passbook out of her purse and noting the number before he could stop me.

Feeling stunned, I wheeled the abandoned walker into the branch for safekeeping. Had I helped? Maybe, maybe not. Would we ever know?

Excitedly, the teller next to me told of her grandma needing CPR at a family Christmas dinner in past years. After they'd revived her, she gave them all hell, insisting 'Next time just let me go'.

Would this 82-year-old victim have the same regret when she woke up, *if* she woke up? What was I doing, interfering in a total stranger's fate? My feelings and misgivings mounted. Thankfully, I learned from another teller that *my* lady had recently fought her way back from a slight stroke – a good sign. Everyone, staff and customers patted me on the back.

"Good job," they said.

But I wasn't so sure. We waited in vain to hear.

The following day was a beautiful first day of spring. I was 'off', washing my car in the driveway, when I heard the phone ring. I ran like mad. I had a feeling...! It was my boss, telling me my lady's niece had come in to collect the walker and had thanked everyone who helped. She mentioned her aunt's heart had stopped *again* on the way to hospital. The ambulance guys got it going once more and she would be all right! She was sitting up already!

***

It was close to 90 degrees in the old Armoury downtown that June evening, but the old lady was cool and pretty in a soft pink suit that matched her rosy cheeks. She said she felt thrilled and lucky to be here, having survived another heart attack and stroke since I had revived her over a year ago.

They read out my award "The Most Venerable Order of the Hospital of St. John of Jerusalem" as I made my way to the front. I happily accepted the certificate and introduced my guest, the amazing Mrs. Harrison. She came up and stood proudly with me for a picture. She was beaming.

***

21

It is this picture of her that greeted me as I signed the book at her funeral today. It had obviously been cropped and enlarged from the original I had sent to her in a Christmas card. Both the St. John's uniform and my prettiest summer dress were only slightly visible on either side of Mrs. Harrison. No one except me would have noticed that we'd been edited out of her final picture.

I had a hand in extending her life for an extra 30 months. For reasons I shall never know, it was important that she 'stand-up' her maker that day. Now, it seemed she had finally finished the important challenge of living that 'Mr. Fate' laid out for her.

Goodbye Mrs. Harrison.

HE CALLED HER ART
R.L. Diebolt

When I was just a little girl
I'd draw upon the sand
Dreams and thoughts and pictures
They drift from head to hand.

The years have passed and I've grown up
Still child comes through, you see
I now love paint and paper
And draw from land to sea.

God's beauty all around us
Strife and torment too
A need to visually express it
With line, pentimenti and hue.

So many thoughts and pictures
Events of passing time
Tragedy and paradox, a laughing comic line
Must register on paper
And free a restless mind.

ARBUTUS COVE: VICTORIA
Jocelyn Wood

I made my way down the steep path,
A shower of sunbeams cascaded me in its warm wrath.
I couldn't wait to finish my flight down the five sets of stairs,
As the tunnel of trees thinned, an ocean breeze tossed my hair.
My feet hit the rocky part of the beach,
I'd never seen the tide so far out of reach.
A plateau of ocean-beaten sand stretched to meet a never-ending
sequence of waves,
The water extended its reach along the flat shore, how water should
behave.
Bathing suit bared, the ocean air prickled my skin,
I couldn't wait to get a taste of the skim.
I stashed my stuff and headed to the brim of the ocean
Skimboard under my arm itched to be in motion.
I tested the water with only a toe,
Despite the freezing temperature, I'd give it a go.
I waited till a wave gripped a point high on the seashore,
I ran along side it where the water could thin no more.
I threw my board down and it skipped forward along the water top,
I reached it when it was barely ready to stop.
I jumped onto its surface and I began the ride,
For over one hundred meters I continued its glide.
Adrenaline pulsed through my body, smile on my face,
I licked my lips gathering a saltwater taste.
I threw myself back and forth across the cove,
Every great wave missed I began to loathe.
A group of friends joined me under the blazing sun,
Skimboarding all afternoon was the epitome of fun.
But, as always, all fun must come to an end,
The tide rushes in, bumping us home like an untrue friend.
I head back up the path, skimboard in tow,
I realize my love for Arbutus Cove as the sun sinks low.

Art Gallery of the South Okanagan

David Korinetz

Artist Sharron Middler arrived in the Okanagan in the winter of 2000. She stayed in the Naramata area for a short while and used the bus on occasion to travel back and forth between Naramata and Penticton. The bus route passed right by a beautiful building near the Lake Okanagan beach. Finally one-day curiosity got the better of her and she went to investigate. The building turned out to be the Art Gallery. She spent a few hours, that spring afternoon, sketching and photographing the building.

This watercolor painting is the result of that afternoon's work.

Original by Sharron Middler

Although the building was erected in 1985, its story really began in the 1950s, when an art club for local artists was formed. The club soon developed into the Penticton Art Show Committee, a vehicle for local artists to display and market their works. The committee organized art exhibits where they could.

In 1965 the Penticton Community Arts Centre was officially opened. In addition to housing the museum and library, the new Centre made its foyer and auditorium available to the Penticton Art Show Committee for their art exhibitions. In 1968 the Penticton Art Show Committee became the Penticton Art Gallery with a permanent secure display area in rooms A and B at the Community Arts Centre.

A part-time curator was hired with a grant from the National Museum Association. In 1977, the name was shortened to the Penticton Art Gallery. By 1979, the gallery board needed additional space and the idea of a new facility was discussed.

In 1980, public land on the Okanagan shoreline received approval by the city as the future site for a new art gallery. An environmentally friendly solar powered building, with 3,300 square feet of exhibition space, was to be constructed. It was another five years before the Art Gallery of the Southern Okanagan finally opened its doors.

In addition to having a large main display area, the gallery has a small secondary display area, a gift shop, a tearoom and a library. The gallery's collection consists of mostly local artists work. In the 1990s, one time resident and well-known artist Tony Onley, donated 26 watercolor paintings of the Okanagan to the Gallery.

In the last few years the building has undergone some changes. Since this painting was completed, the colour scheme of the building has changed and a new heating system installed to improve the air quality for storing artwork. But the spirit of all those who were involved with the gallery's creation still resides there.

THE BEE MASTER
Barbara Heaney

WHAT A FASCINATING SIGHT I was greeted with when I first entered their home – a beehive! An active beehive strategically placed in the living room beside their lounging chairs. I thought, "Wow! These people must really like bees, but bees aren't friendly – they don't cuddle; you can't pet them. Why are they in their house?" I had to remind myself that I was visiting a farmhouse – the home of Henry and Sheila Paynter. They would be viewing an indoor beehive as a delightful addition to their living room that would provide an education and entertainment for family and friends, not to mention a ringside attraction for them to observe the intricacies of bee detail.

The beehive is an atypical glasshouse – one can closely observe worker bees scurrying around cleaning cells or making wax. The brood chamber, where the Queen lays eggs, can be clearly scrutinized. A plexiglass tunnel connected to the beehive and a hole in the outside wall provides an entrance for honeybees to come and go as they please without any access to the Paynter's living room. Since 1977 Sheila has toured school children and visitors from around the world, through their home to get a first-hand glimpse at the valuable honeybees. And presently, while Henry continues to farm fruit and vegetables in the Okanagan Valley, he is working on his 83rd year as a beekeeper.

Henry's first interest in beekeeping was tweaked when he was eleven years old. Living in England at the time, during the last year of World War I, Henry caught a swarm of bees and housed them in a butter box. He has since nurtured his interest in bees and after moving to Westbank in 1919 Henry became a full fledged beekeeper.

The year 1920 marked the beginning of Henry's bee career when he ordered packets of bees from Los Malonis, California for $2.45 per packet. Each packet contained two pounds of bees and a Queen. Henry placed the bees in five hives and even extracted some honey that year in a four frame extractor which he set up in the kitchen. From 1926 to 1946 Henry delivered honey to customers in the family's old Model T Ford. He would fill sixty pound cans with honey and charge ten cents per pound. Most often, Henry filled standing orders of two cans per household and on average he would sell one ton of honey per year. After opening a fruit stand in 1946, Henry started to bottle honey and sold jars from the stall. Each August, Henry would begin to extract honey – it would take approximately one month.

During pollination period, Henry used to rent hives to other orchardists for $5.00 per hive. Today a hive will rent for $100.00, but Henry no longer provides a hive rental service.

Hives are made up of supers and frames. The honey super, a wooden box 9½ inches high by 16½ inches by 20 inches, includes ten wooden frames (honeycombs supported by wood and wire) where honey is stored in wax cells. Honey is basically thickened nectar that has been deposited into honey cells via a field bee to a house bee. Tongue to tongue, a field bee, who forages the orchards and fields collecting nectar and pollen, returns to the hive and transfers nectar to a house bee who continuously cleans and operates the hive. After the house bee spreads droplets of nectar on the roof of a honey cell, the nectar begins to dry by bees fanning their wings over the honeycomb. Fanning evaporates the nectar's moisture, which is 80 percent water. All of Henry's honey is unpasteurized and contains less than 18 percent water. Finally, other house bees cap the honey cells with a thin layer of wax and the thickened nectar ages to become honey. The hive is then transferred to the honey hut where extraction begins.

Henry eventually worked up to managing one hundred bee hives and evidence of beekeeping can be seen outside his honey hut. Upon entering the hut, one realizes that beekeeping is really quite complicated. The hut is filled with bee equipment including a wood burning stove, a 30 frame electric honey extractor, weigh scales, supers and frames, ice cream pails, apple boxes, bee tools such as extracting knives and oodles of glass jars. Honey production requires many stages to be completed inside the honey hut such as hive dismantling, equipment preparation, wax straining and bottling and packaging. While performing the many beekeeping duties that are necessary for Henry to have a successful operation, he must always be aware of certain hazards that accompany the trade – bee stings! He has, from time to time, contracted the occasional sting; however in a recent article written for the Alberni Valley Times Henry told a reporter: "I can take 50 stings you wouldn't know I had any. I don't get any arthritis and rheumatism and it probably has to do with the bees."

In 1926 when the population of Westbank was about 350 people, Henry purchased eight acres of property with the help of a partner, for $125.00 per acre. They made yearly payments and had the property paid for in ten years. It was mostly covered in pine trees and stumps. The partners cleared the property by chopping the trees down with crosscut saws. Large stumps were burned and smaller stumps were pulled out with a team of horses. Once the land was cleared and prepared, they planted Macintosh and Delicious apple trees.

Throughout the years, Henry acquired other orchard properties, but he did not rely strictly on fruit farming to earn a living. He also worked in the local packing houses making wooden apple boxes and packing fruit. He would construct 95 boxes an hour for ten hours a day earning

80 cents per 100 boxes completed. I try and grasp the concept of making less than $10.00 per day. Even though the cost of living was relative, it's difficult to comprehend. Henry informed me that coffee was 10 cents a cup: it cost 25 cents for a loaf of bread and a pair of good Leckie work boots were $5.00.

From 1932 to 1942 Henry worked as a Dominion Fruit Inspector throughout the Okanagan for $135.00 per month. He also served as Secretary for the Westbank Irrigation District earning $25.00 per month. He

Westbank swarm 2002. Photo by Barbara Heaney.

worked every Monday evening collecting water rates and attending to bookkeeping in his spare time. Henry had a busy family life as well. He and Sheila McKay married in 1946. Over time they became proud parents of six children and despite many the adversities they faced in a tumultuous farming climate, the family managed to maintain an operational farm. Today, they have taken on other endeavours and continue to farm as well.

After engaging in some beekeeping research as of late and having had numerous conversations with Henry Senior over the years, I have learned several interesting and curious facts about honeybees. For example, the ancient Egyptians are believed to be the first beekeepers – they kept bees in mud and clay hives. In 1926 a Queen cost 50 cents. Today a Queen costs approximately $10.00. Most of the world's beeswax comes form Africa. In warm weather, a healthy Queen lays 1000 – 1500 eggs per day. A honeybee can see ultraviolet light, which is invisible to the human eye. With their ultraviolet vision, bees can see which flowers are full of nectar. To make one pound of honey, a colony of bees collects nectar from over a million flowers!

For centuries honeybees have graced the world's orchards and fields providing essential pollination to flowers for the enhanced production of fruit and vegetables, so it's probably fair to say that the honeybee's greatest contribution is its service. They pollinate more crops than any other insect and without them farmers would produce considerably less fruits and vegetables than they do today. As an end product of their work in the hive, honeybees' endeavours result in more than just honey. Numerous products line our store shelves such as candles, lipstick, artist's crayons, shoe polish, floor polish, sealing wax, buffing wax for skis, snow boards and surfboards. As well, several different forms of honey are produced: liquid honey, comb honey, chunk honey and crystallized honey.

With the abundance of honey that we have available to us and because I find bee swarms absolutely compelling, I have recently taken an interest in bees. Fortunately this past year, I was asked to assist in the capturing of a Queen and its workers by Jennay Oliver, an up-and-coming bee master and granddaughter of Henry and Sheila.

It was early spring and Jennay was on, what I describe as, "swarm call". When a new Queen is born, the old Queen and about half of the workers usually swarm out of the hive and look for a new home. Additionally when a hive gets too crowded the Queen and her workers will look for another abode. Upon arriving at the swarm of which we had been informed, in Westbank, we parked our vehicle approximately twenty feet from the bees, calmly stepped out of the truck and moved toward the swarm. Jennay assessed the situation – the swarm had nestled onto a branch that was accessible to our reach and the ground below was clear of tree stumps and unmanageable objects. We returned to the truck and donned our bee gear. In the past, when working with active beehives, Jennay occasionally uses a smoker to calm the bees – they get quite agitated about protecting their home. If bees smell smoke they gorge themselves on honey and are less likely to sting. However, swarming bees are not usually aggressive because they are no longer defending a permanent home or a honey supply. Consequently, in this instance, a smoker was not necessary. We moved back to the bee congregation where Jennay gingerly placed an empty hive directly beneath the swarm. At her prompt, I was to pull down on the branch swiftly and smoothly, with my hands placed on either side of the swarm, while she tended the beehive below. I followed Jennay's explicit instructions and immediately after the swarm fell into the hive, she quickly capped it with a lid. We hovered for a few moments watching the results of our attempted catch. If a capture is successful, the honeybees left outside of the swarm will march directly into the hive join the other honeybees and their Queen. They may also start fanning themselves outside of the hive, with their bottoms up, in order to circulate the scent of the Queen, which encourages all of the bees to gravitate toward the hive. We were thrilled to observe that our attempted swarm capture was successful: thousands of honeybees and their Queen acquired a new home and Jennay now had an additional hive to place in the orchard.

Very few people live beyond their golden years. Some would argue that genes play an important role in determining life span or that diet is most definitely a factor.

Others, like Henry Senior, believe toiling, pursuing challenges and continuous labour promotes a long and healthy life. When asked by an interviewer several years ago what his secret to longevity was Henry responder: "Hard work!" It is not surprising then, that Henry has been draw to bees for so many years. The honeybee is known to be a diligent worker and has long been a symbol of 'hard work'. Whatever the case, Henry Paynter's stamina is admirable and witnessing his endurance motivated others. He still tends his beehives and continues to supply honey to Westbank residents through Paynter's Fruit Stand. With the help of his son, Henry Arthur, he plants enough corn seed in the summer to produce 1,800 dozen cobs of corn for the season. He also plays badminton twice a week, travels regularly, is the last one on the dance floor at any party, and given the right circumstances, will engage in a feisty debate. To turn the corner of yet another year, a most notable honour was bestowed upon Henry in 2003 – the oldest badminton player in the world – which was recorded in the latest edition of the Guinness World Records books.

Aside form Henry's accomplishments, the most inspiring aspect of his life is the strong network of family support that he receives, particularly form his wife of 57 years, Sheila. Her work ethic generates enough stories to be worthy of a novel and perhaps one day we'll read more about the Paynter's inspirational endeavours.

BEST OF SHOW
Yasmin John-Thorpe

IN 1989, JOHN SALSNEK'S LIFE took a 180 degree turn. After working for more that twenty years in corporate Canada, where he'd spent most of his adult life relocating wherever his work sent him, from Toronto to Alberta to British Columbia, John and his wife, Stephanie, had arrived in the Okanagan and settled in. However, when his employers went through a policy shift and asked him to relocate yet again, this time to Winnipeg, John realized he did not want to move. He had grown comfortable in his new life, so he made his own shift. He took a sabbatical from his job to concentrate on painting.

The decision to take a year off to paint before looking for another corporate job in the area easily slipped into place. John felt guided. Art had always been in his life. John recalled as a young boy, around age seven, starting a science club with some school friends.

"We were just ordinary kids interested in investigating the world of nature," he explained. "We did the usual things, pressed leaves, collected birds nests and insects. We studied them. We drew the things we collected. The art went along with what we were doing like cream with coffee."

John grew up hiking and camping, maybe a little more than the average kid. He stated that the basic imprint in his life had been sketching and drawing.

"Our science club evolved into the art club by the time I was ten or twelve. When the art club emerged we dedicated ourselves to comic book art. We developed our own comic hero and drew them."

Once he had made the decision to leave his job and paint, everything felt right.

"It was amazing how nicely things fell into place with very little struggle involved, so unlike the corporate world where everything was so much of a struggle."

During this sabbatical time John refined his work, branching out to other areas of painting and using subtle variations in style. Since his love of nature came naturally he explored that area. When the year was over John found being an artist had become a full time job.

"It wasn't a decision like 'next year I'm going to be an artist,'" he said candidly. "There was nothing uncommon in what I was doing. I loved horses, always had and never grew out of it. I always enjoyed nature, so I tried to bring that to the canvas. As an artist you have to have a love for the form, it's like an internal mechanism. You see something and you really 'look' at it. Somewhere there is a fleeting moment of time; a beautiful moment and you show that through the art. Like everything in life art requires dedication. You can't just say 'I'm going to paint nature'."

Along with his love of nature, John also loves to paint city scenes and western art.

"You can't just stand still in this business. Your work has to be recognized by a specific style. You have to feel the evolving process."

His art hangs in many private collectors' homes and he now has special commissioned pieces he works on for his clients. John has regular collectors who like to keep on top of new works and clients who are introduced to his work through galleries and specialty locations throughout western Canada and the Yukon. John and his wife, Stephanie, participate in numerous professional art exhibitions each year and John's work has an increasing following of private and corporate collectors across Canada, the United Kingdom and the United States.

John's art continues to evolve. He has garnered himself several awards for his work, including in 1999 *The Best Of Show* for his two-dimensional paintings at the Spokane Western Art. He went to the Calgary Stampede for the first time in 2003 and won the Best New Artist Jurors Choice Award. Some of his other awards include in 2000 - Voted Best Artist in the Okanagan, Okanagan Life Magazine; 1998 - Published - Wildlife Art; 1997 - Published - Best of Wildlife Art - Northlight Books – Detroit; 1996 - Published - Naturescape - Province of British Columbia; 1995 - Published - Brushes in the Sun – coffee table edition; 1994 -

Artist of the Year - Ducks Unlimited; 1993 - British Columbia Wildlife Federation – Honours; 1992 - Art Award of the Year - Ducks Unlimited.

Looking to the future, John has set his eyes on the Prairies. He recently made several trips there and talked to numerous farmers about their life. His thoughts are on developing a whole series, maybe abstract like the impressionists.

"The Prairie pieces are a new challenge I welcome," he said. "I have to take something that is not very exciting, something simplistic and turn it into an interesting painting to excite someone."

John's home sits on acres above Oliver, BC. He rides his horses into the mountains above the Okanagan and gets his inspiration, his 'moment' to put on canvas. He can see himself doing this until he can't lift his brushes any more.

"When you do something you enjoy, when you have a love of life, and when you continue to be excited about what you're doing, there is no retirement. I look forward to old age and to continue painting without ever retiring."

Acknowledgements: My thanks to John and Stephanie Salsnek for their assisstance with this story.

ABBOTSFORD BERRY FESTIVAL
Alvin G. Ens

Berry red, berry sweet,
berry, berry, good to eat.
Berries here, berries there,
berries, berries everywhere.
Berries red, berries blue,
berries, berries, just for you.
Berries blue, berries red,
can't get berries from my head.

A BLACK BIRD TOOK MY TIME
Carol D. Loewen

TO MY SURPRISE I SAW A STARLING breaking thyme branches in my spring garden. He arranged them carefully, considering how to balance them in his beak. Satisfied with his load, he flew off into the bright Abbotsford morning. *Mr. and Mrs. Starling will have a fragrant nest,* I thought.

A few moments passed. Then, the same silver thyme began shaking as though blown by a turbulent wind. Mr. Starling was back, working exuberantly behind the bush. He popped his head up above the leaves searching for the best branches. He chose carefully, looking each over from top to bottom. Was he thinking how thick they were? He appeared to consider which stalks he would be able to yank off. Did the stems have plenty of fresh silvery green leaves? His head bobbed up and down. Was he thinking of nibbling on the slender mint flavoured morsels, savouring the tasty juices? He and his mate would need a comfortable home for their anticipated family. Was he perhaps mentally drafting a dream home made of these pliable twigs?

His shiny dark feathers reflected rainbow colours in the sunlight. I noticed his sharp yellow beak, his stubby tail, his plump body and bright eyes. His jerky movements added to the look of busyness. Did he know I was taking the time to watch him?

The starling found another suitable branch. He appeared to prefer the straight single stems. He tugged and he twisted. The black bird continued to tweak tough offshoots as he selected them, then dropped them on the ground.

Judging that he had plenty of thyme for one flight, Mr. Starling gathered his plunder together and flew to his secret construction site.

I do hope he leaves enough thyme to flavor my next pot of soup.

THE BLASTED CHURCH
Alan Longworth

DRIVING ALONG EASTSIDE ROAD, from either direction, motorists will see a sign with some caricature faces and the words, *Blasted Church Winery*. A short drive up winding Parsons Road and you will come to the grapevine-lined lane leading to the winery.

Built with a commanding view of Skaha Lake, the red roofed and natural timber built winery invites the visitor inside to taste the array of wines produced, by the vines growing on slopes above the lake. These slopes all face west.

Surely the owners, the Campbells, are not so disenchanted with organized religion they are taking a shot at it by giving it such a name? The answer is no. The name comes from a part of Okanagan Falls' sometimes-odd history, and the Campbells have chosen to keep the history alive by using the name. *Blasted Church*.

In the 1800s when gold mining was in full flush at Fairview, now a ghost town above the town of Oliver, volunteers built a small church to serve the miners and their families. When the gold petered out, the miners left for greener pastures and the town fell into decay.

Between fires and nature claiming back her own, the church stood almost alone on the former town site. For all intent and purpose the town of Fairview was dead, but Okanagan Falls had become a ranching center. It was a place for transferring freight to and from the lake's steamboats. The burgeoning residents wanted and needed a church for their community, and one lay idle and neglected at the Fairview town site.

It was decided that they would move the church to Okanagan Falls. The timber-built church had sat and dried in the Okanagan sun for a number of years. To dismantle it in the traditional manner would have caused a great deal of damage to the boards from cracking and splitting.

What to do? An engineer, Harley Hatfield, who was very familiar with dynamite, made the suggestion that by setting off an explosion inside the church all the nailed timbers would loosen, whereby it could be dismantled safely. One can just imagine the skepticism at his idea. It is easy to imagine the church blown to smithereens over the vacant town site.

History records that in 1929, four sticks of dynamite were hung from the rafters and the windows boarded up on the inside. The fuse was lit, and with a sound not normally associated with churches, the building puffed up like a balloon, but did not disintegrate. The boards had pulled the nails out of the church frame making it easy work to dismantle and transport it to Okanagan Falls by wagon.

The church was relocated and reassembled on Willow Street, one block from the Grey Sage Hotel on Highway 97.

One would think an explosion would be sufficient trauma for any church, but the blasted church endured another disaster. In the great Okanagan Falls flood of 1936 the church withstood a wall of water rushing at it from a burst dam high up above the town. Yet it stood firm against the onslaught. Long-time residents tell me there was a nine-foot high tide mark inside and outside of the church walls.

The blasted church is still in regular use today.

I would suggest that one would be hard pressed to find a church anywhere that has a history to equal this one. So as you sip the wines carrying the Blasted Church label... smile. You are drinking a little of Okanagan Fall's colourful history.

EL NINO SPRING
Violet Nesdoly

Worn out from all the push and bluster
trees lean wearily northeast
or lie broken and surrendered
across limb-strewn streets.
Drains are clogged with stubble of pine,
hair of cedar. Curbs catch
once nubile catkins, fugitive leaves,
pink drifts of downed petals.

My poor crocuses
who faithfully held high
fistfuls of closed buds
hoping one day soon to pay
bright homage to the sun
conquered and crushed on soggy ground.

Enough already!

The inspiration for the poem "El Nino Spring," above, came a few years ago when we had a particularly blustery spring, blamed of course on El Nino.

BOUNDARY CREEK ODYSSEY
Sharon Prafke

I WOULD LIKE TO INVITE the reader to take a trip down Boundary Creek in the midst of its namesake, Boundary Country, located in the southern interior of British Columbia.

While the point of origin, Terraced Peaks, is inconsequential to most, the journey southward really piques one's interest as it flows, meanders and sometimes even gushes over turbulent waterfalls.

Let's begin after the wayward path though dense majestic pine, cedar and larch trees where clear sparkling water levels out and meanders lazily though the full length of a beautiful valley just north of Greenwood. Gurgling over the occasional gold flake, Boundary Creek passes by a herd of Morgan horses before encountering a variety of cattle grazing on a patchwork of lush green alfalfa and golden hayfields dotting the open countryside. Coyotes, deer, cougars and the odd grizzly pause to enjoy a refreshing drink and it's not uncommon to observe a bald eagle circling overhead. After all, this is his realm and he reigns supreme over his plentiful hunting ground of field mice, moles and chipmunks.

Flowing gently through several ranches Boundary Creek now swings dramatically to the west before entering the smallest city in Canada, namely Greenwood, boasting a modest population of 700. Not like back in it's heyday , in 1895, when Robert Wood discovered a large outcrop of copper. Added to that was the discovery of gold and silver, escalating the population to 1,500 within two years. By 1907 it had skyrocketed to 7,000 eager, expectant prospectors and astute merchants offering every amenity. To reflect, it now seems staggering that Greenwood was the social and economic hub for the entire Boundary region. Three banks, sixteen hotels, fifteen general stores, three printing offices, four doctors, six legal firms and many other thriving businesses all flourished within the city's boundaries.

At this point in our journey one must pause at the tunnel of flags painted by our previous mayor, Anro Hennig, before continuing onward, paralleling two major arteries. The first is the Crow's Nest Highway while the second is the old Canadian Pacific right of way linking up with the famous Kettle Valley Railway, thirteen kilometers to the west. Once these ribbons of steel stretched from sea-to-sea but now this lengthy strip of roadbed has been renamed the Trans Canada Trail. Muffled footsteps replace the black engines and eerie whistles that once rang out their melancholy sound.

Bouncing and splashing over grey pebbles the crystal waters gently flow under one of two bridges connecting what in years gone by would have been the grand, burgundy, two-story C.P.R. Station. Today it is only a memory but the downtown preserved heritage buildings of yesteryear still stand staunchly against the testament of time. It is a pleasure indeed to gaze at the numerous classic buildings flanking both sides of Copper Street. A quick stroll to the east impresses the sightseer to observe the original City Hall or Fire Station with the Post Office a mere block to the south. The majority of these buildings were constructed over 100 years ago and still loom over the calm meandering waters of Boundary Creek. This might be a good time to pamper oneself by indulging in one of various establishments located up and down Copper Street.

Mouth-watering home baked biscuits with jam; tea or specialty coffees, perhaps accompanied with succulent, piping hot bread, tarts - or maybe a burger and fries? - luscious ice cream, or a full-ourse meal all wait to appease those rumbling appetites. If thirst whets your appetite then perhaps a brew at one of the local bars would help to soothe a parched throat. Hunger and thirst aren't especially a prerequisite, you say? Then possibly various local merchants might pique your fancy with their antiques, art, trinkets and souvenirs, to name just a few.

Onward Boundary Creek flows, linking us once again to the past as it twists and turns, skirting the haunting memories associated to the skeletal remains of the unique B.C. Copper Smelter. Today one can still rummage around in the old ruins located in Lotzkar Memorial Park, containing the cylindrical red brick smokestack that originally stood 36 meters tall. Although it doesn't tower quite so majestically today, since some of the 250,000 bricks have been lost, it continues to shadow the gargantuan black, glossy slagheap at its side. To this day a curiosity seeker can walk over the molten black shiny glass or sit inside one of the bell shaped "Hell's Bells" that were formed inside the large bell-shaped slag cars during the smelter's heyday.

Progressing, Boundary Creek flows zigzagging westward towards Anaconda, the once formidable rival of Greenwood that has now slipped into near obscurity. Maintaining its gentle journey across flat fields of a countryside that gradually grows wilder the water meanders past a second slagheap, demonstrating the dated prosperity of the region.

Forging ahead the creek now picks up speed as it tumbles over the turbulent gorge at Boundary Falls. There it races downward through a narrow valley alongside those two main arteries to enter Midway, eight kilometers to the southwest. At this juncture the odyssey ends when Boundary Creek merges its waters with the beautiful Kettle River that lazily winds through the land of the legendary Dewdney Trail.

A BRAVE LITTLE BOAT
Pamela & Martin Garrity

THEY ALL SAID, "That was a brave little boat."

Well maybe, but not in my mind. I was given a task to do, so I had to uphold the tradition of all those before me and all those that would come after. This was my story. It's there, in the history books. But nobody asked me how I felt!

I am going to tell you in my own words my short, but eventful life. How with the help of my friends I achieved what nobody before me - nor any other since - had ever achieved. I haven't even told you who I am.

SS Skuzzy, used with the kind permission of the Vancouver Library, special collections, vpl 390.

My name is *SS Skuzzy*. Funny name, isn't it? I like it though. It means, "jump" or "jump across". It comes from one of the North American Indian languages.

I was a Sternwheeler in the year of Our Lord 1882. What a time this was; so exciting. There was the gold rush in British Columbia and the Hudson Bay Company was hauling furs back east.

40

Mr. Andrew Onderdonk, an American of Dutch decent, was chosen by the Canadian Government to build the roads and railways through the Fraser Canyon in British Columbia. Premier Walken placed a $10 toll on the movement of goods by road or rail. Mr. Onderdonk was determined to get his goods and building material from Yale to Lytton without paying the tolls.

Of course there was only one other way to do this journey and that was on the mighty, muddy and treacherous Fraser River. Andrew Onderdonk lived in Yale. He knew how the river behaved. It was not any ordinary peaceful river. There were two problems: a river determined to win and a man who had equal determination to succeed.

I was to be "Born" (well I like to think I was born. Okay then, I was commissioned) or built in a yard just outside of Yale by a very good boat builder, Mr. William Dalton. I was 40 meters long and weighed about 254 tons with an eight-meter beam. I was not big, but I was beautiful and I was very proud to have such a famous owner. On May 4, 1882, Mrs. Onderdonk and Mr. Dalton launched me and named me "*SS Skuzzy*." It was a big affair and Mr. Onderdonk was there.

He stated, "My intention is to sail the Skuzzy up river through Hell's Gate Canyon, continue on to Boston Bar and transport supplies by boat to Lytton." I should have taken more notice of the looks of shock on the faces of the crowd, or perhaps I should have realized that anything called "Hell's Gate" got the name for a reason, but it was an exciting day. All I really wanted was to meet my Captain and get on with my job. You see, I knew I was going to save Mr. Onderdonk a lot of money in taxes and tolls.

It took a while to get a captain, so I spent some time finding out about this place "Hell's Gate" and its problem. I would listen to the men in the boat yard as they chatted about the Fraser River. I have to say what I heard frightened me a bit, but I wouldn't show it to anyone. This was why I was built, so I was determined to do whatever it took to do my job.

Sometimes at night when all the workmen had gone home I shuddered a bit and wondered if I would live to a ripe old age. This was what I learned about Hell's Gate:

Hells Gate stretches from Yale to Boston Bar. This part of the Fraser River was the most turbulent. Simon Fraser, who first discovered the River, said it was like the 'gates of hell' and would never be navigated. And, it was to be my maiden voyage!

It gets worse - just listen to this. I then found out that the cut called Hell's Gate was 300 meters long, but only 34 meters wide. The river had to force itself through the narrow gap at the speed of 32 kilometers an hour. Shall I go on? *That is nine meters a second. That is faster and more water than goes over Niagara Falls.* And there are rocks that we can see (and some that we can't see) jutting out of the water at all angles. (By the way, I am trying not to get hysterical!) That is not all: there are huge trees - yes, trees - that have fallen into the river and are rushing downstream. Any one of these could damage my stern wheel or worse, they could pierce a hole in my hull and I would sink beneath the water.

Mr. Onderdonk was a kind man and would only get the best for me. My first Captain was a man called Nat Lane Jr. I had heard that he was a very experienced sailor and was used to navigating in white water. The fact is I never actually saw the man, because off he went to look at Hell's Gate and without ever setting foot on my beautiful new deck, he up and left. I waited patiently. Well I tried to be patient; by now, I wanted to get this over with.

Very soon another captain arrived: Mr. Ausbury Insley. This man looked at Hell's Gate and stated that he would not be daunted, or beaten by a 'river.' This was my type of man. I set out May 17th with Captain Insley and his equally experienced crew to sail from Yale to Boston Bar on the first leg of our journey. We navigated the waters from Spuzzum, but to tell the truth I didn't see much. The waters were fierce and treacherous. We sailed from dawn until dusk and then it got too dark to see. The canyon got narrower and narrower as we approached Hell's Gate. I was straining against fierce currents and the white water.

Steam screamed from my engine. Thick black smoke poured out of my chimney. My paddle was straining against the white water. I could feel all my joints creak. I was being tossed from side to side. I don't know how I missed the rocks. If one of those had pierced my side, we would be in serious trouble. I was being battered and thrown.

I struggled now. I was tired, but I kept going. I kept fighting against the current. We went on and on. I could not believe there could be such turbulence. Captain Insley shouted his orders, trying to be heard above the noise I was making and the roar of the river. We entered the canyon. Water raged around me, mud swirled about in the bubbling eddies and even more rocks jutted out. I don't think I had time to be frightened.

I went on, but slowly the river was winning. The current was running at the highest it had been in forty years. This was much faster than I could go. I knew deep in my heart that we could not get much further. Captain Insley finally had to give up and he took me back to my mooring.

WE HAD FAILED. The river, the mighty Fraser River had beaten us. Perhaps, we should have listened to Simon Fraser perhaps this river could not be navigated. I stayed in my mooring.

I heard about the other sternwheelers doing their work lower down on the river. It seemed that I would never complete my maiden voyage. I felt a little sad, but I should have known Mr. Onderdonk would not give up that easily.

Spurred on by the fact that the $10 tolls were now mounting up, he needed to save money. Of course, I was keen to get going. With all this in mind, Captain S. R. Smith and his brother David were employed. They knew it would be an awesome task, but these two men appeared to be as intrepid as Simon Fraser himself. I waited patiently and on September 7, 1882, the water in the Fraser River had dropped as low as they thought it ever would. With these two men and a experienced crew we set off.

This time we were determined to conquer the muddy waters of the Fraser River. The current was no less than it had been earlier. There was silt and mud swirling around. I plied my way through this water once again. Oh yes, I was battered. I was being pushed from side to side, but I was not beaten. Let the river throw as much as it could. I would go on. They would have to tear me to pieces before I would give in.

My captain, Captain Smith, was as determine as I. We respected each other. We battled together for ten long weary days against the river. Andrew Onderdonk now decided enough was enough. I was so frightened. I thought he was going to order us back. Was this to be the end for me?

No, he had another plan and what a plan it turned out to be!

He ordered the rock face along the gorge be drilled and ringbolts fixed in place. Long towropes were then threaded through the ringbolts. Whatever were they going to do? When I heard, I was so intrigued that for a while I forgot how sore and tired I felt. I watched the work being completed. Chinese workers, 125 of them, balanced along the rock face and threaded ropes through the ringbolts down onto my deck.

Hell's Gate. Photo by R.H. Truman & Co.
Courtesy of the Penticton Museum.

I was then pulled majestically through the boiling waters of Hell's Gate.

This was very exciting and I was so proud. No other boat had ever passed through this spot in the river. The rocks were very slippery, which made this a very dangerous operation. I was so pleased to hear later that nobody slipped and there were no accidents or loss of life that day. The turbulent water did not claim a single soul.

WE WERE WINNING! I left Hell's Gate behind me, although battered and injured. I went on to Boston Bar for my well-earned rest. My journey had taken sixteen long, hard days to get from Spuzzum to Boston Bar, a total of sixteen miles. I heard that my exploits were even reported in the newspaper and sometimes when I was at my mooring I would look back at my adventure and wonder if Simon Fraser could have seen what happened would he have smiled a little?

I expect you want to know what happened to me. Well, I was never to do the journey again and nor has anyone else. I think we are all in agreement that the Fraser River is the 'Master of Hell's Gate.' I did work for a further two years, after my repairs (I had been damaged quite badly). I went from Boston Bar to Lytton.

I am afraid to say that I needed repairs quite often, so Mr. Onderdonk thought it would be better if I were dismantled, so that is what happened. My engine and machinery were still good, so they put them in *Skuzzy II*. She was much larger than me and much sturdier, but she never attempted Hell's Gate. I know she was a nice boat but she was never … **A BRAVE LITTLE BOAT**!

HOMEWARD BOUND
Eric Linden

Where majestically forested mountains,
Stand with cliffs in deep indigo swells,
Where bald eagles soar high in the heavens
On patrol over coastlines and dells,
Where the grizzlies and caribou wander
Thru their rangelands that seldom see man
Still the swimmer* fights rivers and rapids
To return where his life once began.

Where white trumpeter swans rest in winter
Blending whiteness on colourless snow,
Where the deer and the moose roam the woodland,
Bighorn sheep graze the grasslands below,
Where the call of the loon haunts the silence
And the larks sing in joyful delight,
That's where apple trees blossom in springtime
And I'm heading for home yet tonight!

The salmon is the swimmer in coast Indian lore

B.S. or Bull Stories
Johnny Eek

Elmer observed his new Montana bull wasn't getting his job done.
The rancher that raised the bull said "Come on down and get another
    one."
So his first stop was at Rock Creek to let his friend know what he
    was going to do,
The next stop was at Midway Hotel 'cause he had lots of friends
    there too.
He stopped again at the Greenwood liquor store.
So he could take his Yankee friend some drinks.
As he headed east he said, "I'll pull over and get me forty winks."
The police woke him up and asked if he was all right,
And where was he going alone?
Elmer rears up and said, "If the truck is empty I'm going to Montana,
But if there is a bull in the back I'm going home."

***

When Kenny found his bull was sick and looked like it was going to
    die,
He called in a Vet to see if he could discover why.
A Veterinarian costs lots of money so after a day or two, he said,
"It's best that you shoot the bull, I've done all that I can do."
So Kenny up and shot the bull just like he didn't care,
Then hauled it up the mountain and then just left it there.

***

When I first heard the story I thought it seemed a little strange,
Someone said they had found a Limousine bull dead on Stephie's
    range.
Her bull had not been seen since they had turned him out,
So a dead Limousine bull was surely hers, no doubt.
She thought she'd like to get her money back you can bet;
The one thing in the way is HE WASN'T ALL PAID FOR YET.
Now whoever's bull it was it didn't suffer too much pain,
Because the range detectives found the cause of death was a bullet in
    the brain.
But when the truth came to light, they took it in their stride
It wasn't Stephie's Bull at all; it was that neighbour's bull that died!

45

CAMELS IN THE CARIBOO
Helen Wyatt

IN 1857, WHISPERS OF GOLD along the Fraser River attracted prospectors to the area from around the world. They needed transportation to get their food and gear up to the dig sites. This proved yet another bonanza for teamsters hauling in freight by barge, stagecoach, donkey, oxen and pack-mule.

One type of freight enterprise along the Cariboo Road doomed to failure was a camel transport service. With freight rates at fifty cents a pound from Lillooet to Quesnel, three enterprising northern men formed a syndicate to import camels from Manchuria. They expected to make a large profit using camels as freight carriers. These ungainly brutes could each pack 500 pounds and go without water for a week. Living on practically nothing, they would be easy on fuel!

Photo courtesy of the Penticton Museum.

In 1892, the twenty-two Bactrian camels imported at a cost of $250.00 each, arrived from Manchuria. Bactrians are the elite camels, having two humps to the Dromedary's one.

However, bedlam broke loose on the Cariboo Road when the camels met their first mule pack train. The mules got a sniff of the strange scent of these kings of the desert from a long way off and began stampeding. In the ensuing melee, supplies for the miners flew in every direction.

The pungent odour of camels on the trail continued to cause havoc with the other pack animals. When stabled nearby, the stinking, imported animals spooked horses and mules whinnied, snorted and brayed uneasily all night. In addition, the desert beasts were inclined to bite any animals or men who came too close.

Continued lawsuits and accidents made trouble for the camel syndicate.

Then another problem arose. Their tender feet, while fine on soft desert sands, soon became sore on the rocky mountain trail. As a remedy, the owners tried fitting them with boots of rawhide and canvas.

Though unpopular, the camels continued treading the Cariboo Road for about a year before they were taken off duty. A few were sold for around $35 each and the balance were turned loose around Clinton, where they continued to terrorize the local horses and mules.

When the last camel died in 1905, it marked the end of a business venture that "never panned out."

BILL MINER

AROUND 1904, A SOFT-SPOKEN southern gentleman came to Princeton in search of peace, quiet and a climate compatible to his health. 'George Edwards,' as he called himself, settled in at the Mount Baldy ranch of Jack Budd, whom he'd met in Texas. Throughout Mr. Edwards' stay in Princeton, he became well liked by all who knew him. He was noted for kindness and generosity to children and his charm with the ladies, and he was reportedly a good dancer and skilled at playing the fiddle. He didn't seem to do much, but he never lacked for money and had a strange habit of disappearing for short periods of time.

No one suspected the soft-spoken gentleman was actually Bill Miner, infamous train robber and prison escape artist. Jack Budd's ranch was used as a place to plan their train robberies. Other members of the gang were Louis Calhoun, a quiet unassuming schoolteacher from Ontario, and 'Shorty' Dunn who worked as a clerk in Princeton's hardware store. They were all eventually captured and sent to prison.

The people of Princeton who knew them had a hard time believing they were outlaws.

Submitted by the Princeton Chamber of Commerce

CANADA HERE WE COME!
Margaret Ann Hayes

AFTER TWENTY-FIVE OR MORE YEARS living and working as writers in Kenya, East Africa, the time had come, we decided, to take a look at another part of the world. Taking a three-month vacation my husband and I, with our fourteen-year-old daughter, left Nairobi for Vancouver in August 1979.

Over the next few days we looked in awe at British Columbia's city in the sun; so clean, and with flower-filled gardens and parks well manicured. Yet it was in sight of a glittering sea and the tallest mountains. Within a wonderful sightseeing week, during which time we had met many welcoming Canadians, our seats were booked on a Greyhound bus, (we couldn't imagine ourselves driving on the Right side of the road) and were soon on our way to Penticton, a city in the interior of British Columbia.

With eyes open wide, probably our mouths also, 'country cousin style', we were thrilled with everything we saw on route: rushing, clear, mint green waterfalls, tumbling with abandon down impossibly steep slopes; flowers peeping from hedgerows, varieties we hadn't seen since leaving England for the tropics so many years ago; wild pink roses and thorny blackberry bushes clambering along roadsides where, at times, bright green ferns swayed in the breeze and dark pine forests stood close and sentinel-like, reaching up and up towards a non-stop, unbelievably blue sky. The whole journey was thrilling.

And I had thought Canada was a land of snow and icebergs. How foolish of me!

With our arrival in the Okanagan Valley, Canada had begun to weave its magic. Already we had fallen in love with this wonderful country. Lush fruits and vegetables were displayed at fruit stands along the way, the air was sweet and pine-scented and there were gleaming lakes, sandy beaches and plenty of sunshine to enjoy.

With peach juice dribbling down our chins, we decided to look at property in this 'land of milk and honey'. With excitement mounting we were introduced to an undeveloped property on Hawthorne Mountain, above the village of Okanagan Falls. With bonus of a turquoise-green lake lapping below us, we bought the whole quarter-section of land overlooking it.

Of course we had to return to Kenya in order to apply to live in Canada. A very nerve-racking time indeed, but after seven months, with a clean bill of health in our hands and Kenya property sold and taxes paid, the squeaky clean Hayes family arrived in Canada as legal, landed immigrants.

Walking through the village one morning, an elderly couple waved with a cheery "Hi". I stopped to chat for a few minutes when suddenly they said, "Hey, you talks funny. You must be from England?"

"Yes and no," I replied. "I am recently from East Africa."

"What?" they cried. "Thought people from Africa wuz black!"

We laughed together, already friends, and as I continued my walk they shouted after me, "See ya, have a nice day."

This to me sums up in a nut shell the easy, friendly spirit of British Columbians, who, from many different ethnic backgrounds, blend together to make the unique Canadians they are.

I asked one old man what his tree with the large white flowers was called.

"Oh, that's a *Catalpa* tree. The pioneers in this Valley used to plant them next to their outhouses. The large leaves are very soft, you see," he grinned, shyly.

Soon we had a house built overlooking Green Lake. Although no fish live in the clear waters, painted turtles sunbathe on floating logs, flamboyant yellow-headed blackbirds nest in the reeds and California quail rush about on the shore. We found life idyllic.

In 1981, my husband Charles, an old-time editor, started a small weekly newspaper in Okanagan Falls. We published *The South Okanagan Review* for fifteen years, all the while learning and enjoying much about the area and its people.

Coming to live in Canada was the best decision ever.

A CLOSER LOOK AT MISSION HILL WINERY
Darcy Nybo

I SEE IT EVERY DAY on my way to work: this monumental building high atop one of the many hills in the Okanagan Valley. Every week day, twice a day I see this sand coloured stronghold and wonder what the heck is in there. Curiosity got the best of me and I headed off Hwy. 97 and up to Mission Hill Winery. The fortress-like entry gates slowed me down the moment we entered.

We park the car and enter the winery grounds through contemporary arches held together by a single keystone. Once we step through this arch, the outside world fades away and we enter into the audacious world of Anthony von Mandl, owner of Mission Hill Winery.

A spacious courtyard awaits us as we stare at all the buildings and the views. At the centrepiece of the courtyard is an impressive 12-storey bell tower. The time to inspect the bell tower will come later, for now we are taken to the Estates Room. The secured doors are opened and we step into a room with double vaulted ceilings. We are told that should we book this room we can sample a wide range of Estate and Library wines. While viewing a collection of 17th century bottles my eyes are drawn to what appears to be gaps in the construction. The gaps are actually windows. These 4-inch wide windows run from floor to ceiling, giving you a glimpse of what is outside, but only a glimpse. Our host guides us out onto the Vineyard Terrace.

The terrace overlooks rows of Pinot Noir and Chardonnay vines and has an impressive panoramic view of Lake Okanagan. It's a great place for lunch, but today there is no time and we are off to the Amphitheatre.

This gently terraced outdoor amphitheatre has served as a venue for Shakespeare, opera and jazz. I can't help but think of how it must have been to be enjoying a performance while the hills of Kelowna burned in the background in the summer of 2003. Today the hills look greener, healthier than I imagined they would.

Our guide has moved on and we follow into the Loggia, which is Latin for outdoor room. The Loggia is a great place to get out of the Okanagan sun, or less frequently, the rain. This too offers incredible views of the lake, valley, vineyards and mountains of the Okanagan. I never imagined this from my quick glimpses from the highway!

We leave the Loggia and enter a small Piazetta that overlooks the private Loggia garden below. We discover a Hungarian Oak tree that stands 45 feet tall and a 17th Century Renaissance fountain. All this and we still haven't reached the winery.

Now it is time for the bell tower. The 12-storeys tall bell tower has four bronze bells inside, all varying in tone and weight. We are told they were handcrafted in Annecy, France by the Paccard Bell Foundry. Each bell is dedicated to a member of Anthony's immediate family; his late father Martin, his mother Bedriska, his sister Patricia and himself. There is a miscast bell outside the bell tower. It offers a great opportunity to see these grand bells up close.

The sun is telling us it's time to move on as we listen to the bells peal through the courtyard and across the lake. We are taken to the Education Centre, an ordinary name for an exceptional building. Its wooden doors stand over 24 feet tall and open wide to welcome us to a museum-style reception hall, known as the Chagall Room. On its wall is one of only 29 Chagall tapestries ever made. There are two doors on either side of the room, which lead into the theatre. Here we learn of the grapes, the vineyards, the man and his dream and the award winning wines that are the result of that dream.

Now educated on the fine art of wine making we are taken into the deep volcanic rock cellars. Among the hundreds of barrels of Mission Hill wine is a gated wine vault that houses Anthony's personal wine collection. The only source of natural light into the cellar is from an oculus that sits above ground. Having never heard of an oculus I am intrigued. It is a long tunnel that literally funnels light into the cellars and in Latin it means eye.

After touring the cellars we arrive at the wine tasting room. Once your tastebuds sample the wines, you'll understand why everything is the way it is at Mission Hill. From the beautiful and carefully groomed vineyards to the unearthly quiet of the wine cellars, the grape has made its way to its final destination.

The retail store has a complete selection of wines for you to take home, as well as cookbooks, wine education tools and gift ideas.

We leave the retail store and head for the arches. The bells are ringing again and I can't help but walk slowly, somewhat reluctant for our visit to end. As I drive out the gates and back into the world I smile, knowing that should I ever need sanctuary from the hectic pace of life, Mission Hill Winery is but a short drive away.

Mission Hill Winery is located off Boucherie Road in Westbank, BC

Cowboy Up!
Laurena Typusiak

IT'S ALL PART of the cowboy way.

A dusty rodeo arena. A cowboy scrambling up the nearest fence rail with a Brahma in hot pursuit. The pounding music and booming announcer encouraging the crowd to cheer - especially for the local boys.

"C'mon, Oliver! He's one of yours!" roars announcer Tony Acland Sunday, inciting the audience to shout once more for fifteen-year-old novice bareback rider, Jeremy Risling. But, Risling doesn't hear the crowd until his feet are back on the ground.

"I just block it right out, I just get on my horse and think about what's going to happen next," says the blue-eyed cowboy.

The novice category is for less experienced horses and cowboys who are younger than twenty-one. Oliver born and raised, this farm boy has

ridden in about eighteen professional rodeos since the age of twelve. He's found some recognition in the sport - last year he took third in Washington for Junior Rodeo - but so far, he hasn't won any prize money.

But it's not money that spurs Risling to ride.

"It's the adrenaline. I like it because of the power. You get the horse between your legs and your horse gets bucking and you're sitting on 'em and it makes you feel good 'cause you're staying on and riding him," he says.

The goal is to stay on until the buzzer marks a successful eight-second ride, and during the eighth annual Oliver Kinsmen Pro Rodeo, Risling doesn't make eight in front of the hometown crowd. Knowing that's part of the ride, he jumps to his feet and waves his hat at his cheering fans.

He's not afraid of getting hurt when he's thrown, though he's earned his share of knocks. On Sunday night his hand stuck in the rope rigging, and Risling thinks he broke it. Will it deter him from riding in future rodeos?

"No! Uh-uh, no way," he insists, sporting a bandaged hand. Though he's not concerned about injury, Risling admits he feels nervous before each performance.

"If you're not nervous, you're either stupid or crazy," he says with a grin.

The cowboy's father, Lloyd Risling, isn't worried about his son getting hurt.

"It's all part of the sport, you just give 'er and then you worry about the other part later," he says. A former bull-rider, Risling's father understands the attraction of the bucking broncs, the dusty arena, and the cheering fans.

"It's to preserve the past, it's to keep doing the cowboy way."

Originally printed in The Penticton Herald *August 27, 2003*

A BULL-RIDER'S COMMENT
Johnny Eek

If you're riding Brahma bulls, this is what Kaylan said,
So you won't hurt your feet, practice landing on your head.
'Cause when you're on the ground and a bull is after you,
You might not get the speed you need if your feet are black and blue.
Or if you are heading for the fence and the chips are down,
You might feel a little safer if you can outrun the clown.
Now if a bull is following you and looks mean and grouchy,
You can't get going fast enough if your feet are sore and ouchy.
Sometimes we have to go by how high the barnyard stuff is piled,
And I watched his face and he never even smiled.
So if you are bucked off a bull this is what Kaylan said,
You can't afford to hurt your feet, so practice landing on your head.
I don't think my grandson would string grampa a line,
But then you never know 'cause some folks seem to do it all the time.

COWTOWN OKANAGAN
Alan Longworth

WHEN THE HUDSON BAY FUR traders first came through the valley we now know as the Okanagan Valley, they reported that the grasses here were so lush and thick that it came up to their horses' bellies. In later years, in the mid eighteen hundreds, when the lure of gold brought men surging northwards, cattlemen quickly followed, driving their herds ahead of them. Many established ranching operations along the entire length of the valley. Others chose the Similkameen or Kettle River valleys. In short order there were cattle ranches from Princeton to Merritt and Rock Creek to Salmon Arm.

Long, arduous cattle drives were the only way to get the livestock to markets. But when the CPR built a rail link from the boundary country to the markets on the Coast and in Alberta, Okanagan Falls turned out to be a focal point for the shipping of cattle by rail. Once given the dubious name of Dogtown, it was situated at the south end of Dog Lake, which has since been renamed Skaha Lake. Okanagan Falls became a gathering point for herds of cattle from all over the neighbouring valleys. The cattle were held in the stockyards ready for loading at the CPR siding between what is now Cedar Street and the now tamed falls on the Okanagan River.

While eliminating the long cattle drives all the way to Kamloops or Hope, the system had other problems to contend with. The ranchers had to ship their livestock on faith and they found themselves being cheated by the cartel of slaughterhouses. Some unfortunate ranchers ended up with no financial return for their livestock.

In 1942 a meeting of ranchers from the surrounding valleys was held in the shade of a large cottonwood tree at the Okanagan Falls CPR stockyard. In order to fight back at the inequities they faced, the ranchers formed the Southern Interior Stockmen's Association.

The CPR donated some building materials and the ranchers set about building their own sales ring and cattle pens. They purchased a cattle weigh scale and installed it at the sales ring and got ready for their first sale. A day or two before the sale, when hundreds of cattle were already assembled, the government scale inspector arrived and condemned it, claiming it had not been installed properly. To avoid a financial disaster the cattle were sorted into boxcar lots and herded across Shuttleworth Creek up to the Thomas ranch and weighed on the ranch scales there. As one bunch was driven back down to the stockyards, another bunch had to pass them on the way up to the scales. Man and horse were tested to the limit, by cows following their herding instinct and not wishing to go in two different directions. Despite all the problems, the first cattle auction in Okanagan Falls became a reality.

In the early days, there was no eating establishments nor a hotel or other accommodations in Okanagan Falls. Saddles became pillows and the hard dry ground a mattress. The music of the Okanagan night was the bawling of herds of disgruntled cattle in the confines of the stockyards. The OK Falls community at that time rallied behind the business of the stockyards and it became a gathering place for people as well as cattle. The women of the community became involved with feeding the ranchers and ranch hands. Eventually the stockyards began to develop better facilities and added a covered, enclosed sales ring and later, a concession stand. The local ranchers' wives, the village Women's Institute and church groups all pitched in to run it and help feed the hungry cattlemen. It was a time of sharing that regretfully seems to have passed into oblivion.

Okanagan Falls has a heritage unique in the history of the Okanagan and yet unlike other communities the length of the valley, in some ways it has changed very little.

Yes, we have a hotel and couple of motels and several cafes. There are condos and apartments, stores and fuel stations. But some things never change. On spring and fall Sunday afternoons, right through until the following Tuesday, the bawling of up to a thousand head of market ready cattle singing their mournful song echoes across the narrow valley between the high rock walls. On Mondays the open land around the stockyards is filled with giant two decked cattle-carrying trailers and the cars and trucks of the ranchers and hands.

The long overland cattle drives to the Falls are now just a distant memory of those who took part in them. It is a part of our heritage and history that is not often told. But there is no doubt of the economic impact resulting from a group of ranchers 60 years ago sitting under a cottonwood tree and making hard decisions. Driving through Okanagan Falls today the motorist has no inkling of the significance this little village has played in the development of the entire region.

Thanks to Morrie Thomas, Okanagan Falls Rancher, for some of the facts on the cattle auction gleaned from his book Fifty Years – Three And A Half Million Cattle.

CRYSTAL CLEAR:
NEW YEARS NIGHT IN KITS
Darriel Dawne

SO BEGINS the Year of the Monkey

I went to the movies tonight, a double-bill for $5.00, that's a deal you can't beat. It's one of the things I love about my neighbourhood. It's got neat things like an old movie theatre, organic produce stands, funky clothing shops, kids books stores, flower shops, and of course Starbucks. Everything is within walking distance, all along one street.

I live just one short block away. But it's like a different world when I turn the corner to go home. My house is an older home on a tree-lined street. It was built in 1912, and like many of the other houses on my block, it's been divided into suites. It's beautiful and peaceful. We have block parties in the summer, and neighbours invite you over for barbeques and Christmas parties. It's a good place to live. And, only a 15-minute walk to the beach!

As I'm walking home from the movies, taking in the night air, glad that it's stopped raining for a while, I see this couple running down the sidewalk towards me, playing "catch me if you can".

At a distance, I think maybe they are in love, the girl is laughing and doesn't seem to be trying to get away. It's the kind of thing you expect to see; there are lots of students living in the area, what with it being so close to the University of British Columbia.

My thoughts change when she runs into traffic, trying to flag a car to stop. Then she runs past me screaming, "Help me, help me. HELP". I try to grab her, but she keeps going. The man in pursuit looks apologetic and says, "She's coming down off of meth".

Sadly, this is also something I've seen in my neighbourhood. I follow the pair. This girl is in trouble, and I don't know who this man is. I don't know if he is here to help or to hinder. He catches up with her. I catch up with them. He's holding her and she's screaming and crying, desperately trying to escape. He asks her about the drugs and she tells him her friend threw them away. She's not on drugs. She turns and begs me to help her.

We sit. She is restrained in her father's arms on the risers the florist uses to display simple acts of beauty. She escapes, but he catches her before she can run into the street. He brings her back to where I sit. A crowd gathers. Someone asks if they should call for help. The father says, "Yes, please call."

This is all happening so fast.

He's holding her now, so I call 911 and ask for police and an ambulance. The ambulance comes first and I tell them, "There is a young girl here, she's hysterical and is being restrained. I think she's coming down from crystal meth."

"How old is she?" Her father tells me she is 17. "She's 17. Yes, she's on crystal meth."

There is nothing left to do but wait. I hold her hand and wait. She screams and begs, cries and struggles, and we wait. I take off my gloves to touch her, to give a human connection. It's all I can offer. I wish for something more to give her, but all I can do is brush the hair from her eyes, tell her I know she's hurting, and listen.

A man comes, offering water, to calm her down. I think he may have bought it for her. It ends up thrown in my face and I am a bitch. She screams for me to leave, for me to help her, for anyone to please, please help her, so she can go to John, so she can see her boyfriend, so she can get away from her father. Anything, just please help her.

A couple stands watching, silent witnesses. Her father apologizes to me, but it's only water, and she is so hurt, so terribly damaged, there is nothing to apologize for.

She's so young and lovely, her tear stained lashes so close to my face. When she breaks from us again I have to grab her. She feels so light, so tiny. She says she can't run anymore since she has no muscles left.

When I hold her, she is all softness. Her skin is flawless, her eyes deep brown wells. She is so strong. As her tears abate and I look into her eyes, I see my niece. This strung out young woman reminds me of what I have, and what could be lost. She wants help so badly and doesn't know where to find it. It breaks my heart.

Her father wants her to go to detox. "Please, so you can think clearly". She begs me to make him stop. I tell her I'm trying to help her, that no, I won't let her father take her, that I'm helping her the best I know how. The ambulance is coming and I'm staying with her until it arrives.

Waiting. The waiting is endless.

Her spirit flames. She is so scared and doesn't know why. Over and over she screams, bolts and struggles and rages. Her father and I do our best not to hurt her when she tries to flee. She cries and begs. She is calm. Then it starts over again. We sit and wait. We talk. She tries to run. We wait some more.

It finally arrives. I flag the ambulance down. The watchers all wander off. I have let her go. I stand back as the paramedics talk to her. She tells them it's been two days since she used. Before that, she hadn't used in weeks. She's trying to stop. Calm now, she's getting help.

As the police arrive I too take my leave to the end of the block. To my block. But, I don't turn to go home. I sit and wait and watch. I need to know they take her away. I need to know she is helped. All of a sudden I am crying and I can't speak. It was all just so hard. Not a bad experience, just hard.

The ambulance pulls away and I see her father running towards me, coming to thank me. He tells me the police won't take her to detox. She's 17 and they can't force her. She is being taken to the hospital, so maybe she'll choose to admit herself.

I tell him I know she's strong, that she'll be okay and that he'll be okay too. I believe in them. If a stranger can believe in them, he should too. I hug him, and take my leave.

And with every act of kindness I am seeking redemption.

ON WAKING
Marguerite Fry

Good Morning, World,
> This new day another gift
> In my brief share of infinite time.

Good Morning, Tree
> Your russet branches warming in the sun
> Holding your gift of bright berries
> For hungry birds and all who look
> To wonder at.

Good Morning, Surf,
> Softly today you whisper
> Of rainy days to come
> No shaking crash to send logs pounding
> When Squamish winds whip sea to foam
> And sky to crackling blue.

Good Morning, Man
> The peaceful hand of sleep
> Still smoothes your brow
> Sleep on a while in these warm folds
> Life's burden soon enough will plow
> Their furrows, Sleep on.

Good Morning, God.

DEA EX MACHINA
for Josi Abata
David Herreshoff

Arriving in a basket from on high,
lowered to the stage, a deity
performed then left again.
That's how Greek dramatists resolved
an impasse between actors in a play.
But your appearance was a solo one.
Your presence wasn't actually required
at lake level, three hundred feet below
the highway you were driving on.
And yet your drama seemed traditional.
Alone in your machine you lurched through air.
hurtling, tumbling toward your landing
You might have been Athena looping down
to Earth to meet Odysseus, except
nobody was waiting for you on the beach
and Athena always makes perfect landings.
Like every actor and immortal you
survived catastrophe and earned applause.
But before you could acknowledge accolades,
dea ex machina, you had to crawl
out of your wreck and wait for stage hands
to lower a basket into which you climbed
and made a glorious departure skyward,
as though returning to Olympus.
It is to be hoped your fans' enthusiastic response
to your theatrical triumph will not tempt
you to offer a repeat performance.

(Nelson Daily News *Editor's footnote): This poem was written for Josie Abata of Kaslo who hit black ice on Highway 31A north of Ainsworth while on her way to Nelson. She and her Ford Tempo flew off a cliff and plummeted about 100 meters to the lakeshore, she says. "It was really just about complete surrender, because it was obvious there was nothing I could do to change the situation. When you surrender that completely, there's nothing but beauty and grace around," she says. "I remember the flight because it was a really beautiful day, and I remember how beautiful the sky was." Abata was unhurt.*

DISCOVERING THE OKANAGAN
Klaus Sturze

THE YEAR WAS SIXTY-FOUR, only four years after my immigration to Canada. I was living in Saskatoon, yearning to find a place, similar to Europe in climate and scenery, at which my family might spend the holidays. There was no such place in Saskatchewan.

A colleague working with me, had been born in Osooyoos, and he told me if I were willing to travel for two days across the prairies and mountains, I would find such a place in B.C. called the Okanagan.

Needless to say our desire to spend a holiday on lakes with beautiful beaches, wooded mountains and orchards, overcame the worry of traveling such a distance with two little girls, a wife and a dog.

Driving along Highway #3, I got my first look at this wonderful place. Standing high on Anarchist Mountain overlooking the southern Valley, my wife and I were overwhelmed with the beauty of what we saw. We made camp a few hours later in Summerland. The evening found us already in the lake.

Later, sitting around the campfire that evening, my wife and I decided this would become our new homeland. The valley had much which resembled the country where we were born. It would make our transition to live in a new country so much easier.

The following day was spent job-hunting, which was unsuccessful. Thirteen years and many holiday trips later, the day came when I packed all our belongings in a rental truck, along with my wife, girls, dog, assorted other pets, a store full of business furniture and headed out of Regina on the day of the first winter snowfall.

We arrived in Penticton on the fifteenth of October 1975. We have never regretted our decision to live in this magnificent valley.

The community has sustained our business now for twenty-eight years. I retired from professional life on the first of January 2003 and I'm fulfilling my lifelong dream of becoming a writer.

We raised our girls in relative safety away from the big cities. The people are friendly and forever helpful. Often, I have been asked, 'What is so special about the Okanagan Valley?' For me, it was finding it and having no desire to ever leave it.

DOUG COX:
BRINGING THE PAST TO LIFE!
Ken Larson

EDUCATOR, AUTHOR, HISTORIAN, photographer. That describes Doug Cox of Penticton, retired schoolteacher, who has been recording Okanagan history since 1982. He's authored eight local history books and is researching his ninth, *Ranching Now, Then and Way Back When* for publication in late 2004.

Doug and Joyce Cox in front of their kiosk at the Farmers' Market on a Saturday morning in Penticton.

A farm boy at heart, Doug lives on a small acreage with three breeding ostriches, several emus, three alpacas, some horses and Jenny, 17, one of three children still at home, and, of course, Joyce, the English born teacher he met while teaching elementary school in Penticton.

Doug was born in Wadena, Saskatchewan and grew up on his grandfather's old-fashioned farm—it had a smokehouse, an icehouse, a blacksmith shop, horses and cattle. While he was learning his ABC's, his mother was helping the Second World War effort by making Bren guns and his father was serving in the army. Doug left the farm for Vancouver to get his Bachelor of Education degree at the University of B.C. He taught in Hope and Kamloops before teaching local history in Penticton and meeting Joyce, also a teacher, and getting married in 1973.

Joyce and Doug are a tall, attractive, energetic couple who have been active in their church and community. At one time they did well raising cattle, buying in the Spring and selling in the Fall. When the price for fattened cattle dropped, they began breeding ostriches (from South Africa) and selling eggs and feathers, and for a while marketing the meat from these 750 pound birds to selected restaurants.

Doug began writing history as a contributor to the Penticton Western, a local bi-weekly magazine. During the 18 years between 1982 and 2000, he contributed over 1000 historical photos and captions. These were part of one of the largest private photo collections in Western Canada, many transferred to 4x5 negatives, but now scanned on his very efficiently organized computer system.

How does he acquire them? Many came from old-timers who read the stories and saw the pictures in his publications: Okanagan Roots, Rodeo Roots, Wagon Train over the Monashee, Heritage Tours, Pioneering the Peace, Best of the Western, S.S. Sicamous, Mines of Eagle country: Nickel Plate & Mascot. Doug has taped and transcribed the reminiscences of over 200 early valley pioneers. After reading one of his books, a man from Castlegar was so impressed that he sent him a box of 300 old pictures to use in his future publications.

When Doug first started writing and publishing his books, a B.C. Heritage Trust grant was available, but that is now finished and he has to finance his new publications by profits from sales in selected outlets in the Okanagan and Similkameen. He sells up to 90 books per month at the Farmer's Market in Penticton during the summer months. Each Saturday you'll find him in their kiosk, he with his books and Joyce with her ostrich eggs and feathers, and alpaca fibre. Drop by sometime and talk history!

DOWN HOME WITH ROSIE
Helen Wyatt

THE TROUBLE BEGAN WHEN BUD, (I call him that since they held the naming contest, and he calls me Rosie) started enlarging our underground dwelling. He insisted on burrowing more tunnels to make these big vent holes in the roof, smack up into the middle of the Penticton Rose Garden.

Naturally, these strange, pancake-sized holes marring the lawn alarmed the groundskeeper, Liz Smiley, a lady we'd observed for some time, and at all hours, lovingly tending her roses.

At first, we figured Liz assumed the rose thief had struck again. Bud and I had spotted this rose-napper, early in the morning and late at night when few people were around, carrying a plastic shopping bag and garden snips and stealthily and swiftly denuding whole bushes of flowers and buds. Bud thought it was a man but I voted for a woman.

Liz probably suspected this vandalism to be the work of some craft's person. I understand it takes a lot of dried petals to make that potpourri, and you need to dry a lot of roses if you're planning to make wreaths or some such dried flower arrangement.

Now, on top of the pilfered flowers, having these weird holes appear in her turf must have made Liz Smiley take note of our humble beaver lodge. Our home looks kind of messy from the top, just a pile of sticks and sun-baked mud, partly supported by the wire-link fence separating the rose garden from the lake.

Suspicion finally switched to us, both for digging holes and consuming roses. We beavers have sharp hearing, and we overheard plenty of the ensuing conversations. The powers-that-be got all worked up about the damage: Liz, the Rose Society people and the Park's Department. That's when the City Fathers hired the trapper to eradicate us. "Eradicate" being a polite term for murder. If they couldn't trap us they would tear down our lodge to persuade us to re-locate. Imagine the hostility!

"Not 'eradicate', 'evict' us," Bud corrected me. "They plan to catch us and move us someplace else," he said, then added, "I think."

"And lose my lovely home... Start all over again," I wailed, slapping my tail against the water.

"I never promised you a rose garden," Bud whined. I could have nipped him in the tail with my sharp teeth, joking at a time like this.

Bud is a big beaver, about four feet long I'd venture to guess. That's one of the reasons I chose him for a mate. That and his giant incisors, chisel-sharp I tell you, the better to fell trees with, good teeth being an important attribute if you're planning to raise a family. We had the two kits last year and two kits again this spring. That's why we need more room. Kits don't leave home early. It takes two years at least to train our offspring in beaver lore; how to cut down trees, store food, groom their fur, build lodges and everything else a beaver needs to know before setting up a home and starting his own family.

Bud even takes them over to the concrete dam to inspect it for leaks, gives them an idea of what's required in a dam. Bud and I take parenting seriously and now this. Our family's game plan, was being threatened by an uncaring, homicidal trapper!

We located here in Penticton at Riverside Park on the south shore of Okanagan Lake about two years ago. We're near where the S.S. Sicamous, the old sternwheeler that plied the lake, is beached.

This site is a paradise, a lakefront view on one side, and the rose-garden in our backyard. Well, actually we built our lodge right under the wire-link fence at the edge of this garden. Those roses smell heavenly on a June day!

A question people ask, and they've written a book about it, is *"Do animals act out of instinct or intelligence?"* Well, we built right beside the dam on the Okanagan River Channel that connects Okanagan and Skaha Lakes. In fact, some of our relatives, who live along this water-way, say this all drains into the Columbia River at Pateros, Washington. The point is, we didn't need to build a dam to make a beaver pond - we have 75-mile-long Lake Okanagan here, ready-made.

Instinct or intelligence?

It had been a wonderful life until Bud attracted the attention of the authorities with his beastly vent holes, and now it might be all over, with that trapper on our tail, so to speak.

I've heard horror stories of how our ancestors were almost wiped out by trappers. There were those brave *couriers-de-bois* hunting us, and also those 'Gentleman Traders of the Hudson Bay Company', not to mention the Indians.

At one time the natives sort of revered nature. They called us their 'little cousins'. I guess they too were lured by all those European trade goods - guns, blankets, as well as sugar and so on. It became a consumer society and our beaver pelts were the currency.

They made my forebearers into hats, and sometimes coats. You've seen pictures of those Europeans wearing tall hats? Apparently, at that time if you didn't own a beaver hat, you were a nobody.

Those fur-traders made a fortune off my forefathers' backs! Fortunately, laws were passed before our species became extinct, giving us beavers protected status.

Now here in our hometown, a trapper was out to get us and our family. Bud, that wily rodent, managed to outsmart that old trapper though. All six of us, laid low whenever he was about. We're nocturnal creatures anyway - we work and play at night and sleep in the daytime. We always saw Mr. Trapper before he saw us and could just duck back into our lodge or into the secret underwater swimming channels we'd had the foresight to dredge, or we'd just dive under the S.S. Sicamous. No problem.

Weeks of this threat of capture began to take its toll, however. Always having to be alert for that trapper and getting ready to dodge him made me jumpy. I feared our family might develop some stress-related diseases if the constant living in danger kept up.

Despite all his crafty tricks the frustrated man failed to catch us. Also, the powers-that-be figured that if they tore down our lodge, the fence would collapse and a good section of the rose-garden topple into the lake.

About that time it dawned on someone at City Hall that a beaver is atop the City of Penticton crest. I could have told them the beaver is a national icon of Canada, right up there with the Maple Leaf and the NHL. We're even on the nickel!

"You know what Archie Long, the Parks Superintendent said about me?" Bud said one evening. The way he puffed up his fur I knew it would be flattering.

"Mr. Long said, and I quote, 'This is one guy who, through all kinds of adversity, seems to be able to survive, to raise a family, and even build a home. He's hard-working and he's smart. You've got to give him credit, really."

That Bud, he always seems to come up smelling like a rose! The upshot was, they grudgingly began to admire us for outsmarting them. Also in a tourist town we were quite a draw, a decided asset. They opted to 'leave it to beaver', as they put it, and to leave us undisturbed. They even held a 'name the beaver' contest with prizes.

A girl of ten won with "Bud" for him. Someone got a prize for 'Rosinbloom' for our family name. Then they threw in "Rosie" for me, the choice of a lot of contestants.

"A rose by any other name would smell as sweet, I always say," Bud remarked, quite pleased with our new status. "They're even going to put a little fence around our lodge with a plaque with our new names on it, maybe a little mailbox."

This whole thing inspired me to name our kits. Of the two-year-olds, the oldest male, an earnest little fellow, I call "Igor" ("Igor Beaver," get it?), and the light-coloured female, "Honey." The two we had in the spring, I'm calling "Thorne" and "Roseanne". Appropriate, I think.

Now that the dust has settled and we feel safer, Bud is getting quite bold. During the recent Rose Garden Tour he swam around out in the lake to the delight of the local entourage and the Asian tourists with their cameras. Talk about getting excited when they caught a glimpse of him!

They knew we lived here, but few people had ever seen us. The way things are going I'm afraid Bud is in danger of becoming a show-off.

Let me tell you, lately everything's coming up roses. We're going to enjoy the rest of the season playing, swimming, diving under the S.S. Sicamous, or just plain loafing around now that the addition to the lodge is completed. Later, we'll begin stockpiling our winter's food supply: We'll cut these willow branches and stick the pointy end in the mud, in case the lake freezes over - not likely but it has been known to happen, I hear.

Then we can just swim out our plunge-hole and have dinner-under-the-ice, then back down the plunge-hole into the comfort of our snug lodge.

On dark days as a special gourmet treat I've stored up a nice little cache of dried rose buds. I'm sure Liz Smiley can spare a few from her precious rose garden.

"Any comments to add?" I ask Bud.

"Tell them we Rosinblooms really 'dig' this Okanagan lifestyle," Bud, that perennial joker answers with a sly wink.

A Day At The S.P.C.A.
Janet Burkhart

I was helping out the other day,
Down on 8th at the S.P.C.A.
The fires had caused this frantic need,
To clean, and walk, water, feed.
A sign that said Aggressive cat,
I really couldn't imagine that.
I put my head inside its cage,
'Twas then she acted out her rage.
She hissed and growled and in two quick slashes,
Clipped me just below my eyelashes.
These faithful workers, heroes all,
Had exceeded far above their call.
So please remember these volunteers,
When donation time comes each year.
Employees who work at the S.P.C.A.,
All deserve extra danger pay.

THE DRAGON CHANGES SHAPE
Sonni Bone-Freeman

FROM THE TIME SHE WAS 'VERY LITTLE', Jeanette Beaven loved dragons, so her mother, Jill, not only drew them for her, she became a dragon every Sunday. On these Sundays, Jeanette would sit at the bottom of the stairs leading to the attic bedroom, where her dragon mother slept.

Jill worked six days a week. Jill's mother, who lived with them in their small house, would not allow Jeanette to climb the attic stairs on Sunday mornings until the dragon let out a giant roar to say she was awake.

"She would come bolting up the steps and hide under my bed," Jill recalled. "I would draw dragons for her whether she was upset, ill or happy or if she had done something good. Any excuse."

Out of those drawings and Jill's imagination came *Ms. Wiz* – the dragon who oversees the **Dragon's Den**, which started out as an off beat boutique, on Front Street in Penticton.

"She is a very feminine creature," explains Jill. "She loves to eat chocolates and get fat. She drinks pink tea, eats ripe Okanagan fruit, and wears pure silk. She doesn't live here all the time she just floats in and out. Even a nomadic dragon has to have a place to call home."

Jill, a single parent, managed Stocks, a former camera and gift shop on Main Street, for 14 years. Jeanette worked with her after school from the time she was 13. In 1987, the two decided to buy the old Murk Building on Front Street – accomplishing the long-held dream of having a place of their own.

A few old-timers may remember Front Street when its focal point was the Empire (later the Empress) Theatre. Next door to the theatre was the Murk Building, built in 1911 by Tom Murk, the barber. In one of the lower shops, Tom snipped, shaved and sheared. Above him the Empire Rooms took shape. The sign outside read: *Special Rates by the Week. With connections* – meaning (it's presumed) there was running hot and cold water, versus the jug with a bowl usually found in most hotels of the day.

For six months, mother and daughter, with volunteering friends, stripped the building – a maze – connecting what was once three separate buildings (joined in 1931).

"Anyone else would have ripped down the place," recalls Jill.

As the stripping took place a dirty but exciting adventure into the past unfolded. Doors and windows that looked onto nothing were uncovered. For 50 years various owners had done their own thing.

In some places we took off as many as seven layers of plywood paneling, lathe and concrete. Every time we took off a layer, we discovered another. I thought it would go on forever."

On top of those layers the spiders had done their thing for years, weaving the rooms thick with cobwebs – "some of them creations in themselves."

As the Murk Building shed its scales, another revelation showed itself. Under one of the many roofs being removed a brick courtyard was discovered, a very continental 'old English mews type' of courtyard.

Slowly, as renovations proceeded, the new-look Murk Building emerged – centered by the wondrous **Dragon's Den**, which was to change shape over the years. Over the deck above (once the old Empress rooms) separate suites were built for mother and daughter. The courtyard became a zocolo – Spanish for 'the center of any little Spanish town.' If Jill or Jeanette needed a breather, they sat in the zocolo and oversaw the whole store.

"I designed it like that. That's why my fountain is here," explained Jill, pointing to the re-circulating water wall, completely covered with silver lace vines and housing a fish pool at its bottom.

"We created a place where people could come and feel they were on holidays – where they could pick a country and almost revel in it," said Jill.

At times the den displayed all kinds of riches – hoards of silver and crystal jewels, masks, bedspreads, little 'worry' dolls from Guatamala, and Panama straw hats. Jill, who dealt with over 200 worldwide merchants, couldn't resist anything that intrigued her. Every time you walked into the den you found something new.

Jill is also a realistic businesswoman. "If a change can further sales it is done now." And she means it. The building has housed everything, a café, a hair salon, a dress shop, a shoe store and many others.

Today the den is the only complete artists supply store in Penticton. It houses racks of wondrous greeting cards and paper products from all over the world. Through it all, *Ms. Wiz* watches with her dragon's eyes. She goes into all the advertising and brings back dragon-size results. Her image appears on T-shirts and a line drawing of her etched in glass, stares out the store's front window, beckoning to all who pass.

Although Ms. Wiz would cringe at the very notion, she would not be a footloose, tail-flicking dragon if it were not for Jill's nimble fingers and wild imagination. Proof is in a special folder which Jill will show you – should you ask or not – filled with a collection of exquisite drawings of the dragon at her best.

Twelve of the drawings show *Ms. Wiz'* antics for every month of the year. In January she goes skiing. In February she devours chocolates (since they are sweeter than people). In March she house cleans, while in

April she starts garden pots. In May (mother's day) she is up to her ears in bubble bath and in July she books a cruise.

Children entering Jill's shop also get to meet her. Kids love dragons – they love to colour them. "So I make up different drawings of *Ms. Wiz* for different occasions – Hallowe'en, Christmas, et cetera – and hand them out as colouring sheets."

Another reason kids love dragons?

Jeanette has the answer, "You can always blame everything on them."

In most everything, like mother like daughter. What else should Jeanette call one of her business enterprises but *The Dragon's Daughter.* She opened another shop, *Jett Shoes,* adjacent to the Dragon's Den, selling shoes that are every colour of the rainbow – or of every dragon.

"Dragons," said Jill, "wake up each morning any colour they feel like being – blue, yellow or green. The fat ones are sometimes a pale mauve or pink."

When you ask Jill about her endless energy and her ability to always keep smiling, she announces, "It has something to do with not growing up."

With the revitalization of the Murk Building, gradually came the revitalization of Front Street – once the hub of Penticton's downtown core. Jill and Jeanette would like to see it that way again. The merchants on

Jill & Jeanette Beaven

Front Street helped with new lamp posts, cobblestone sidewalks, trees now grown taller, decked out nightly with brightly coloured lights. The atmosphere draws people, who enjoy strolling along the street at night.

"The revitalization has been a great success. It has certainly paid off for us."

Mother and daughter continue to work hard. They enjoy it. It is in their blood. As for *Ms. Wiz*, she too pulls her business weight and changes shape as required.

"We just don't know very much about her private life," said Jill.

DREAMS REALLY DO COME TRUE
Yasmin John-Thorpe

AS SOMEONE WHO HAS WATCHED the British Columbia wine industry over the years, one pioneer in particular deserves recognition.

Anthony von Mandl started Mission Hill Family Estate over 20 years ago and his unshakable determination and belief that the Okanagan Valley could produce world calibre wines has helped to put our province on the world wine map.

It all began when Anthony opened his wine-importing agency in Vancouver, British Columbia, in 1972. His first office, a 10x10 room next to the stately Queen Elizabeth Theatre went for the princely sum of $29.95 per month. His first desk was salvaged from a yard sale and refinished in his parents' garage. That first office was situated beside the men's washroom and he remembers sales calls being especially challenging because every time the toilet flushed, it sounded like Niagara Falls.

Despite that auspicious beginning, six years in, his Mark Anthony Wine Merchants started to grow in earnest and he expanded into California. But he still had a dream and that dream eventually brought him home. He wanted to own a winery and he wanted it to be in his native British Columbia, not Napa or Washington State.

"I knew I couldn't afford to build my own winery," he recalls. "I knew I'd have to find a winery in distress and somehow make it work." In 1981, he risked everything to buy a rundown winery high atop Mission Hill overlooking Lake Okanagan. What came next challenged him to the core.

"The conditions were deplorable. Everywhere I looked there was filth and it appeared as if everything needed to be repaired," he remembers. "The first thought that went through my mind was that this was the worst decision I'd made in my life. Basically, in my mind it was over."

Not one to give up, Anthony chose that moment to re-commit himself to his dream. He removed his suit jacket and tie, grabbed a hose and started washing down the flea and dirt covered fermentation tanks. So began his precipitous uphill climb to turn things around at Mission Hill.

Using the resources from other businesses, he set about upgrading the winery, but quickly discovered one almost insurmountable obstacle. Wines from British Columbia had an image problem.

"People weren't willing to open their minds to the possibility that decent wines could be made in the Okanagan," he says.

The advent of North American Free Trade in 1989, was to Anthony's mind, the saviour of the Okanagan's wine region. Two-thirds of the vineyards were ripped up. Classic grape varieties were planted and wines from British Columbia were, for the first time, on a level playing field with the rest of the world. For Anthony, 'the game was on and those key changes opened the door to the future'.

Mission Hill began to win awards, but Anthony knew if he was going to take the winery to the next level, he would need to find an experienced winemaker willing to accept the ultimate challenge of putting a young, unknown wine region on the map.

He found that person in John Simes, then chief winemaker at Montana Wines, New Zealand's most recognized winery. Simes was at the top of his game, but he was getting restless and wanted a new challenge. It took Anthony ten months to woo Simes to British Columbia, but his effort paid off handsomely from the outset.

His first vintage, a 1992 Chardonnay, stunned the wine world by winning the International Wine & Spirit (IWSC) trophy for *Best Chardonnay Worldwide* in 1994. Anthony recalls the judges were so shocked by their choice, they insisted on re-tasting. Mission Hill won again and after a quick lesson on how to pronounce the word O-k-a-n-a-g-a-n, the prize was announced.

Entering Mission Hill Family Estate   *Photo by Brian Sprout*

"John and I were in a meeting when the call came through and we were both thunderstruck," he recalls. "It was the first major turning point for Mission Hill, and I believe, for wines from the Okanagan Valley."

That pivotal win gave Anthony the confidence to begin a series of unprecedented investments in vineyards and winemaking. With those areas in hand, he continued to press ahead with his vision. It was time to anchor the valley by creating a destination winery.

"Building a winery, which would draw visitors from the world over was absolutely key," he says. "It had to be an architectural statement unlike any other."

Proprietor Anthony von Mandl (right) is joined by his mother Bedriska (center) and his sister Patricia (left) at the winery's opeing in 2002.

During the winery's official opening, 21 years after he purchased Mission Hill, Anthony reminded us all that dreams are never far from his mind. Quoting Henry David Thoreau, he said 'If you have built castles in the air, your work need not be lost; this is where they should be. Now…put the foundations under them,' and that is exactly what Anthony did with his beloved Mission Hill Family Estate.

What strikes me most is that despite a host of incredible achievements, Anthony insists that he's not done yet. He remains determined to see wines from Mission Hill Family Estate considered among the very best in the world, despite the region's relative infancy. He is resolute in his commitment to increase awareness about the Okanagan and its wines, both domestically and internationally.

But, in the end, what ultimately drives him is the fact that 200 years from now, someone will visit Mission Hill Family Estate and wonder what inspired the creation of such a special place and perhaps even begin to realize a dream of his own.

My sincere thanks to Corinne Kovalsky for her valuable input to this story.

ECHO LAKE SUMMERS
Dawn Renaud

I WAS THIRTEEN the summer of '73. It was the season that marked the end of my childhood, and among the lessons I learned two stand out: how to work, and how to eat bread.

From the time I was eight, my family lived on a nine-hundred acre ranch at the east end of Echo Lake. The power line ended about where the school bus stopped, some seven miles closer to Lumby. Our only neighbours for miles around were Eve and Ray Hodge and their teenaged children, Ralph and Charlene. The Hodges had come regularly from the coast to camp at Echo Lake Resort, and eventually bought the business. I don't really remember the original lodge, other than it was an older log structure, quite dark inside. I do remember Charlene showing me the facilities: a large bowl with a handle that was stored under the bed, appropriately known as a thunder-mug.

The lodge had burned down around '70, taking with it a lot of history and virtually everything the Hodges owned. Mrs. Hodge had managed to rescue Charlene's pink formal gown so she'd have something appropriate to wear in the upcoming Miss Lumby contest. As far as I know, there's still a portrait of Charlene wearing that dress in the village office.

By the summer of '73, the lodge had been rebuilt as a roomy building with a small store-front off the kitchen, a small dance-hall, a real bathroom, and, upstairs, three good-sized bedrooms for the summer help.

That was where I came in.

Our family was typical of most in the Lumby area: long on kids and short on cash. My friends and I were happy to get clothing that was brand-new, never mind designer labels. And when it came to school supplies and pocket-money - well, you just made do. So although Mr. and Mrs. Hodge had never hired anyone as young as thirteen, they were good people and, knowing there was really no other way for me to 'find work,' they kindly offered me a job.

I was something of a hopeless case from day one. On the Friday afternoon of the July long weekend, Mr. Hodge pulled into our yard. He quite patiently explained that I was late for my first day of work. No, I wasn't to start on *Monday*: This was a *long weekend. Long weekend* plus *summer* plus *resort* equals *work*. I threw some stuff into a suitcase and hopped in the truck. I was off to join the ranks of the gainfully employed.

Although the resort was only a couple of miles away, I was expected to live-in with the rest of the staff. Work started at 8:00 a.m. and carried on into the evening, until the last guests had arrived and been properly taken care of. Proper care consisted of "greeting" each carload of guests as they arrived, determining whether a campsite, a cabin, a boat or a picnic table was sought, and sending the traveler-in-charge to the office for further information, registration, or, on rare occasions, so that a person of authority could explain that rabble rousers were not welcome. 'Greeting' required a cheery disposition and a good knowledge of what we had to offer and at what cost. I was shy. I got over it. I knew nothing about the resort. I learned fast.

Mrs. Hodge handed down the work ethic she had learned from her first boss: you are paid for your time. You do what the boss asks you to do. And you do it right.

There were some unusual communication problems. "Dawn," she would say, "bring me that thingamabob."

Thingamabob? I'd stand dumb and idle, trying to think what on earth she wanted, until she'd notice my usual blank stare and follow up with an exasperated: "The doofer. It's over there, on the whatsit!"

I learned to translate.

I learned to tie up tomatoes, to weed, to water properly. The power generator was turned on one day each week. During that time water was pumped up to the gravity-feed holding tank at the top of the driveway. While the pumps were running the gardens were thoroughly soaked, so their roots went deep to where the ground stayed moist through until the following week. While the power was on, the two wringer-washers were pulled out and put to use. Laundry was hung from long clotheslines, accessed from a high platform that doubled as a roof for the compost heap - a low wood-sided bin which also housed the dozens of worms my brothers sold to the lodge for re-sale to the guests as fish bait. As needed, we'd dig the worms up and drop them into a bit of dirt in a clean tin can.

The cabins needed to be cleaned to a state of spotless perfection: no dust on the baseboards, no fingerprints on the windows. Although my mom had instilled in me an appreciation for 'hospital corners,' I learned that a bed was not made correctly unless a quarter dropped flat onto its surface would bounce back off it. There were nine cabins of varying configurations and ages, some quite old and some brand-new, but all were rustic. Translation: woodstoves, oil lamps and water that 'ran' only if you trotted while carrying the bucket up from the lake. Each cabin had an outhouse, and an ice-box: a small metal refrigerator kept cool by a block of - you guessed it - ice, placed in the top compartment.

The ice came from Echo Lake. Each winter an ice-cutting day was proclaimed. Dad would drive his tractor over to the resort, and then down onto the ice of the lake. Hanging from the tractor's bucket was a heavy set of tongs. Chainsaws roared all day; Dad used the bucket to pull block after block from the lake. The men cut each huge cube into smaller ones and loaded them into trucks, hauling them up to the ice house, which was a shed-within-a-shed, the space between the walls filled with insulating sawdust. The ice blocks were unloaded onto a layer of sawdust on the floor, then the blocks were covered with another layer of sawdust for good measure. Come summer, guests would pay five cents a pound for one of us to chip a good-sized chunk to keep their fridges cold.

The kitchen in the lodge was equipped with two propane fridges and lights, and - thank heavens - real genuine running hot water. Much of my first couple of weeks were spent in that kitchen, helping to prepare meals for the crew, and cleaning up afterward. I shone at neither. Years later, Mrs. Hodge still casts her eyes toward the heavens in mock-supplication as she recalls how very long it took me to wash a single dish. Apparently I had a propensity for daydreaming.

Sometimes, though, the amount of time it took to clean up had nothing to do with my lack of skill. Sometimes, it was simply a consequence of someone having broken that most significant of mealtime rules: thou shalt fold thy bread.

Woe betide the fool who forgot this rule. Mrs. Hodge watched over the table with an eagle eye. An open-faced slab of bread slathered in jam, or peanut butter, or honey, or any combination of delicacy, never approached anyone's lips un-noticed. If that careless diner sat within reach, Mrs. Hodge herself would reach over and, with a perfectly-timed upward flick of her wrist, smear the sandwich dressing all over the unwary eater's face.

Because she sat at the head of a rather long table, she often noted a rule-breaker beyond her reach. In these cases she would deploy an enforcer. If you were sitting next to her, a sudden kick to your ankle would get your attention. A raised eyebrow, then a slight tilt of her chin would indicate the target.

While one seldom retaliated against Mrs. Hodge herself, her enforcers were considered fair game, so any smearing-by-proxy always resulted in an all-out food fight. Food could be supplemented with other less-tasty stuff: shaving cream, for example. And once all this mess was thoroughly worked into the girls' long hair – well, the boys figured it was only chivalrous to help wash it out.

They did this by throwing us in the lake.

We showed our appreciation by giving their laundry some nice finishing touches. We stitched the flies on their underwear shut. That was when we learned that many boys never use their flies. However, almost everyone puts on their jeans one leg at a time. We folded their jeans as usual, then hand-stitched an almost invisible seam across one pant leg, about knee height. When the young man's foot hit the extra seam, there were interesting results. Sadly, as the boys shared quarters, this only worked once per summer. When one had toppled, the gig was up.

Applying plastic wrap to the toilet bowl was successful too, but since we girls had to clean the bathroom the boys had the last laugh. So, we short-sheeted their beds.

Streaking had become popular in the cities, and a couple of the guys decided to bring this trend to our neck of the woods. In the semi-dusk of the Saturday-night barbeque and dance, the assembled crowd observed two full moons slip out of the garage and drift quickly over the hill and around the back of the lodge. Meanwhile, Charlene trotted into the garage and collected the heap of temporarily-discarded clothing, cannily locking the door to the lodge before running the cast-off undershorts up the flagpole.

Good times.

We worked hard, we played hard. I learned much.

By my third summer, I was "head girl." This meant I checked the cabins to see if they were up-to-standard, and if not, took responsibility for re-training the new girl. I was left in charge of the operation on a long weekend. And I was impressed with the new boy's trick of removing every stick of furniture from the girls' room. (He'd even dismantled the beds and tucked them into the rafters of the attic.) That was my last Echo Lake summer; the Hodges sold the business, and I moved on to work a summer at Pinaus lake, outside of Falkland. But that's another story.

AN ODE TO THE OKANAGAN SUMMER
Klaus Sturze

Summer, oh summer you're here,
we need hardly anything to wear.
Not a single cloud and all the girls are out
who seem to have nothing to wear, here, here.
Oh summer, you're here,
what a wonderful time of the year.
The sun rises so warm and bright,
pushing away the coolness of night.
Let everyone have fun, in the sun,
in water or sand, all over the land.
Boats crisscross the lake, trailing a glittering wake.
What fun in the sun.
Oh summer, oh summer you're here,
what a wonderful time to drink some cheer,
and watch the poor girls who have nothing to wear.
Oh summer, oh summer you should always stay here.

A Feathered Lake Friend
April Fortin

Last summer when my dad, Pat, my sister, Ayla, and I headed out from Peachland for a four-day sailing trip on Okanagan Lake, I didn't know I'd find a new lake friend. One who would swim right up to me. (No, not the legendary lake monster, *Ogopogo.*)

We planned to head up through the Westside on our sailboat *Catspaw*, enjoying the scenery along the lakeshore, before continuing on to Kelowna and Vernon, where we would spend a couple of days, before heading home. *The wind was with us*, as my dad would say, and we arrived in Kelowna in just a few hours.

Before we could go any further up the lake, we needed to pass under the Okanagan Lake Floating Bridge. But our mast is too tall, and the bridge's lift span only goes up at certain times. If you miss it you're out of luck until the next time. So we reduced sail and motored around nearby for about a half-hour, waiting.

Suddenly, the bridge buzzer rang out alerting us that the bridge span was about to go up. Dad turned the boat around and heading straight for it, when suddenly something dropped straight down into the water next to us — *Splash!* It began to flap around wildly. Ayla screamed, "Wait, Dad! There's something in the water! It's hurt!"

"Turn around!" we both screamed.

"But we'll miss the bridge lift," he said.

"Turn around!"

Reluctantly, Dad swung the rudder and we headed back in the opposite direction.

"It's a bird!" I gasped.

I leaned over the aft port side of the boat and held out my hands and to my surprise the struggling bird flapped across the water, using its wings as oars, and fluttered straight into my open hands! I lifted it into the boat.

"It's a pigeon!" said Ayla, and we both stared at the dark grey bird.

"Okay, hang on!" shouted Dad as he swung the boat back around and headed at full speed under the raised lift span. We made it just at the last second.

Once on the other side, Dad raised sail, and we headed up the lake while my sister and I checked out the bird. It seemed to be happy for the rescue. We quickly found it a box and gave it a small bowl of water.

For the next few days "Pidgey" became my best friend, cooing at me and climbing into my arms every chance it got. We had a great singing duet going. *"Cooooo cooooo cooooo!"*

Unfortunately, we didn't have any birdseed, so we searched the cabin of our boat for something for it to eat. We found hotdog buns with sesame seeds on them. Pidgey enjoyed pecking off the seeds.

Sometimes when it was the hottest part of the afternoon, I would sprinkle water on the bird and it would dance around under the shower like a happy kid, bobbing its head up and down and cleaning under its feathers. When I would relax on the deck under the sun, Pidgey would jump onto my lap and enjoy the scenery.

April, 13, holding Pidgey & Ayla, 15, coming out of the sailboat's cabin.

Photo by Pat Fortin

In Vernon we anchored near a swimming bay and camped there overnight. The other kids were very interested in my new pet, which loved to swim with us. When it was time to get back onto the boat, Pidgey flapped aboard too, like he was one of the family.

He seemed to be getting better, and was able to fly a bit, but stuck close by anyway. Maybe it was the good food. Sometimes when the sailing was smooth, we put him in the dingy trailing behind us and other boaters would look puzzled as we sailed by. At night, we only partially covered his box outside, so he could leave if he wanted to. But, he was always there in the morning.

Then a strange thing happened as we were heading home. We were approaching the floating bridge in Kelowna again, when Pidgey suddenly lifted his head. He seemed to recognize the area. Before we knew it he lifted up his wings and flew off.

I guess he was home.

I was sad to see him leave, but happy he was home. We think that he was probably injured or stunned when the bridge span lifted up on the

78

first day of our trip and it knocked him into the water. He had recovered now.

Pidgey left us a special little gift before he flew off. But that was okay. Dad cleaned it up with a paper towel. My dad thinks this is probably what Pidgey said when he joined his old bird friends, staring down at us from their roost on the bridge:

"You'll never believe what happened to me. I went on a boat ride with some very nice humans. They fed and bathed me and we rode all the way up to this place at the far end of the lake. It was beautiful. But I couldn't believe it...they had no bridge there.

"But I'm glad to be home. What's for dinner? Not worms and dry grass again!"

THE ROUGH EDGE OF THE MOUNTAIN
Elizabeth Woodford

The swirling wind
flows through my hair
The sun shines high
I feel the air

The pale blue sky
with clouds fluffy white
The soaring eagle
takes flight

The rough edge of the mountain
The trees flow in the wind
The dust flies around
Birds fly by without sound

The silence as day
Passes thru to night
Night rodents appear
What a sight

The moon is full
Shining bright
Now is the time
I say Goodnight.

FIRE IN MY OWN BACK YARD
Faye Rothlander

IN THE AFTERNOON OF August 22, 2003, I was leaving my house to visit some friends when I saw on the Okanagan Falls horizon the ominous tell-tale smoke clouds of a wildfire. The enormous fire cloud from Kelowna had marred the previous day. But this was so much closer. The weather had been extremely hot and dry the last few months and I knew right away how dangerous a fire would be.

When the electricity went out at 4 p.m., it was not too hard to cope with that.

I arrived at my friend's house, where I was surprised by a group of ladies who wanted to celebrate my birthday. The conversation turned to the fire. My experiences with a similar situation in Alberta came to my aid. I think when you have gone through the experience of selecting what you absolutely want to save from the fire, it is easier the next time. After about two hours we all went home.

One of my friends was very distraught. Her house was very close to the fires; her street was on a high evacuation alert. She had a very valuable doll collection. They would not fit into the small camper they would take if they had to move away from the fire. I asked her to bring the dolls to my house. Being in the town proper and somewhat farther away from the flames, they would be safer. That was the plan, but when she went home, she almost could not get to her house. The streets were all closed. We changed plans. I went as far as I could and she came from the other side. We exchanged the suitcases full of dolls and said goodbye. I had now seen exactly where the fire was.

When I came home I decided to use the daylight and get at least some suitcases out of the corner where they were hidden and get the cat transport ready... just in case. After four hours the electricity came back on and confidence rose. A while later there was a knock at my door. An official person handed me the evacuation alert paper. After some thought I decided I had done enough so far and would wait to see what developed.

I had a good night's sleep.

The next morning an enormous airplane surprised us by flying over our roof. When we went outside, there they were five yellow water bombers from Quebec. They came down so low I could not believe they missed the trees or our roofs. I called them 'Buckaroos' and quickly found my camera for some very interesting pictures.

They would dip into Skaha Lake right behind our house to fill up with water to fight the flames. Each one had a certain flight path. Number 242 came the closest to my balcony. They worked hard, long hours. I found it very exciting. I felt so helpless against nature's fury. The water bombers were like powerful fighters. Somebody said it felt like in the war and he was right. My memories from the Second World War were very fresh those days. It was, after all, a war too.

On Sunday word was out that the firefighters, who erected their tents in the schoolyard, needed some dessert after their meals. Somebody went around and asked everyone he could find to bake or buy something for them. Everyone who knew about it did something for the firefighters.

That made me very aware that the communal danger had brought us closer together. Neighbours who before hardly said 'Hello' began to talk. We were out of our homes, watching the planes and talking.

As the firefighter camp increased, the real danger to the town decreased. When I visited my friend on the hill we could see the flames jumping from tree to tree and the trees surrendering to flames. But the fire moved away from the town. At least that was good news.

On the next day I had to spend a few hours in Penticton. I had a great wish to thank those pilots for their work. It must be very dangerous to fly so low, and so precisely. How could I get in contact with those lofty guys?

I spent part of my time in Penticton at the airport. I asked around if anybody could tell me how I could get to the water bomber pilots to say a thank you. Nobody knew. But I was sent to a group of buildings at the beginning of the street to the airport where the fire people were housed.

The first and only person I spoke to was the fire Chief himself. I had no idea who he was. I put my request to him. He must not have had much sleep or something, because he complained bitterly the pilots got all the glory, while the ground crews did so much more … and so on. I told him he should thank the ground crews from me and now, how could I get to the pilots? He told me to go to the end of the road, past the airport tower. But he also warned me there would probably be nobody there and that I should come back about noon.

Somewhat deflated and disappointed I went back to town. But when I thought it over, it became clear if I didn't do this right now, it would not happen. I would lose my courage. So I drove back to the airport. This time I went right towards the area where the planes stood. I reached a chain link-fenced area. 'Authorized personnel only' was written on a big sign. I parked my car just inside and got out. I entered a building where a very friendly young man listened to my request and gladly agreed to go with me. I was lucky. One of the yellow planes had just come in. The young man beside me assured me he was looking forward to me thanking the pilots. He expected them to be very embarrassed. I assured him that I did not believe that, since I was no longer a young woman.

The men had just climbed out of the plane when I gave my impromptu 'Thank you' speech. "And especially number 242," I said. "He comes especially close to my house." Several pointed to him. I gave him, and his co-pilot, a quick hug.

The next day the Canadian Army moved into Okanagan Falls. They also came to help. I do not think I will ever again be as close to the army as here. I went around to their camp. The nurse and the doctor sat outside the hospital tent. They were very eager to talk. I was shown around the field operating room. It was all very interesting.

Ten fire engines from the lower mainland also came to our aid. Now the fires are out and everything has settled down to a dull roar.

5H

Sharon Ward

THERE ARE A LOT OF DREAMS which somehow never come to fruition. Others give even greater rewards than expected. This is such a story.

Billy and Maud Whiting's dream began in 1919 with five Leghorn chickens. Billy had served in World War I and Maud was a nurse in Queen's Hospital, England, where they met. In 1919 they moved to Canada to a five-acre plot of brush in then remote Port Kells, in what is now Surrey. Out of this bush they carved a farm. The sign above the gate read:

NO DRONE
BREEDERS OF HIGH RECORD
SCW LEGHORNS
ROP REGISTRATION
W. WHITING, PROPRIETOR

It was here ten years later that 5H was hatched. She had spent twenty-one days in a crowded, warm incubator, where loving hands turned her twice daily and held her egg to light for candling on regular occasions. Once out of her shell, she joined hundreds of other hatchlings under bright, heated brooder lights. When feathered and able to withstand colder temperatures, she found herself in the large whitewashed room of a hen house. Even better, as she grew her time outdoors foraging for bugs and seeds increased. By the time she was a pullet, this was her regular daily experience. But that would soon change.

The chicken farm that had begun with five birds had by this time swelled to around 500 birds. It was, by nature of the business, necessary to keep only the best of the birds for laying. Some were shipped for meat, some, including breeding pairs, were sent world wide to other poultry farmers. Eggs were sold in Vancouver and across Canada. Of course the best breeding pairs were kept at No Drone.

5H was one of those kept for laying. Already the farm had won honours for a cockerel in the Ottawa Poultry congress of 1927.

Just one short year after her birth, in 1930, 5H participated in a government trap nesting program. As the term suggests each bird was trapped so the eggs could be picked up and counted daily. Special agents from the Agassiz Experimental Farm would come regularly and monitor the whole process and even take over the trap nesting of the up to 300 birds in the program. This program ran from October to October.

In the trap nesting program year, 1930, 5H laid 356 eggs in a 365-day period, setting a world record that may never have been broken. Certainly it hadn't up to around 1980. But then chicken farming had radically changed in the ensuing years. In any case, at the time, great honours were bestowed upon bird and farm alike.

In 1934 when 5H died it was decided to have her mounted and displayed in a local museum, where she resides to this day. Her stuffed form was taken to Rome, Italy that year and put on display at the World Poultry Congress there.

Many years after Billy died, in 1943, Maud, having reached an age where memory fails, couldn't recall where she had donated 5H. She wrote long and tirelessly to several museums to try and locate the bird.

The bird was not at the Provincial Museum, nor like all the other information on the farm, at the Surrey Museum. She resided instead at the British Columbia Farm Museum in Fort Langley, B.C. She has now been in that facility's care for almost 70 years. She resides in a glass case, and while there are few who grasp the significance of a Single Comb White Leghorn from a five acre farm in old Port Kells, making it to the top of the poultry world, this does not lessen her glory.

ODE TO A FINCH
Ken Larson

I have a little friend
His breast is red as red can be,
He sits upon a rail and keeps me company.
He trills a merry tune in such sweet harmony,
I hear the praise of heaven in the song he sings to me.

FLY AWAY
Helen Wyatt

I LAY IN AGONY on the highway amid my scattered feathers for hours. Then, just before dark, two women in a jeep stopped. *"This poor owl has a broken wing, I think,"* I heard the driver say. *"We must get him to the Owl Rehab Centre."*

She threw a towel over me and wrestled me into the back seat, though I did my best to claw her. Once she removed the towel, I gradually calmed down and actually basked in all their concern. That ended when the driver cried out:

"Look! There's the hawk I got the phone call about."

They pulled over. Then, to my chagrin, they put this gross-looking hawk in back with me. Tattered feathers. Blood all over him. Totally disgusting.

"Yeuch!" I hooted. "Just watch where you're stepping, Buddy." He glared at me out of one beady eye. The other eye seemed swollen shut.

"I got rights," he finally squawked. "Don't try pushing me around."

"I'm warning you, Hawk," I sternly said, " keep your big, dirty talons at your end of the seat."

"Listen," he said. "I don't want trouble. Being shot today's enough grief."

" Indeed! Well a speeding car hit *me*. Do you hear me whining?"

"So, wise old owl," he had the nerve to sneer, "you didn't see the car coming?"

I gave him a fierce look. Up front the women seemed unaware of our little squabble in the back seat. "Say, Owl," the hawk said to me, "why do you keep staring at me like that? Don't you ever blink?"

"When I choose to. Tell me, you miserable little bundle of feathers, just who shot you, and where?" I shifted my position to ease the pain from my broken wing.

The hawk answered in a plaintive voice, "A hunter took aim at me back there in that big orchard. His idea of sport, I guess."

I shook my head. "I mean, where on your sorry carcass were you hit?"

"Left leg. You weren't wise enough to notice my limp?" Now, in the dim light, I could make out his wound.

"Listen, I couldn't be less interested in a scruffy bird like you," I said. "Especially one who smells so foul. Ha, Ha. Get it? Smells so *fowl*!"

"Hunh! Very funny, Professor." He paused, then said, "Where are they taking us, do you know?"

"Some sort of bird-hospital. Seems as though this woman Sharon runs it, and the other one must be a volunteer helper."

"Bleeding-heart do-gooders, eh? I hope they have food at their pad."

For the rest of the trip I gave him the silent treatment. If he stirred near the invisible line dividing our territory, I ruffled my feathers menacingly. They unloaded us at this little cement-block building. Then they filled out admittance forms for us, just like for human patients going in hospital.

"Is this a Pygmy Owl?" the volunteer asked Sharon.

"Look on the wall-chart," Sharon instructed, *"and compare the wing shape and length."*

Of course I could have told her, 'I'm a Saw-Whet Owl, and this other ratty bird is a Red-Tailed Hawk.'

They disinfected us, dosed us with painkillers, medicated the hawk's gunshot wound, splinted my wing, and gave us a bit of food and water. Then they placed the hawk and me in separate cages. Cages! Were my nights of flying free in the woods over? After a night of misery, next morning I glowered at the hawk. "I hope you don't plan to squawk like that all day long too, Red! I need rest."

He stared back, evilly. "Well, my leg doesn't just tickle, you know. Think you're a tough old bird, don't you, Professor?"

"I'm no cry-baby. Too much character and pride." I tried out my best, unblinking, contemptuous stare on him.

He cocked his head to one side, a sneer on his face. "A wise old owl sat in an oak," he began reciting the nursery rhyme. I merely shrugged, tucked my head under my good wing, and went to sleep.

For days, as our wounds healed, we both felt low and droopy. Sometimes we exchanged insults. Of all the

obnoxious companions to be stuck with in a bird-clinic, this bedraggled hawk rated high. The caretakers began feeding us more solid fare. Tasty little white mice, in fact. In back of the clinic, I learned, they raised cages of them for food for us bird-patients.

One morning Sharon said brightly: *"Well, boys. I think you two are ready for a little exercise. Today we try the flight cage."*

I perked up. I saw a glimpse of freedom! The flight cage provided us a more open-air experience. Built of upright wooden bars spaced apart, inside it had log perches. When Sharon let Red go first he just hip-hopped along the ground. Afraid to step down on his bad leg, it looked like.

"Who, who," I said, "You call that flying?"

"Oh, shut your flat little feathered face," he snapped.

When my turn came I could just manage little wing flutters that carried me about two inches off the ground. Red preened his feathers and chortled. I felt like flying at him and pecking out his eyes. Except that Sharon stood there, watching. After a few more of our feeble tries at flying, Sharon took us back to our cages inside the bird-clinic.

"More practice tomorrow," she promised.

The flight cage training became the highlight of our days. Progress was slow but in time we got promoted to the log perches for our take-offs. Now the hawk and I competed to see which of us could fly well enough to be released first.

"Everyone knows hawks soar way above owls," the hawk claimed.

"Just watch me, Red," I shot back. "I'll shake the dust of this place long before you do."

Two days later, I was proven right. The girls staged a little ceremony to see me off. "Who, who!" I said to Red who sat sulking on his perch inside the flight cage watching, his expression mean and sullen.

They took me out to a little knoll where I could smell the piney woods beckoning. *"Bye, bye, little owl,"* Sharon called.

With one last triumphant glance at that Red-Tailed Hawk, I flew boldly off to freedom, dipping my wings in farewell to the waving women below who had saved me.

FORGET ME NOT
Charlene Friesen

WHILE LEANING ON MY SHOVEL one hot Abbotsford afternoon, I surveyed my landscaping project to date and made a mental list to self. Grass planted? Peat moss mixed with the soil? Muscle toning rock border in place? Major shrubs planted?

Still, something wasn't quite right. The dirt was too clean and tidy, the plants looked too regimental. I needed a few rambunctious plants to kick up their heels and loosen up my sensible and solemn garden.

Unfortunately, I had just pruned my money tree so a trip to the plant nursery was not an option. I drove to the next best source for plants - my parents' garden.

Armed with my spade and a box, I spied some alyssum and a blue weed like plant. "What's this?" I asked my dad, pointing to the weedy specimen with my muddy shoe.

"Those are called Forget Me Not," he said. "It's a self seeding plant and a super rockery filler."

Sold! I grabbed my shovel and eagerly dug up about twenty-five tiny, tender plants.

Once at home, I was pleased to see the sun had now side stepped my garden. I went right to work baptizing my new little flower friends with dirt and water. I dubbed the Forget Me Not "my ladies" and indulged them like a grandma who has nothing but time and chocolate bars for her

Photo by Steve Johnson of Alaska Essences

grandchildren. I unselfishly gave my attention, encouragement and healthy applications of fertilizer.

Soon, my ladies were perking up. They threw their shoulders back and in time were saluting me with their tender blue flowers. I enjoyed watching them spread their arms and twirl in the breeze. Their dance even spilled onto the rockery border.

As winter approached, I wondered how my ladies would cope. As the wind and rain fought for position, I anxiously peered through my window and hoped they were keeping warm.

In time, the sun nudged the winter rain aside and I wandered through my garden once again. My crocuses winked and nodded their colorful, smiling faces. Spring was open for business!

I stooped over my garden and nosily poked around in the soil. The ladies in blue were back with a vengeance! Not only had they hunkered down over the winter, they had flourished in the spring. It looked like my Forget Me Not had hosted a Christmas party and the guests never left!

In time, my sculpted, uptight garden developed a cheeky attitude. The shrubs relaxed and kicked off their shoes. Through the spring and summer, the Forget Me Not tirelessly filled my garden with vibrancy, chaos and a definite style of their own!

I want to be remembered as one who had a style all her own. I have already placed my order for a big bunch of Forget Me Not to be planted on my grave. Hopefully, family and friends will chuckle and remember me as a resilient little lady who willingly ventured onto the rocky, less traveled path.

Until that time, I will continue to give friends and family a tour of my garden and ample cuttings of Forget Me Not.

"Here," I'll say, as I stand amidst colour, delightfully dirty soil and endearing disorder, "let me give you something to remember me."

IMAGINE
MaxineRae

September on Sudbury Beach
Life no longer on fast-forward
A time with no stress
Relax into sun-warmed sand
Eyes half closed, watch fluffy clouds
Slow dance to the rhythm of the waves
Float content in the irrelevance on time
Alone at last on Sudbury Beach

GATEWAY TO THE MONASHEES (LUMBY)
Katharine L. Kroeker

OR AT LEAST THAT WAS LUMBY'S SLOGAN. To me, Lumby is the gateway to paradise. As a new reident of this beautiful little village, I've had much to learn about my new surroundings.

Lumby is nestled among the beautiful Monashee Mountains, in the north of the Thompson-Okanagan region, in the interior of British Columbia, Canada. Monashee means 'of peace' in Gaelic, and the mountains certainly live up to their name, protecting the tiny village of less than 1800 from the outside world.

You'll find Lumby twenty-four kilometers east of the city of Vernon. As you travel down Highway 6 anticipating your destination, you might get the feeling of driving down a long, winding driveway - one that has cattle grazing along its sides, and in places grain fields and cornfields. It's a relaxing drive. One that gives you time to unwind from the hurried pace of the city left behind.

Like many places, Lumby was named after a person. Moses Lumby was born about 1840 and came to British Columbia from England at about twenty-two years of age.

Some thirty years later, Mr. Lumby became a government agent in Vernon, also covering Lumby and the surrounding area. It was during this time, so one story goes, that Loris Morand applied for a liquor license for the local hotel. If granted, Lorand agreed to name the town after the then government agent, Moses Lumby.

Another story is that Mr. Morand was a friend of Moses and that he and his partner, Quinn Faulkner, having great respect for the man, named the town after him.

Which version is correct? Maybe we'll never know for sure, but one thing we do know is that by all accounts Moses Lumby was a man who was well respected and admired by many. Some might say he was an ambitious man as well, holding such offices as Gold Commissioner, Vice President of Shuswap and Okanagan Railroad Company, Justice of the Peace, President of the Okanagan and Spallumcheen Agricultural Society, Assistant Commissioner of Lands and Works, not to mention being a farmer and a mail carrier at one time.

In 1893, less than two years after having the village named for him, Moses Lumby died in Victoria, British Columbia.

As you come into Lumby, you are greeted by several of the many murals that grace this village. One such mural depicts the village in 1914 and hosts a portrait of Moses Lumby in the upper right hand corner. Michelle Loughtery painted this mural and many of the other ones in town.

Tucked within and protected by these majestic mountains of peace, the Village of Lumby is also a peaceful place, with side streets so quiet children can ride bikes carefree all day without much thought of danger. With little population change over the last five years, I believe Lumby is a well-kept secret. And I, for one, would like it to stay a secret. That may be selfish, but it's true, nonetheless.

I moved to Lumby from a much larger, noisier, hectic city, and it took some time to get accustomed to the slower pace. This pace however, was not totally new to me; I grew up in a village in Southern Ontario, very similar to Lumby. Moving here, I almost feel as though I am returning home.

I believe Moses Lumby would be proud of the village named after him. It is a place where neighbours know each other. They talk over the fence and share a laugh or two in the evenings, asking how the garden is doing and if all is well. I haven't heard any talk of wars or the latest burglary or drug bust; things all too common in the city. I love the fact people know each other here. Maybe more importantly, they really care about each other. Now, that isn't to say people don't care about each other in big cities. I'm sure they do. It's just that it's much easier to feel in a small town.

Living here, it doesn't take much imagination to feel that I have been transported back in time; to a time where communities worked together for the good of all, supporting one another in times of need, rejoicing together when things are good. It's much like it must have been in Mr. Lumby's day. The new slogan for Lumby is "Simply the

Best." I find it difficult to argue with that. Even though Lumby is a bit larger than the village where I grew up, I often have to remind myself that the two are not the same.

I feel blessed to have grown up where I did and I hope the young people of Lumby will feel the same way about growing up here, where it is, "Simply the Best!"

THE MONUMENTS WE BUILD
Esther McIlveen

Craigdarroch Castle, Victoria, "rocky oak place" in Gaelic.
Home of the Dunsmuirs; two sons and eight daughters.
Built in 1890 - 26,000 square feet, on an estate of 28 acres.
Four floors, 39 rooms, 17 fireplaces and 87 stairs to Tower.
Dancing floor, billiards room and maids' rooms.
One of North America's treasure trove castles,
built for men who grew wealthy by the
industrial transformation of a continent.
Robert Dunsmuir's climb to the pinnacle
of power on the backs of countless miners.
Thirteen years before Craigdarroch, a militia was
marched in to restrain striking miners.
Son, James, became Lieutenant Governor of B.C.
and built his own castle three times
the size of Craigdarroch on 650 acres,
Even though hundreds of workers had perished
in his father's dangerous mines.
Robert Dunsmuir never lived in Craigdarroch,
he died a few months before the castle was opened.
What gravestones we leave.

This piece appeared in the Richmond Review, May 2001.

GEARMASHER'S LAMENT
Shirley Dobie

A trucker's life is woe-be-gone cruel.
To do it at all he must be a fool.
In winter he freezes, in summer just fries.
His schedules get later the harder he tries.
Tires go flat, waybills in Dutch
'Bout all he can do is just double clutch.

The snow is swirling, he slides every time.
He'll have to chain up to make the next climb.
The pilgrim ahead won't let him by.
It's snowing so hard he can't see the sky.
Keep plodding on, you'll soon be at Trutch.
'Bout all he can do is just double clutch.

There's a jackknifed rig on Steamboat.
Some tourists tangle with a mountain goat.
The rhubarb is right where Lynden sits.
Bob-tailing in slime, don't call it quits.
Some coffee and pie won't be too much.
All we can do is just double clutch.

Mud's to the axle on the Edmonton run.
Got stuck out of Smith, he'll never get done.
The reefer has croaked, what a treat,
While hauling a load of hanging meat.
Chain up and gear down, the ruts are such
All he can do is just double clutch.

He's making a dollar, spending two.
Sometimes held up, other times gets through.
Roads like a circle, life is a loop.
Hang onto your hat and never droop,
'Cause curse or blessing it isn't much.
All you can do is just double clutch.

GREENWOOD'S
LEGENDARY COURTHOUSE
Sharon Prafke

TALK ABOUT YOUR ECHOES from the past to footsteps of today and you'd be referring to the stately Courthouse/City Hall dominating the corner of Government Street. For 100 years and counting this building has stood the test of time and the rigors of a rowdy few. From marriages to divorces, petty arguments to full blown fights, government appointed judges have sat on the raised coastal cedar dais to look upon the various faces of the spectators and those guilty as charged.

From the mid 1890's pioneers were eager to fell the magnificent old growth forest in their zest to stamp their names into the pages of Greenwood's past. That was over 100 years ago and from then until this very day the eight sweeping concrete steps greet visitors, prisoners, barristers, judges and mayors alike through the double glass panelled doors.

A wide spiral cedar staircase invites the casual observer to investigate the auspicious interior of the courtroom occupying the entire second floor. Above, on a balcony, a spectator's galley overlooks the courtroom drama below while a semi-circular stained glass window at the back bears the Coat of Arms of the existing seven provinces of Canada back in 1902.

If one lingers long enough they may hear the echoes of the Supreme Court of Yale, which once sat in session with the judge rapping his gavel insistently on the hard surface of his desk. Filtered light prisms cast extraordinary light through the circular stained glass ceiling panels, symbolizing the Saints of England, Scotland and Ireland, thereby comprising the Flag of the Union Jack.

Snapshots of frozen images flash before one's eye as an imaginary judge, garbed in his elegant black robe, presides over what once must have been a tremendously vibrant scene.

Perhaps the guilty offender was one of the 1200 forced Japanese internees during the Second World War. Or possibly a mischievous young man arrested for disorderly drunkenness in one of the sixteen notorious saloons. Nevertheless, as the sitting judge gazed up at the twenty-four-foot-high native cedar ceiling to ponder while staring at the hammer beam roof trusses constructed from Douglas fir, justice always reigned supreme for the young and old alike. It should be pointed out that numerous unruly individuals have occupied one of three prison cells down in the bowels of the dark, dungy basement.

Whereas the courthouse prevailed on the second floor, private rooms for the government agent, gold commissioner, mining recorder, registrar and sheriff's office originally spanned the majority of the main floor of this flawless structure.

Twenty-three mayors and their council members have sat adamantly in the dark cedar chambers to continue preserving the rich traditional debates and controversial meetings that perpetuate to this very day.

HER PEOPLE'S STORYTELLER
Yasmin John-Thorpe

TRACEY JACK BELIEVES her ability to be a storyteller has led to her career in making films.

"Being in that environment," she stated, "growing up in isolation and with close relatives, has contributed to the person I am today."

She can vividly recall life on the Penticton Reservation. Although a part of the community, the family lived rural and isolated from that community. Tracey talked candidly about the home with no running water or electricity, but of the place full of laughter and most of all, a time with grandparents, sharing stories about their people and their community.

"It was a really simple but creative time," she explained. "These were shared visits, where we ate together, not only with family, but with extended family – uncles, cousins and elders. We've adapted not only as a people, but as a culture."

It was through this adaptation of culture that Tracey found a new tool to embrace, a new medium to grasp as a storyteller for her people. She found her voice through film. Today, Tracey is a teacher, creative writer, producer and editor of cutting edge films and documentaries as well as a wife and mother.

She knows the exact incident, the turning point in her life, which steered her in the direction she stands at presently. Her uncle, August Armstrong, was a 'techno whiz' (she recalls). He had hooked up an old radio to a generator to listen to a program in Penticton on CKOK radio called 'Access.' It was a local show where listeners could call in, but since their home boasted none of the equipment to participate in the show, Tracey remembered as children they created their own Access show and her uncle recorded their performances.

In the 1970s, when the Band purchased a video camera to tape community programs and events, Tracey became fascinated by this new medium and volunteered to help tape anything happening, just to get her hands on the camera. She remembers taping her own skits at this time… she was only ten.

In the summer of 1983, when she was sixteen, the En'owkin Centre got an editing machine. Tracey worked on a drama "Cause For Alarm" about drugs within the young community. She produced and acted with ten youths age 16 – 25 years old. At eighteen, when she graduated from the Penticton Secondary School, Tracey had no idea of the future. She had no goal, but she knew she wanted to work. The Friendship Centre in Vernon hired her to host, produce and write for *Klahowya,* a current affairs weekly program. At the same time this evolved into a business, marketing and training others, while covering community weddings and conferences. Tracey obtained some large business clients for the show, but she needed and wanted to understand the technological side of everything.

She applied for and received training given through the Chief Dan George Memorial Foundation at the CCMA Program (Capilano College Media Arts). Tracey found the entire experience amazing and thrilling, "...but it was an unrealistic goal," she stated. "Who would hire me? Where would I get a job? I would not be able to make a living from what I had learned. So I did the next best thing... I took a Hospitality & Tourism course. It was something I could fall back on. It would help me to be a good manager and it would help the business side of producing."

Tracey moved back to the Okanagan and got a job catering. While working she volunteered for the next four years at local Shaw Cable studio, just to keep her hands in that medium. She now had the business skills but wanted to tap into her creative side. At that time Margaret Atwood was one of the Canadian authors invited to lobby the governments to let the En'owkin Centre offer a Fine Arts Program through the University of Victoria. Tracey registered at the International School of Writing at the Centre. She fondly recalled picking up the famous author, who had come to see the school and meet the students, at the Penticton airport with not the cleanest of cars.

Tracey, now twenty-two, realized she had a voice and issues, which were important to her and her family.

"That's when I figured I grew up," she said.

Tracey freelanced for CHBC TV in Kelowna. She began to produce one story a month for the television station. Her first piece featured her grandmother explaining the 'Bitterroot plant'. She recalled being both nervous and excited. At the same time Tracey continued to hold a full time job for a local band owned business in the resource industry.

"I took this very seriously," she explained. "I was not in the big leagues."

She eventually left the full time job with the Band and went to work for IASO (Indigenous Arts Service Organization) as a volunteer. At the time they were working on programs with the provincial government. After the person representing Penticton moved to Vernon, Tracey applied and was given the job. She has been the Program Director since 1999. It is a year round, part time position, which allows her to teach at the En'owkin Centre and concentrate on making films.

"At the end of the day I know why I'm doing what I'm doing," she said. "I want my children not to hang their heads, but to hold them up high."

Tracey continues to find her voice. She teaches a first year media arts course 'Preserving And Developing Our Traditional Storytelling Skills in Contemporary Media' at the En'owkin Centre to twenty students. She's won both first and second place in The Native American Journalists Association 2003 Best Documentary Award for *Crying in the Dark* and *REZcovery*, and won The BC Association Of Broadcasters Award Of Excellence. In 2003 she won the prestigious Gold Ribbon Award from the Canadian Association of Broadcasters for her riveting documentary *Crying in the Dark*. Tracey continues to receive nominations for her realistic cutting-edge films and documentaries.

In 2003 she also received a scholarship from Ryerson Polytech School of Film and Television to begin freelance programs on CBC Radio. Recently, her five-minute short film was selected in a National Competition, and was accepted for development by CBC Television.

Tracey resides on the Penticton Reserve with her husband and children. Her long-term goal is to produce a feature length documentary, which is currently in development. Her dream is to encourage aboriginal filmmakers to engage in modern story-telling filmmaking, which will be of the highest caliber and which will become the 'must see' films of the future.

Acknowledgements: My thanks to Tracy Jack for her assistance with this story.

HILDA LEHNER:
WAR, LOVE AND A MAIL ORDER BRIDE
Ken Larson

THEY WERE TWO WEARY, hungry girls who only wanted a few potatoes to eat. The farmer didn't care that they wore German army uniforms and had walked five days without food from Prague, Czechoslovakia, trying to keep ahead of the advancing Russian army at the end of the Second World War. He was German, too, but still he chased them away with his shepherd dog.

Hilda Lehner (nee Ruppert) and her co-worker, Fanny, were heading home to Berching in southern Bavaria. They had turned down an offer by a truckload of young German soldiers, who wanted to give them a ride in a crowded military truck. Some ride that would have been!

Hilda is unique. Five feet tall, and now 80 years old, she has been a resident of Penticton for 13 years. She still goes for fast, energetic walks and coffee at Walmart in the Peachtree Mall five days a week. You realize how spunky and resourceful she

Hilda, 30, in Germany.

was in her youth as you listen to the stories of how well she coped during the massive bombing raids by the Allies or of life as a conscript in the German army. She trained to become a nurse before the army recruited her to be a spotter of incoming Allied aircraft. The way it worked was this – a circle with numbers one to twelve was marked on a large field and as the enemy aircraft passed over, the staff would phone ahead to the main command post to tell them which direction the planes were going. There were many of these circles around Germany and they aided the artillery and air force to respond to the attacks.

Army life was harsh. Rations were skimpy. "Half the time," Hilda said, "we had nothing to eat. Sometimes we got a little extra. In Bulgaria we noticed that when a person died and was buried, the custom was to put food on the grave. So we would take the food for ourselves."

"When the Russian army was sweeping toward Germany," Hilda explained, "we were ordered to leave immediately. Our superiors had no time to issue passports to us. Without them we could be accused of being spies. The SS shot two of our army girls because they didn't have passports. We wrapped them in plastic and with the help of soldiers who were deserting, and we carried them for fourteen days across the mountains to Serbia. Others met the same fate as we discovered at the public fountain in another town. There we saw thirty blankets spread around, covering dead German soldiers in hospital clothes. The SS soldiers had shot them – their own countrymen – because they didn't have passports."

"When we were in Austria," Hilda continued, "the German soldiers said we couldn't cross the river because they were going to demolish the bridge to stop the Russians from using it. We didn't want to be caught by the Soviets, so Fanny and I ran as fast as we could and made it across the bridge just as it blew up. Then we had to get off the streets quickly to avoid being shot by the partisans. We had warned a friend not to ride a streetcar, but he did, and the partisans shot him and threw him onto the road as we watched."

Hilda finally met up with several dozen soldiers, who were amputees, needing medical care and not sure where to go. She had no money, so she offered to take them to a hospital if they paid her fare on the train. She took them to her hometown of Berching and after settling them in a hospital she was reunited with her parents.

On arriving home, she discovered her father had rescued a U.S. army lieutenant who had been captured by the Germans and had been hiding him in the house. Hilda delivered him to the U.S. force in the area and they asked her to serve as a translator in dealings with the villagers. When the Americans learned she was in the German army and hadn't told them, they jailed her for two weeks. Later she was jailed a second time, for a whole month, when she took an unauthorized ride in a German aircraft.

Several years after the war Hilda embarked on her next adventure: that of a Mail Order Bride. Hilda answered a classified ad in a German magazine placed by a former German paratrooper and prisoner of war who had moved to Canada and was living in Squamish, B.C.

Joe Lehner chose her letter from thirty-six others, and corresponded with her for three months. He travelled to Germany to meet her and married her in 1955. The couple spent many happy retirement years in Penticton before Joe passed away in 2001. This ended an ideal marriage full of love and without a single argument.

HISTORY OF FILM: HORNBY ISLAND
Gayle Nicholson & David Kilmartin

WE BY NO MEANS CLAIM to have written a complete and painstakingly accurate history of film on Hornby Island. There are holes in our timeline. Important figures may not have been unearthed in our loose research. The following are moments dug from deep ridges of collective gray matter and pulled together to remind us of the great value movies have played in the social foundation of the community and the contributions of those who gave us the viewing pleasure.

There is something about the social scene of attending a movie at the Hornby Hall that draws people to come early. There is a mixing of generations, from the babe put down to sleep to the octogenarian discussing how Woody Allen took up where Charlie Chaplin left off. The silver screen has been on the island for about fifty years.

Bertie Stonehouse and Bill Arthurs started bringing Islanders together for screenings at the hall back in 1951. Through a connection of Bill's, Rank movies were shipped from England every two weeks. Standouts from this time were the "Carry On" series and "Waterloo Bridge".

With no electricity on the island, Bill would arrive early to fire up the generator that powered the lights and projector. The films came on three reels and when one was over, the lights would come up, while it rewound and the next was set up. A few of the fellas would spend these intermissions in the parking lot drinking beer. "Everybody"(about fifty or sixty people) came to the movies. Admission was $1.50. The seats were long wooden benches.

Ginger Slade ran movies from the late 50s into the sixties. She was known to be an intense collector of movie fan magazines, amassing a veritable Hollywood archive. Problem was, Ginger had a higher love for Elvis and everything rock'n'roll, and as a result, she seemed bent on showing nothing but the King's flicks and various other forgettable films such as "Beach Blanket Bingo". Attendance dwindled, while Graceland-hate-mail postmarked Hornby Island skyrocketed.

Later on when the effects of "Blue Hawaii" were fading and the shuddering had ceased, Carol Quin and Richard Martin took a new approach to showing films on the island. They brought in films as part of the school program. The success of this grew into adding Canada Film Board shorts made by notables such as Norman McLaren. The fall of '73 saw Judy Cross step behind the projector. Judy brought in mostly artistic, alternative type films, such as those by Goddard and Cassavettes.

So basically, every second week, the hall was filled with French Existential Angst and/or working class New York City Columbo meets Gazzara testosterone driven absurdism.

Many from this time remember the deliciously, heady reek of the hall emanating from the old oil burning stove, which served to heat the room. A noisy 16mm projector ran from a table set up at the back.

Seeing the need for some wholesome children's entertainment, Nora Laffin introduced matinees for kids. The windows of the old hall were covered over with sheets of plywood to shut out the daylight. Parker Laffin was in charge of running the school's borrowed projector at just twelve years old. Youngsters were happiest when Charlie Chaplin or the Marx brothers were in the house. Nora has a constant reminder of those days in the form of a 14k gold tooth that resulted from a run in with a falling cinema screen. Make her smile sometime and you might catch a glimpse of it.

From 1978-1983, Steve Roberts took on the challenge of being the movie man. Technical changes made during his time greatly improved the viewing experience for islanders. He used two projectors, eliminating the need for a lights up/rewind pause in between reels, but necessitated Steve to be on the ball for cuing the transition from one reel to the next. It seems Steve must have had moments of burn out (he also traveled to show films on Denman Island, in Courtenay and on Cortez). There was never any great fortune to be made, but Steve's straight- forward, "I did it to contribute to the community" answer to the question, "Why bother?"

Many islanders have played a part in the evolution of movies on Hornby. During the transformation of the hall, Lloyd House suggested a storage closet be made into a projection booth. This would shift movie mechanics and their operator out of view for the first time. A window was cut to show the film through, and glass was set in later to buffer the racket produced by the projectors. Bob Thompson, who owned the pub at the time, donated the first "in house" popcorn popper. The wafting smell of hot, buttered popcorn is now cemented as part of the traditional movie going experience, as we know it today.

Which brings us to the present stalwart, who took over from Steve in 1983 and has been lighting the screen at the hall practically every Saturday night (and more) for the last eighteen years. Gabriel Zoltan Pius Cyrilus Christopher Peus David Guido Benedict Jeroschewitz was born in Munich, Germany "sometime after the war". He arrived on Hornby in 1972 in need of a bath, a job and the love of a loose woman. Unable to locate a tub, Gabe concentrated on being a house builder/carpenter/fix it dude/ferry worker/ice cream peddler/philanderer/ goat wrestler/tofu manufacturer, until his cinematically charged DNA led him to the projection booth.

The first film Gabe showed at the hall was Bertolucci's *1900*. In his first year alone, film classics such as *Tootsie*, *Raiders of the Lost Ark*,

E.T., *Diva* and *The Conformist* were shown. Growing frustration with the quality and limited selection of films available on 16mm film, prompted Gabe to look into procuring a 35mm projector. In 1990, the leap to upgrade was made. This piece of equipment, which markedly improved the quality of picture and sound, transformed the community hall into the equivalent of a professional movie theatre.

Three summers ago, Gabriel established the Hornby Island Film Festival. This week long showcase was born to draw attention to more eclectic, artistic films, often from other countries, that many on this island would not have the opportunity to see otherwise.

No movie at the hall is complete without the opening announcements. Carole Chambers first walked before movie audiences to make known upcoming Hornby happenings, fund raisers, etc. in 1983. Carole would open with a Hitchcockian "Good Evening" and end with a "Thank You For Coming", whereupon the lights would go down and Joe Pesci would start cursing. It was about seven years ago that Gabriel became the evening's announcer. He brings the crowd to attention by waving a handful of papers and yelling the now familiar "**Hello! Hi!** Anybody's birthday tonight?" which can lead to a full crowd singing out *Happy Birthday* to complete strangers.

There is something about the lights going down and the chatter dying away as the opening credits roll and the room is filled with moving images. Okay, so Mr. Chakra Sprout, who chose to sit in front of you at the last minute, is 6'7" and Frieda Peeple, on your right, has legendary body odour and Pinhead LaLeisure, in the middle, talks through the whole movie, but this is all part of the group experience. The darkness carries us all.

HOME IS

p.j. flaming

This piece was written online for Canadian Geographic *magazine's discussion about what home means to people, months before the massive forest fires of Kelowna summer 2003.*

HOME IS INTERNAL and external space, an abode, a domicile, a place to hang your hat, to take off your boots, put your feet up, a place to go inward or celebrate with friends. Home is a wandering spirit come home to roost, a glance out the window, a bald eagle overhead, the ponderosa pines moving, and squirrels in the attic. Home is the sound of cats meowing and the clatter of domestic life, a pot gonging here, the whir of a washing machine there, the tip-tap of fingers on keyboards, or an accordion blazing through the house with Celtic furor. Home smells like old linen, good coffee, snow on its way. Home is here, where we live, home is where we have lived, home is where we are going to live. It is all these places rolled into one, yet disparate, hanging by our narrative thread, stuffed into boxes, pasted between pages of photo albums and the minds' eye. Home is of our choosing, not a difficult choice, when home speaks you can hear it calling, speaking your language. Home has a center a sense of balance that persists through acute angles, high ceilings and arched windows. Home is organic. Home tastes of curry, of cinnamon toast, of sushi, of bannock, of bacon and eggs on Sunday. Home still lingers on the farm in the Creston Valley, a big open land we shared with 250 species of birds and an apple eating grizzly bear. Home is now in the Okanagan, where everything is milder, where everything is available, where the flow of life is relentless, where you have to remember to climb a hill, or walk along the forest trails leading out the back door. Home is a garden, a tent under summer sky, or a place on a plane. Home feels safe, but can be swiftly blown away by invasion, accident, war, or acts of nature. Home is always and absolutely defensible. Home is autonomy; home is sovereignty, the right to denounce intruders posing as friends. Home is the 'true north strong and free'. Home is Canadian, welcoming with open arms, and 'the right to security of person, the right not to be deprived'. Home is for everyone not just the imagined few. Home is right here, where I lay my head beside you and dream, home free.

HOMECOMING
THE SALMON'S JOURNEY
Jill Webb

From stream to ocean, the time, four years.
    Protection, shelter, nourishment, the waters gave,
        Struggling, struggling to survive
           Always, just a swish away, form a hook or net.
The trek home begins
    Instinct tells what must be done,
        Its' will pushes onward and forward
           To find the stream that started its life.
Scales darken, their time it slows
    Journeys' end comes closer,
        The waters rage, the push is on
           Leaping up, then down, until ….
A rocky ledge is found, to rest awhile
    To start again to leap, to fall,
        Never veering from the goal
           Home is near, pebbles glisten and invite.
Fall colours all around
    Leaves turning red and gold,
        They float and swirl and gently land along the bank
           Peaceful now, fulfillment met.
The eggs, at last, lay nestled in a sandy bed,
    The fish flip, a final splash,
        All movement, now, can cease
           Their time ….COMPLETE

IMAGES TOWARD A PLACE TO GATHER...
Tracey Jack

THE LEAVES WERE PAINTED ochre and banana-yellow, scattered piles of gold surrounded by huge trees, whistling songs from the lake. Mom shouted, "Tracey, Lyle, it's time to come in! I think a storm is blowing. Anyway it's time to eat."

Inside the cabin my brother and I maneuvered our way around her art prints, charcoal drawings and large acrylic paintings. Pages torn from her sketchbook were also scattered about. I loved looking at them. They were magical symbols mom had created. I always found them interesting and stared at them. Her brush strokes seemed to rest so intricately on the canvas. I watched her, two long braids crowned by a silk flowered bandana hanging down, stirring steaming chicken noodle soup as she hummed a stick game song.

We loved the songs because it reminded us of the summer that had just passed. Her voice grew louder and she belted out the song beating the stir spoon on the counter. I sang with her as I remembered eating bologna in our tipi, getting covered from head to toe in dust while being crooned to sleep at night by the drums as the muggy summer's air drifted in. The best part of the pow wow was getting to hold the bones during the stick game and scoring a stick for the team. When the pointer would point and not be able to guess my bones, mom and the rest of the family would sing real high and she would let out a whoop of approval!

"Eiiiii Eiiiii Eiiiii."

Sipping on my hot soup I looked up at mom.

"Mom, I can count my age in Indian! Naqs Asil Cathlis moose Chilx tuqwumqx!"

Mom laughed and said "Yep, your're six years old." She always slid Okanagan words into my memory bank and would test me whenever she had the chance. We were staying at the summer cabin for two winter seasons, while she earned her visual arts credits at the local college. In the summer months we returned to our ranch in the hills.

Two seasons passed and an even greater passage occurred. I was nine years old and mom told me we were going to be living where the parliament buildings were! We were at the ranch that summer when mom told us.

"We are moving to Victoria, I'm going to another school," she explained at supper one night.

Confused and a bit afraid I asked her, "Where's Victoria mom? What does it look like?"

She then explained to me at the wooden table lit by a kerosene lamp. "It's where the parliament buildings are." She then grabbed the bottle of HP sauce and said, "Here, look at this picture."

I stared at the bottle and saw this fancy building of what seemed like a castle to me!

Grandpa laughed and said, "Pass the HP. I'm gonna put some on this good deer roast your grandma cooked."

On a late summer's day, we piled our clothes, dishes and a black cassette tape recorder in our small green station wagon and began to drive for hundreds of miles in endless sloppy rain. Giant raindrops bashed down on the windshield as we watched the rhythm of the wipers, while listening to the scratchy AM radio. It was all very exciting. I was so excited about this new place because it was like we were moving to a fantasy city with it's own castles. The most exhilarating part was that it was on an island!

Getting to the ferry, my heart pounded. We loaded on the ramp and piled out of the car. Seagulls screeched and joked with each other, while gigantic waves splashed against the big ship. The teal blue ocean had no ending in sight. It was late when we arrived on the Island, and Lyle and I fell asleep. The next thing I heard was mom waking us up.

"Tracey, Lyle, wake up! Look at the lights around the parliament buildings."

I looked up and was in awe of the outline of white lights that traced the brilliant building. Mom drove really slowly to our new house. To our surprise, it was only two blocks from the parliament buildings! Later that week Lyle and I raced to the parliament buildings. We ran our bare toes through soft velvety lawn, landscaped so perfect with odd shaped giant trees. Lyle and I climbed the weird shaped trees and played tag for hours on the huge green lawn of the legislature.

Later that warm fall, I ran back to the house from the mailbox and my heart was racing! We got mail from uncle Auggie! I ran in the house "MOM...MOM...we got a letter! Where's the tape recorder? Do we have batteries?"

Mom smiled and grabbed from the top cupboard the little black cassette deck used to record stick game songs during the summer. I ripped open the envelope and inserted the cassette in the tape recorder. We sat around and played the tape. Uncle Auggie taped our dog Tuffy barking and I could hear everyone saying hello on the scratchy tape.

Grandma was telling us she won 15 dollars at bingo in the band hall and grandpa got a big buck behind Charley's place. Uncle Chris said they were drying the meat and would have some put away for us when we came home at Christmas time. I rewound the tape over and over and over until mom finally said, "Not too much Tracey, the batteries might die and we can't get batteries till next month."

As she turned the recorder off, I looked over at her arm and saw its muscle was bigger than on the other arm. "Mom why does one arm have a big muscle and the other so small?"

She laughed and said, "It's my welder arm, tweetie! I'm welding big pieces of steel to create sculptures!"

I was so amazed. "Wow, mom, you're pretty tough!"

Two more seasons passed and mom graduated from University. I stared at her picture with the cap and gown admiring how pretty she looked. We left the magical island and came home back to live on the ranch.

Mom started working with all the kids on the reserve. She had a project with the local school district and the Penticton Band and invented an Indian cultural camp program. It was so much fun. I always looked forward to camp day because we got to miss school for a day to go up in the mountains.

We learned to cut up dry meat, pick berries, make baskets and swim, telling horror stories at night about the giant turtle in the lake. Mom planned lots of meetings. I remembered finding scribbled notes on napkins, brown paper bags and pretty much anything she could write on, was filled with ideas about how she was going to work in the community.

"Tracey, help your Uncle pack the PA system over to the ball field we are gathering the elders to talk about our language and history."

Feeling high-tuned I gathered the cords and followed my uncle Auggie. He knew everything about electronics. To me he was a wizard!

By the time I was sixteen, Mom was working at an office downtown. It was such a cool place because only Indians worked there and they were all working on such neat ideas. Once, as I waited for her to get out of her meeting, Linda showed me a colorful kids book mom just wrote. She wanted me to tell her what I thought of it.

Graduation came and I was off to college in the big city of Vancouver. One day the phone rang.

"Tracey, it's me, Mom. I'm doing a reading downtown of my new book."

I jumped on the bus and headed into the city core. Mom was getting very well known and respected for her literary work and I loved it when she came into town. The room was filled with so many people. It was crowded. I listened as her words echoed gentle notes. Some people were crying others were just amazed by her grace of words. I waited for the crowd to die down and went over to her. I laughed and teased her and told her, "I took some of the fancy teas 'cuz I'm a starving student!"

She laughed and said, "Well tweetie, let's go eat then!"

Her good friend, Lee Maracle, came over to say hi and mom invited her to eat with us. She had daughters my age. So we all decided to go together. We sat in the Chinese restaurant laughing and sharing stories for at least four hours. I think the owners got nervous about us not having money to pay because we were having such a good time.

College ended and I came home and had my first baby. Mom was so excited about her first grandchild. For her it meant her blood would carry on.

"We'll have a dinner and Grandma will name her. We'll put out our Indian food."

The following year after almost twenty years of hard work the poles went up at En'owkin Centre on the reserve. Not long after the poles went up, students from all across Canada drifted into the En'owkin Centre. Wanting to share in the magic and dream of a place, where, as Mom had said, "We can do our best thinking, learning and sharing about who we are as Indigenous people."

Today, as I walk back to my desk to finish this story the answer hits me as to why we need this gathering space. I realize now what Mom's vision is. Indigenous student artists are painting, carving, welding, performing and writing about themselves. They are practicing this so they can return home to their communities and build something just as evocatively wonderful for our nations.

IN SEARCH OF THE
CAMP MCKINNEY GOLD BARS

Wolfgang Schmidt

IT IS SUMMERTIME AND UNDER the porch roof, a light breeze makes it very comfortable. I am lying in my hammock, which is attached to two of the porch posts. The book I am reading is all about archaeology and history: *The Sumerian Clay Tablets.* It's an interpretation of them suggesting that alien space beings have been here on earth for at least 35,000 years.

Time flies by, but business is slow. I had read a number of chapters when a car drives in.

We are a guest ranch with Bed & Breakfast and a craft shop. Our specialty is local crafts, native hand-made leather items, beaded jewelry, gold panning and canyon tours. Customers drive in and out. There is no line-up here.

The car is a bit too fast for normal tourist traffic. It stops with a screech and the doors fly open. Out leap a couple, visibly upset, and they rush into the shop. They did not notice me in the hammock and when I get to the counter, they demand something cold to drink – and look at me quizzically. Then the woman touches my arm, she says, "Hurry, I need something cold."

Only later did I find out that the touch on my arm was to check to see that I was a real live person.

I serve the cold drinks, ring in the cash, but I can see that the customers are not relaxed – something unusual in my shop, because I have so many interesting things to look at that people normally browse around whispering, "Look at this," and, "Look at that."

"Do you have a washroom?" the lady asks.

I point her toward the outhouses.

She says, "I think I am going to be sick."

The man looks at me and whispers, "We have had a very harrowing experience just now and you have to forgive my wife. She is still very upset."

"What happened?" is my question.

"Wait 'til my wife comes back and we will tell you the story."

The lady arrives and points nervously to the picnic tables. "May I sit down?"

"Of course," is my answer. I pour myself a coffee and join them. "What is the problem? By the way, may name is Wolfgang and I am the owner of the ranch." I say this in my calmest voice, hoping that it will have an effect on them.

A couple of sips on the pop and then she bursts out, "You probably won't believe me, but we saw a ghost!"

"Well, try me," I say again calmly. "I wrote a book about unexplained phenomena, so I don't 'spook' easily, so to speak."

The words come out of her mouth like a machine gun: "I was driving down Mt. Baldy and my husband was looking at a map, when suddenly I noticed a man at the side of the road. He had a long-handled shovel and was digging into the ground. But there was no dirt on his shovel when he threw it over his shoulder. He was working frantically, without noticing us.

"I stopped the car. My husband looked up and said 'That's strange.' And with that he opened the door."

She takes another long sip of her drink. "May I have another one?" she requests, handing me the empty can.

I go to the fridge to oblige. When I sit down again, she continues with the story.

"This business about the shovel without dirt made me look at the person more closely.

"While he was dressed like a cowboy, with hat and boots, he some-how looked strange. He ignored us stopping. My husband walked towards him and I could hear him saying, 'Is there anything we can help you with?' but he was ignored."

The husband interjects "I thought that maybe he did not hear me and I went closer to get his attention. He was working very hard but did not get any dirt on the shovel. I looked down at the ground and all the effort so far had been for naught. I moved out of the way of his flying shovel as I did not want to be hit, yet he still did not notice us."

"This is how fast he was moving the shovel," says the lady. She stands up, pretending to have a shovel in her hand, and rapidly imitates a dig-ger, but with such a speed that it was definitely not normal. Obviously, he was not very efficient either, as he apparently got no dirt on the shovel.

"I touched him on his right shoulder," says the man. "I should say 'I tried to touch him', because my hand went right through his body and what was even stranger the man just evaporated."

"Yeah, I watched from the car and saw Ken touching him, and the man just disintegrated, disappeared, vanished..!" The woman's voice trails off. "We had an encounter with a ghost."

Her body trembled and I was the one to place my hand on her arm and say, "Just relax, I probably have the answer for you."

Ever since I had published the book, *Psychics, Crooks and Unexplained Phenomena*, people in the neighbourhood revealed to me that they too had some very strange experiences. Most of the neighbours kept the encounters to themselves, as they did not want other people to think that their minds had snapped. With my publishing a book about those things, they felt comfortable to talk.

One of the stories I had heard was about a ghost on the Mt. Baldy road, near the McMynn Meadows. I did not pay much attention to it; just another ghost story, and I had heard many of them before.

Then another neighbour reported a similar story. This time a 'ghost' was trying to fill a hole in the ground - I paid more attention. The location in both reports was the same. I deduced that maybe it had something to do with the gold bar robbery, which had happened at that place many years ago. The famous Camp McKinney gold strike properties were very close by.

I had read in two different books about a robbery of a gold transport travelling from the mine to the bank and the subsequent shooting of the robber, without the booty ever having been recovered.

Could it be that the ghost of the robber was looking for the gold bars he had buried? The history books said that the robber fled and that he must have hidden the saddle bags with the gold, because otherwise he could not have eluded the posse that quickly. All attempts to find the treasure had so far been unsuccessful.

When the robber came back to get his loot, he was shot. There is also a conspiracy theory about that fact, as some people believed that the shooter might have been a partner in the plot. Whatever the real facts, many people have come to the ranch with metal detectors and enquired about the exact location of the robbery. We never heard of any success.

Now, this was the third time I heard the ghost story. So, I relate my knowledge about the robbery and the prior sightings to the couple.

The man, Ken, is the first to respond. "It sure was a shock to us. However, I thought right from the beginning that there was something strange about the person. Somehow, the figure was a bit fuzzy. Also, when I stood right behind him and my hand went nowhere – wow. I could feel my heart beating in my throat. I looked at Evelyn and saw her sitting in the car with her mouth wide open, staring at me with eyes as big as toonies."

"This gives me something to think about," says Evelyn. "I touched you when I came in, because I wanted to make sure that you are a real person."

Ken and Evelyn relax a bit. They now could take their mind off the ghost and I learn that they are staying in Osoyoos, visiting from the lower mainland. They had taken a drive, wanting to make a circle tour via Oliver and Mt. Baldy, and back to Osoyoos via Highway #3.

This vacation is certainly a memorable one for them, I can see as they begin to smile. Both decide to buy a souvenir in my shop. Both regret not having taken a picture of the ghost.

"But then, who could have dreamed that the guy wasn't real," says Evelyn.

As I wave 'good bye' to them, I get back into the hammock. Until the next guests arrive, I read more about the Sumerian clay tablets and wonder what other unexplained phenomena might be explainable a hundred years from now.

SUFFERING IN SILENCE
Barbara M. E. Bonthoux

Dim, Dark Days of times gone by
Wars of survival and heart
Watching as her family falls prey
To Huntington stealth
One by One a member cries
"I'm losing control of me!"
Anger bites as neurons misfire
She is forced to watch as...
First her husband...
Then his two sisters
Start their downward spiral
Descending into oblivion where
They see and understand,
Unable to move or speak.
Afraid for her children
For the question is not if...
But how many?
Will they choose to know...to test?
Son does not...So...
She waits...She watches
As along with her family...
Suffers in silence.

Insect Espionage
Naomi DeLury

THE CODLING MOTH (Figure 1), a worldwide pest of apple, pear and various other crops, has become infamous in the interior of British Columbia. People in the Okanagan have become accustomed to hearing about the damage this "worm-in-the-apple" causes as incredible attempts are made to control its numbers through sterile insect release, mating disruption and insecticide use.

But man is not the only enemy this small moth faces in its daily battles, and at least one of its natural "enemies" has found a way to use scents generated by the codling moth itself to hunt it down.

The "enemy" in question is also an insect: a small

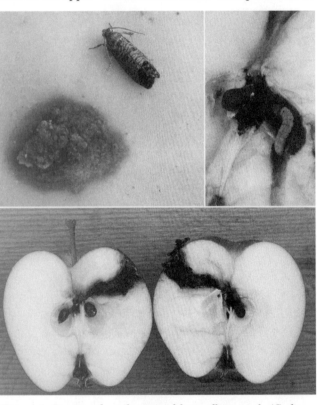

Figure 1. Damaged apple caused by codling moth (Cydia pomonella) larva: (top left) adult codling moth beside a larval entrance hole with frass; (top right) codling moth larva feeding on seeds in the apple core; and (bottom) a cross section of an apple showing larval damage.

(4.5 mm), black, nondescript, non-stinging member of the Order Hymenoptera (Figure 2). *Ascogaster quadridentata,* as the human world has christened it, is a parasitoid that uses the codling moth larva as a food source for its young, and in doing so, causes its host's inevitable death.

114

The initial attack is quite subtle. *A. quadridentata* targets one of the few vulnerable stages of the codling moth life cycle: the egg. (Codling

Figure 2. A female parasitoid, Ascogaster quadridentata, has just laid an egg into a codling moth egg. Her ovipositor is still extended. The codling moth egg appears as a white disc below her abdomen. Notice the presence of codling moth scales on the substrate and the parasitoid's antenna.

moth eggs are laid singly near or on the fruit. Soon after hatching, the codling moth will burrow into an apple and remain protected by the fruit until it is ready to pupate).

An adult female *A. quadridentata* lays a single egg into the codling moth egg. The parasitized codling moth continues to develop, with slight modifications in its behaviour, until it has spun a cocoon[1,2]. At this point A. quadridentata launches its "second", more deadly attack, this time from within the host. First the parasitoid chews its way out of the codling moth, then consumes the entire codling moth larva with the exception of the cuticle[2,3]. Once it has finished eating, *A. quadridentata* spins a cocoon within the existing codling moth cocoon, pupates, and emerges as an adult 8-12 days later[3].

A.quadridentata can lay several hundred eggs[3,4], but in order to do so, she must find an equal number of codling moth eggs! As mated female codling moth disperse their eggs throughout an orchard, *A. quadridentata* must be good at searching to find enough eggs before she becomes too old, or before the codling moth eggs hatch. How does she do it?

Fortunately for the parasitoid, the codling moth female leaves a clue, or should I say clues, behind at the egg site. During the egg laying, the female codling moth will brush the surface of the leaf or fruit with her abdomen. Scales from her wings and body fall onto the wet egg and as the egg dries the scales become trapped (Figure 3). *A. quadridentata* associates the smells released by these scales with codling moth eggs. And each time she encounters a scale-covered codling moth egg, her preference for the scale-smell becomes stronger. When the female de-

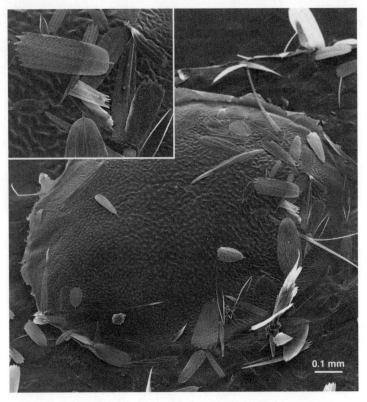

Figure 3. Scanning electron micrograph of a codling moth egg, depicting moth scales embedded in the surface of the egg. Eggs were sputter-coated with gold, then viewed with a Hitachi S-2500 scanning electron microscope at 10 kV accelerating voltage.
Photographs courtesy of Michael Weis and Mark Gardiner, Agriculture and Agri-Food Canada, Summerland, BC.

tects the complex scale odour, she becomes excited, remains in the area and conducts a thorough search, which usually ends in a successful egg laying.

This parasitoid is using information left behind by the codling moth adult as a guide to focus her searching behaviour on areas with high probabilities of encountering host eggs.[5] Some might say *A. quadridentata* is a successful spy.

[1]*Brown,J.J., J. Ahl, and D. Reed-Larsen. 1988. Endocrine communication between a host and its endoparasitoids in relationship to dormancy, pp 443-447, in F. Sehnal, A. Zabza, and D.L. Denlinger (eds.). Endocrinological frontiers In Physiological Insect Ecology. Wroclaw Technical University Press, Wroclaw.*

[2]*Brown, J.J. and M. Friedlander. 1995. Influence of parasitism on spermatogenesis in the codling moth,* Cydia pomonella *L. J. Insect. Physiol. 41(11): 957-963.*

[3]*Boyce, H.R. 1936. Laboratory breeding of* Ascogaster carpocapsae *Vier. with notes on biology and larval morphology. Can. Entomol. 68: 241-246.*

[4]*Swan, L.A. 1964. Insect parasites: the Braconids, pp. 156-158, in L.A. Swan (author). Beneficial insects. Harper & Row, Publishers, New York.*

[5]*DeLury, N.C., R. Gries, G. Gries, G.J.R. Judd, and G. Khaskin. 1999. Moth scale-derived kairomones used by egg-larval parasitoid* Ascogaster quadridentata *to located eggs of its host,* Cydia pomonella. *Journal of Chem. Ecol., 25(11): 2419-2431.*

THE SIMILKAMEEN
Fred Leard

THE SIMILKAMEEN IS ABOUT as close to heaven as one can get in their lifetime. If you've led a good, clean life come and a sneak preview of what is in store for you in the hereafter. If you haven't done so well, come anyway and you'll get to see what you're going to miss.

IT SEEMED LIKE A GOOD IDEA AT THE TIME
Wesley Nicholson

MY DAD WAS ALWAYS THINKING of ways to either save money, make money or, at best, create work to keep us kids out of trouble.

He had some good ideas and some not-so-good ones. The not-so-good were the ones people always remembered saying, "Well it seemed like a good idea at the time."

One of those infamous ideas struck Dad when he was working for the Department of Highways, mowing the sides of the roads. He figured the dead grass would make good hay for our horses, so he devised a way to collect it one weekend.

It was sunny and sweltering hot that day. Dad rigged up a hitch so he could pull our old steel-wheeled, horse drawn hay rake with his 1949 Ford pickup truck. (the hay he wanted to get was too far from our farm to take the tractor, and besides, we needed the pickup to haul the hay home.)

The rake extended out to the right. That way, the truck could stay on the road while the rake did its job in the ditch. It was my job to ride the rake and trip the teeth when it got full. That would make nice neat piles of grass that we'd load later with pitchforks.

This looks a bit dangerous, I thought to myself. But Dad knows what he's doing — he wouldn't do anything to kill me… not intentionally, anyway.

I was wrong. Dad thought nothing of driving the pickup 10 to 15 mph on the smooth gravel shoulder. Meanwhile, I was sitting on an unpadded steel seat, going like mad through the ditch, running over culverts, through mud holes, bouncing over rotten fence posts, tin cans, rocks and whatever else is found in ditches along rural back roads.

I hung on for dear life, trying to stomp down on the tripper, which would flip up the teeth so fast it scared me. But I stayed with it, gritting my teeth and trying to prove to Dad I was a man.

After my cap blew off and the rake got all tangled up in some rusty old barbed wire, I finally had to yell and wave my arms to get Dad to stop. We sat down for a drink of water, and I explained the situation like this:

"How about I drive the truck and you sit on the rake and do everything you're supposed to while being pulled along like a bullet through the ditch?"

Dad got the message and we went back to making hay… a little slower.

When it came time to load the truck, Dad pitched in the hay while I drove along slowly, stopping every so often to get back into the box and stomp down the hay.

As the load got higher, I couldn't see the sides of the box. A few times I stepped over and took a tumble off the truck. Trying to keep up with Dad kept me hopping.

With sweat running down my neck, hay in my pants and dust all over me, all I wanted was to get that truck loaded so we could go home.

But sure enough, the fates were against me. My mistake was forgetting to set the emergency brake when I'd parked on an incline.

The truck rolled backward – with me in the box! I jumped out, hit the ground rolling and got to my feet without missing a step to run and catch the truck.

I made it to the running board, but had all I could do to hold on while the truck went bouncing into the ditch. When it stopped (by running into an electrical pole) I went flying head over heels onto the ground.

Luckily I wasn't hurt … and the heavy steel bumper kept the pickup from being damaged. Dad drove the truck out and we went back to loading more hay.

Still a little sore form all the activity, I wasn't moving as fast as I should have. When Dad tossed up a load of hay, his pitchfork poked me right in the foot. I was wearing work boots, so it hurt a bit, but didn't draw any blood.

We finally got the hay loaded and tied down with ropes. Then we headed home. Dad had devised a system for unloading the hay using the ropes and the tractor. I was eager to see how it worked.

I tied the ropes together, then stood behind the truck to observe. But I wasn't ready for the ropes breaking. The hay headed right for me. I

Wesley, sister Marilyn, & Dad at home in Pouce Coupe, 1968.

started to back up, but tripped over an old oak bucket. Before I could get up, the load of hay came right down on top of me!

As I crawled out from under, Dad got off the tractor and asked if I was okay — for the third time.

"Yes," I answered. "But I'm getting a little tired of everything happening to me."

The rest of the unloading went as planned. We finally went into the house, where I got a chance to examine my injuries.

Nothing serious. I was fine after a warm bath. Compared to that first day, the rest of the haying season went very well.

TOILING FOR PIPES - THEN AND NOW
Dawn Renaud

My daughter tells me I've got pipes -
And this is bad, which means it's cool.
(At least I *think* it does. She learns
Her speech from peers while she's at school.)

Those 'pipes' are muscles, on my arms.
"How'd you get them, Mom?" she asks.
"I guess by piling fresh-baled hay
Those golden summers long since passed,

And chopping wood to heat the house,
And growing veggies for a meal
And digging rocks and feeding cows..."
She sighs. My answer's lost appeal.

She likes kickboxing at the gym
Or playing rugby- ouch. And I
Hope she'll have pipes much grander than
My own, her 'toils' to justify.

JAKE'S JARDINIERE
R.L. Diebolt

JAKE, LADY AND THE KID lived in the city of Esormac on College Street. Their residence was a large, lofty spruce tree with a spectacular view of the area. With fall here, and winter fast approaching, Jake soared freely on his daily excursions for family food.

Watercolour by R.L. Diebolt.

Jake especially liked Mr. D's peanuts in the shell. Mr. D. would place seven peanuts on the back porch every morning, and the blue jay family was swift to fly to the occasion.

Jake was first on the scene. One peanut beaked-in lengthwise, and a second one in crosswise, and off he went. Then Lady and the Kid followed suit. Beaking the peanuts quickly, and locating a hiding spot for later recovery, was their intent.

Jays have numerous hiding places to store their winter food. Jake's favourite spot was Mr. D's jardinière. It was a little tricky to fly into the restricted area between the fence and the garage, but a super spot for peanut hiding.

One day he poked a little deeper, and his beak hit a hard object. Jake's curiosity took over. Tap-tap-tap. He tapped and poked and beaked-out a gold chain with a pocket watch attached. Jake knew this hole would make room for more peanuts, so flying quickly, he delivered that pocket watch right to Mr. D's back porch. Then home he went to tell the story.

Sadly, Lady was not well and Jake knew he must find more food to feed her. The Kid spent more time with Lady while Jake searched morning, noon and late day.

Two days later, as Lady lay sick and frail, Jake flew to Mr. D's yard and what a glorious sight to behold! A spread of peanuts, sunflower seeds and water awaited him.

Soon Jake, Lady and the Kid were well and happy.

Mr. & Mrs. D were very, very happy and the choice spot of Mr. D's garden was "Jake's Jardinere."

THE JEWEL WITHIN OUR MIDST
Sharon Prafke

IF THERE WAS EVER an appropriate synonym to describe a location, then Jewel Lake is that perfect synonym. The locals of Greenwood know that it's a true *'gem'*, hidden from the unfortunate tourist aimlessly driving by without realizing what's nestled up on a flat plateau of Mt. Roderick Dhu. Sheltered in a canopy of trees, inviting jade and azure waters shimmer on the surface, reflecting back the golden orb that hangs in a gorgeous soft, blue sky.

It's time to share the secret, beginning at the junction of Highway #3 and the entrance to Boundary Creek Road. The paved nine kilometre drive loops up the mountainside in a series of switchbacks with an occasional glimpse of the hayfields and a cemetery just below. Dense towering trees separate, and suddenly the glass surface mirrors a blue heron circling overhead, searching for a fish to pacify his persistent, gnawing hunger.

A quaint rustic resort is perched on the pristine shores of a gorgeous setting cradled by the mountains curving protectively around it. Trout splash, muskrat comb their silky strands of fur while deer meander to the shoreline, occasionally teasing the patient fisherman as he casts his rod.

It's not unheard of to hook a five-pound trout or an Eastern Brook on the end of a bobbing line.

History tells us that Jewel Lake once supported a gold mine, with tailings still evident to this very day. Now four cozy cabins share this awesome view with another three interspersed between the trees alongside abundant private campsites. A picturesque restaurant with an adjoining outdoor patio serves fabulous home cooked fries and my favourite, a mouth-watering roast beef dip. The wine and beer are chilled and the pies are to die for, so I'm told. The owners, Leo and Solange Jacob, are polite with warm friendly smiles to guarantee a delightful visit for whatever duration you choose to stay.

So rent a boat, launch your own, or stretch out on a chaise lounge and listen to the haunting call of a loon drown out the noisy hubbub of the hectic life you left behind. If Jewel Lake Resort is full then follow the main road as it circumnavigates the north side of the lake to the far end, three kilometres northeast, where a Provincial Park offers numerous shady campsites, and sandy beaches are caressed by the warm, inviting waves.

Winter months reveal this gem is anything but forgotten. Christmas is enjoyed by many tucked cosily inside the warm comfort of their cabins. A bright fire and a warm cup of cocoa is a *'must'* following an intoxicating day of cross-country skiing on trails too numerous to mention. The resort takes great pains to clear these trails, at their own expense, as well as the large expanse of outdoor skating the Jacobs encourage on the frozen 'Jewel' at their fingertips.

And so to summarize: snowmobiling, hunting and snowshoeing are just a few more of the popular activities that abound in this paradise hidden in the scenic Boundary Country.

THE KITTEN WHO CAME FOR THE WEEKEND
Gwen Gregg

AT TWILIGHT ON HALLOWEEN NIGHT eleven years ago we arrived in Penticton by car from Vancouver Island with our beautiful three year old brown tabby cat, Babe.

Our brand new show home contained some furniture and the kitchen only needed dishes and pots and pans, so all we had to do was plug in the kettle for tea with our sandwiches.

We carried Babe in her cage to the laundry room. She hopped out and headed for the bedroom where she hid under the bed all night. By morning she found her cat food and water. After she explored her new home. The next day our furniture and household things were delivered and she immediately settled down to be our housecat in the Okanagan Valley.

The first winter in Penticton, Babe let me carry her outdoors to circle our house, but she preferred to sit on top of the piano and watch out the bay window to see people walking dogs or traffic passing through the gates. By spring, she would go outdoors on the steps and let me fasten a tether to her breakaway collar. She liked the front yard and the security of entering the house easily. Twice in the past eleven years she has caught and killed a mouse that was near the bay window. Once she brought a bird into the house and dropped it when we chased her around. She does not tolerate spiders living indoors with us either.

There is a tiger personality there, which developed when she lived with her mother as a stray in a house in Sidney-By-The-Sea. The cat was abandoned by people who had moved away.

On Saturday August 26, 1989, my husband and I walked along Third Street in Sidney, B.C. on our way uptown to buy a birthday card. We stopped opposite an apartment building to chat with a couple, when a tiger stripped brown kitten circled us crying piteously. I picked her up, realizing she seemed lost and frightened. We inquired at the apartment building and new houses on the side street, but no one had seen her before. We left her and continued uptown. When we passed that area again she ran to me crying for help. We decided to take her home for the weekend, so I sat down on the park bench holding her close to me while my husband went for the car. He took us home then he continued to go shopping for cat supplies. Our new kitten was house broken and happy with us. We took her to a vet on the Monday for a check up and to search for her family. Her new doctor said she was healthy and about six months old.

It was over a year before an older woman who was visiting us said she knew the cat, but it was actually Babe's mother who she knew. This cat had returned everyday to the empty house looking for her kitten. By then someone else had adopted the mother who never found her kitten because we had made a house cat of her, only letting her outdoors in the backyard on a tether. Her first owners had lived one street over from our townhouse and she had crossed a busy street to find us.

Babe has lived with us for fifteen years. I just adore her, especially when she permits me to brush her beautiful long fluffy fur with orange and brown colours and a white bib. To me Babe must be one of the prettiest cats in the Okanagan Valley. Whenever we travelled she stayed alone in our house enjoying the care given by friendly neighbours.

My husband says that she is part of our family, especially to our three Kelowna grandchildren, who visit us frequently. She entertains them by playing hockey using a mini marshmallow as a puck and her paws for a hockey stick. Then she eats the marshmallow. (She only likes white ones.)

There have been two other cats in my lifetime, but they were completely independent, coming and going outdoors. Babe is our house cat and she is remarkable. She licks my cheek to say goodnight-I belong to you! It was fate that brought us together.

NIGHTFALL
Maxine Rae

Shadows creep across Green Mountain
Changing green forests to purple
Then black against a fiery sky
Fire dies, day becomes night
Feel the quiet.

Blue now purple now indigo
Twilight arms close around us
Clouds tipped by moonlight
Drift through ebony skies
Hear the quiet.

Moonlight creeps across Green Mountain
Shadows deepen, stars twinkle
Lovers entwine
Dreams take flight
Feel the quiet.

KITTY WILSON OF PARADISE RANCH
Dodi Morrison

BORN TO 'VERY, VERY BRITISH' parents, Katherine Haverfield grew up as one of two children of a gentleman farmer and his wife, in the then rustic countryside of Okanagan Mission. She remembered great stretches of manicured lawn, glowing flowerbeds, fields of wheat and tobacco – plus the endless rows of orchard trees that were her father's realm.

Of her parents Kitty said, "When I think of them, I see them seated at each end of the long dining room table – Father carving the roast and Mother pouring tea out of the huge silver teapot, into a Blue Willow cup." She and her sister Joydie lacked for nothing.

Yet she was born a rebel. Unlike Joydie, her mother's pet, who seemed to do everything correctly, Kitty had a mind of her own. She fought – in vain – the idea of boarding school. Sent first to St. Michael's School in Vernon, she was so unhappy there that she was moved to Strathcona School for Girls at Shawnigan Lake. There she was more content, perhaps because her talent for theatrics was completely acknowledged. The little girl, who had loved to dress up, became a confident young actress. And a passion for theatre was born that lasted her lifetime.

With her usual flair for drama, she felt her future was decided while home for Christmas holidays, and attending a skating party. There she met the new young schoolteacher, Victor Wilson. He was "swooningly handsome", she told me. "All of us girls fell madly in love. I made up my mind on the spot that I would marry him. But it took Victor a little longer."… As a matter of fact, it took him seven years!

Meanwhile, her education continued, and eventually she enrolled at McGill, to achieve her lifelong ambition to become a librarian. Was it coincidence that Victor, now an enlisted man, was stationed on the East Coast? At any rate, romance flourished. They were married before his departure for overseas duty, and Kitty returned to her parents' ranch to await the birth of the child they hoped would be the first of many. Brian arrived in 1942; his father was not to see him for two more years.

Kitty and the new baby moved to Paradise Ranch, which still belonged to her strong-willed mother-in-law who did not approve of her son's marriage to this pretty, pert, dark-haired little miss from a sheltered background. The first years of marriage were spent in the "wharf house", with few amenities. None of this fazed Kitty. Victor returned from the war miraculously unscathed, and their second son, arriving unexpectedly early, was delivered by his father while Kitty read aloud instructions from *The Canadian Mother and Child* between labour pains.

"It didn't help," she told me, "that I turned over two pages by mistake and started on a recipe for muffins!" Victor wrapped the baby in a blanket and placed him in a warm oven as a substitute incubator. At regular intervals, Sandy, Matt, Elaine and Nonie appeared. Six were enough, Kitty decided, "though Victor wanted ten." Meanwhile, the family had moved into the large house which Victor had built.

Life was busy, but highly organized. Sandy remembers her mother sitting down each morning to write the daily list. Then she got right to work. She was a devoted, but unsentimental mother. The wooden spoon was kept

Kitty Wilson at age 18.

handy. Kitty had a firm belief in fresh air. "She was always sending us outside to play in any weather," her son recalls. Determined that her children share her love for reading, she made sure four books for each child were chosen when the Traveling Library visited. And she gathered her little crew around her nightly for story-time.

The cooking, cleaning, canning, the huge meals – their children remember company almost daily – went on endlessly. How did Kitty do it all, and still find time to indulge in her love of the theatre? A picture taken during those early years shows an adorable Kitty as Madam Precious Stream, in a play of the same name – one of the yearly presentations of the Naramata Players. And she was always writing, Sandy says. Columns for newspapers and, of course, indignant letters to MPs or MLAs. For some years she worked as Women's Editor for the Penticton Herald, as well.

There was little money, and the orchard consumed most of Victor's time. Still, Kitty found ways to celebrate all kinds of occasions: birthday parties, Valentine's Day, Hallowe'en, and Christmas. Christmas was Kitty's masterpiece. Her children still remember the mounting excitement; the house filled with delicious smells; the huge tree chosen from their own woodland; the decorating, the mountains of gifts arriving from wealthy British relatives; the torture on Christmas morning of having to milk cows and feed chickens before this wonder could be approached. And the bundling up later to tackle snowy roads for dinner with relatives. It was a magic time.

With the children grown, Paradise Ranch was sold, and Kitty and Victor looked forward to easier times. Victor, however, suffered a long and debilitating illness and died in 1992. Kitty, now living in Penticton, continued her active life. She attended clubs and church committee meetings, and she continued to write scathing letters to MPs and MLAs on justice issues. She remained active in the Arts scene, and was an enthusiastic supporter of young actors.

One day, she confided to me that her old friend, Jack Riley, now a widower, wanted a companion for plays and concerts. "Of course, there's nothing to it!" she hastened to add. Nevertheless, some months later she confessed they were engaged. This was in February, and the date was set for June.

At that time she was seventy-eight, and Jack, eighty-one. "But Kitty," I asked hesitantly, "Why wait so long?"

"Jack has never thrown anything away since Ruth died," Kitty pronounced. "That house has to be cleared out before I live in it!" Sure enough, each Saturday after that Kitty and two of her sons arrived at Jack's door. Jack would disappear. And at the end of the day two truckloads would depart for the dump, or perhaps the recycling centre. Finally Kitty was satisfied. The wedding took place in the small Naramata Church where Kitty and Victor and their offspring had filled two pews many years before.

Kitty and Jack had three happy years together. After his death, Kitty continued to tend the large garden Jack loved so much. She was still the feisty, youthful figure, always on the run. A month before Christmas, in 1998, she suddenly fell ill. The prognosis was not good. Still, she held court, graciously acknowledging the visits of family and friends, as she lay passively between snow-white hospital sheets.

She did not, however, lose her witty tongue. One visitor apologized for having to be absent over Christmas. "I'll come again as soon as I return," she promised.

"Never mind," Kitty told her. "Just watch the obituaries. You'll find me there one of these days!"

She died on New Year's Eve. A line in her obituary read, "She will be missed by her many friends and her worthy adversaries." She was. She still is. There will never be another Kitty Wilson.

KLUB KALAMALKA
ORIGINAL HALF WAY HOUSE?
Anita Ewart

TODAY, HALFWAY BETWEEN VERNON and Kelowna on Highway 97, visitors and locals can enjoy a refuge from the typical bustle of the Okanagan Valley. Found nestled on the western shore of what many call our Valley's most beautiful lake, Klub Kalamalka is a seasonal lease campground, which caters primarily to recreational vehicle folks.

But in 1904, when W.R. Powley came to Half Way House, as it was known then because of its location as the halfway rest stop for stagecoach horses, he was *not* impressed. Having been told of the bountiful life awaiting him in "God's country", one can only imagine his misgivings upon arriving to find a one-room cabin in the middle of nowhere. He remained as the operator until a Colonel McKay took over prior to WWI.

Colonel McKay built the Lodge, which is still in use today. After some years, in order to return to Britain, the Colonel left the buildings to his maid and butler. These two former employees, who incidentally were cousins, married and farmed the land after the site no longer was used as a mail-coach stop. It was one of their sons who eventually sold his share of the family property to the Thompsons, parents of the present owners, a retired orthopaedic surgeon, David Harder, from New Westminster and his wife, Sandi.

Harold and Dot Thompson, together with one of their sons, Duane, developed the campground which eventually had over 100 sites: it quickly became very popular for summer vacations.

Dr. and Mrs. Harder had long been involved in the development and running of the campground and upon the Thompsons retirement, took over the business in the early 80's, changing the campground to a seasonal lease entity.

Half Way House was often, unfortunately, mistaken to be a rehabilitation center. The name was changed to Klub Kalamalka in 1985. In 2004, it is as popular as ever.

2004 marks the 100th anniversary of Mr. Powley's arrival in our beautiful Okanagan Valley. What better way to celebrate than by visiting Klub Kalamalka, just north of Oyama.

The Last Train
Alan Longworth

THERE HAVE BEEN MANY STORIES and songs written about the short lived Kettle Valley Railway. It was a railway stretching from coastal Vancouver, all the way to the Kootenays. The line traversed some of the most difficult terrain on the continent. The route was finally completed in 1916 after some horrendous construction problems.

Eastbound from Hope, the line began the arduous climb through the Coquihalla Canyon. Recorded winter snowfalls in this area reached depths of 60 feet. One such winter, a train took twenty days to reach Princeton despite over two miles of snow sheds and a series of sheltered tunnels. Chief engineer Andrew McCulloch, a Shakespeare buff, named a number of the stops on the line after characters in Shakespeare's plays. Some of these spots are clearly marked on the side of the more recently built Coquihalla highway.

Brookmere, by the water tank.

In 1959 after a series of major washouts the line through the canyon was finally abandoned. Trains to the Okanagan now took a much longer route to and from the coast. At Hope the trains utilized the C.P.R. track up the Fraser and Thompson Canyons to Spences Bridge then reconnected with the old K.V.R. line at Brookmere and from there traversed the Tulameen valley to Princeton. The line snaked up the switchback curves out of Princeton to Osprey Lake, the start of the easy descent down to Summerland and finally Penticton, a city that owes much of its Civic existence to the Kettle Valley Railway. The last official passenger train to Penticton unloaded its passengers in 1964.

On Saturday May 21, 1983 the British Columbia Chapter of the National Railway Historical Society, after much negotiation with the C.P.R., organized a passenger train trip over the remaining operational line to Penticton. It was a sold out event, but I managed to get tickets to ride.

The journey began early at the C.P.R. Station on Cordova Street in Vancouver. The train followed the harbour's edge to the tunnel that begins at the Second Narrows Bridge, and ends at Willingdon Street just below the Brentwood shopping centre. From there the train ambled at a steady pace up the Fraser Valley through Haney and Mission. At Hope we turned north into the Fraser Canyon and stopped for a while at North Bend the C.P.R. marshalling and repair yards, to allow the southbound freight trains to pass.

We continued on to Lytton and the Thompson Canyon. Then at Spences Bridge we changed to a southerly direction into Merritt. I swear the whole town had come down to the depot to welcome the first passenger train to come through town in 19 years. They greeted us with loud cheers and waves. After exchanging greetings we continued on to Brookmere, the site of the water tower for the old steam trains. We tarried for photo ops, and then continued on to Princeton through the Tulameen Canyon. Once again the town turned out to greet the last train. Leaving Princeton we laboured up the switchbacks on the long climb to Osprey Lake, just like all the trains that had made this journey before us. With the climbing over, we rolled gently downgrade and over the 241 feet high Trout Creek trestle into Summerland. The train followed the gardens and orchards on the high banks above Okanagan Lake; finally crossing the bridge over the river channel and coming to a halt and a tumultuous welcome at Penticton's old passenger terminal. A band played, and buses waited to whisk us off to our hotels. An exhausting but marvelous journey had come to an end. We 300 passengers had traveled in rail coaches the youngest one built in 1930, a fitting tribute to a railway that is now just apiece of history, except in the minds of those able to remember the rumbling of a line of railcars pulled by a steaming behemoth, and those who worked on the K.V.R.

In this year of 2003 a massive forest fire destroyed the Myra Canyon trestles, which served as a monument to those who laboured building the K.V.R. line from Penticton over the mountains to the Kootenays. Sadly almost all of the vestiges of the K.V.R. have been removed, but there are memories of an incredible day journey in the minds of those who rode, The Last Train to Penticton, 20 years ago this year.

It is still possible for a railroad buff to get a glimpse into the K.V.R. history. A tourist steam train runs in the summer months on a short

131

section of track north of the Trout Creek trestle above Summerland. It is a short window into what the K.V.R. used to be.

I did get the opportunity to drive on the abandoned rail bed from Merritt to Hope before the Coquihalla highway was built. I recall the thrill of fording the swift running river, and driving through the canyon tunnels with the water cascading over the openings. The K.V.R. tunnels are now preserved as a provincial park and campground, just a few miles out of Hope.

ALONE
Don Conway

Slave to the bottle
I'd change if I could
Abandoned by loved ones
No money for food

Up in the morning
The suns yet to rise
How did I get home?
My mind won't reply

Hand down the sofa
Looking for change
A butt in the ashtray
Relit once again

Outside the tavern
The sun hits my face
Follow the staff in
The usual I say

Alone on the bar stool
Sipping my beer
Looking for talk
But no one is here

As a BC Trainman I am inspired to write about life as I see it along the rail tracks passing through town.

THE LEGEND OF SALAL JOE
Ramon Kwok

JOSEPH WILKOWSKI WAS BORN on March 19, 1919 in Poland. His parents were killed when he was a young boy and he had to live with his Aunt and Uncle. He suffered physical abuse from his Aunt and Uncle and lived a mysterious life ever since. Not much of his early life is known except he was an adult at the time of WWII. He got caught up in the conflict, survived, and somehow made his way to Canada, where he could disappear into nature, hoping no doubt to be left alone.

On the West Coast of Vancouver Island in Barkley Sound, there is a group of Islands called the Broken Group. Local residents enjoyed the convenience of this area and built recreational cabins. In 1970 these Islands became the Pacific Rim National Park. Boaters who had cabins were given a certain amount of time to remove their property. All the cabins had to be removed or destroyed. This group of Islands came under the jurisdiction of the Pacific Rim National Park and no permanent structures were allowed, except one. This float cabin was in the far corner of Turtle Island. It was the permanent residence of Joseph Wilkowski. Boaters knew him as "Salal Joe".

Salal Joe was not receptive to strangers. He lived in the float house year round. He lived alone and was safe. He was a man troubled with an unknown past: a very private person, one who never spoke often, either much of the present and none of his past. He never associated with strangers with the exception of a few fishermen, who would stop by his float. He confided with a friend that he thought there were people looking for him. He was suspicious of everyone.

He lived off the land or sea so to speak. His meager income came from cutting Salal bushes to sell to florists, whence came the name "Salal Joe". Provisions that friends would give to him never were enough. Many an American boater, anchored in the broken Group, were frightened out of their skin to see a bearded man, wearing a green toque, silently climbing over the stern to borrow some sugar or milk.

He was happiest feeding his humming birds that flocked to his cabin by the score. If you wanted to make friends with Joe, bring ten pounds of sugar. He had garden and fruit trees and managed to grow some vegetables. He was the ultimate hermit. Living in a cabin with no power and surviving on the meager money he made, selling Salal bushes, and from small government assistance.

Joe disappeared July 20, 1980. They found his boat on the beach at Dodd Island, not far from his cabin. His body was never found and it is presumed he drowned. The Superintendent became the custodian of all of Joe's possessions. Today Joe is remembered with a short write up on the back of Marine Charts of the area.

THE LEGEND OF SALAL JOE

My nights begin with pain
Of memories I abhor
Sleep is for the innocent
My joy and horror of war

Mine enemy in like desire
Of respect before destruction
Another place another time
No need for this aggression

Solitude is now my penance
Of deeds I proud not do
To take the life of a human being
To satisfy a few

I live among the giant Spruce
My soul I bare to all
I fell away from humanity
Resigned to take the fall

I've become a group of creatures
Of trees and birds and sea
They fill my life with happiness
With peace and company

I leave this world of piety
Of humans I trust not
To drift away on a silent sea
For man was born to rot

I've lived a life of misery
With nothing left to show
Except on Turtle Island
The legend of Salal Joe.

LEGEND OR REALITY?
Penny Smith

My cousin Harold has always razed me,
About my staunch belief, you know,
Concerning the truth of a monster,
Who's known here as Ogopogo

Harold teased me as in summers past
Though I tried hard not to listen
'Twas then I decided it was past time
That Harold needed to learn a lesson.

Two days later we rowed to Squally point
That day, smooth as glass was the lake
When suddenly waves rocked the boat
No crafts created such a wake

I knew what to expect of this sudden squall.
I waited breathlessly till he appeared.
First one hump, then others followed.
His mighty goat shaped head he reared.

Big green Oggie leaned in close to Harold
And snorted as he took a sniff,
Of my poor, pale, quaking cousin
Crouching paralysed in the skiff.

Ogo disappeared as quickly as he came
My cousin stared out upon the lake
He didn't speak for several minutes
Then a sheepish grin he did make

My cousin Harold doesn't mock me now,
He knows the truth about our wondrous find
He spends his time convincing others
To really open up *their* minds

LIFE ALONG THE
KETTLE VALLEY RAILWAY
Lorraine Lindy

THE FAMILY NAME, LAUTARD, has long been associated with the Rhone area, which is located five miles north of Westbridge, B.C. That association is just fine with Paul Lautard, who is known as the 'unofficial' mayor of Rhone, population 28. Paul and his nine brothers and sisters grew up along the Kettle Valley Railway (KVR), in places such as McCulloch, Carmi, Taurus and Rhone because their dad, Edourard, worked for the railway.

Although Paul briefly worked for the railway, trains have always been a part of his life. While living at McCulloch, south of Kelowna, five of the Lautard children, including Paul, hopped on the KVR on Sunday evenings for the trip to Kelowna where they went to school during the week, returning home again Friday nights.

They stayed with the Capozzi family in Kelowna. This handy arrangement quickly changed with the onset of the Depression in 1929. The Capozzi's could no longer help them out.

Accommodation for the children was found at a Catholic Orphanage in New Westminster. They received an education and lived for $12 per month per child. At Christmas, and for the summer holidays, they took the KVR back home. Living so far away from their parents was hard on the children, but there was no choice at the time.

"The orphanage we lived in was known as the 'dump,' because people who couldn't afford to look after their children dumped them at the orphanage," explained Paul.

There were 100 boys and 60 girls living there in separate quarters. The boys lived in a pen about 100 feet long and 60 feet wide, enclosed by an eight foot high board fence.

The girls were about 50 feet away in an enclosure surrounded by chicken wire.

"We knocked the knots out of the boards on the fence so we could see out and we could yell over to our sisters. Otherwise, we had no contact with them," commented Paul.

Between the two pens was a delivery yard where horse-drawn vans brought in food such as barley and oats by the ton, and stale bread. Paul has many memories of the food they were served and said, "Every morning for breakfast we ate crushed oats, the kind they fed to horses. We chewed around the oats and spit out the hulls, got all the bran that way.

We had barley soup everyday, something I refuse to eat today. We'd slice off the moldy ends of the bread and then eat the rest of the loaf. They gave us chocolate pudding once in a while, but no vegetables."

They stayed at the orphanage from 1929 to 1934 before moving back home to Taurus. At age 19, Paul joined the army. He served overseas for three years in WWII and saw action in Normandy.

"After the war was over, I arrived back in Vancouver on the train with 2000 other troops on Halloween night, 1945. Once I was discharged from the army, I apprenticed as a carpenter in Vancouver as I'd been banging nails into boards since I was a little kid," he explained.

Paul retired from his carpentry career twenty years ago and, once again, the KVR figured prominently in his life when he, along with his wife Gloria and family, moved back to the Rhone area.

Nowadays they live in a comfortable home on a hill overlooking Rhone Road. At the bottom of their driveway is the old KVR line, now part of the Trans-Canada Trail, which has become a popular cycling trail for people from all over the world.

When the Trans-Canada Trail Committee decided to use the old KVR as part of the trail, some people in the West Boundary area weren't too happy with the idea of cyclists riding through or past their property. Always looking on the positive side, Paul welcomed the cyclists by building a shelter complete with a picnic table, chairs, hammock and an outdoor washroom for the two-wheel travelers.

Paul Lautard standing on the steps of the caboose he built to scale.

In 2001, Paul completed an authentic replica of a CPR caboose beside the shelter. It contains three bunks, where weary cyclists can spend the night. When the cyclists stop to enjoy a cold glass of fresh water, supplied by the Lautards, they also admire all his railroad memorabilia.

Paul loves to share his knowledge of the history of the Boundary area and the KVR. Since he added plywood sides to the shelter in 1998, all the visitors have been signing their names and hometowns on the plywood, the roof trusses and any other available surface. Currently, there are thousands of signatures from practically every county in the world, a fascinating collection to read.

Although the Kelowna fires and subsequent loss of many of the Myra Canyon trestles last August slowed down the number of cyclists on this portion of the trail, Paul is confident the trestles will soon be rebuilt and his summers will again be filled with company.

Besides the cyclists, Paul has many other hobbies and interests to keep him busy. Each fall he and Gloria cut and stack fire wood for the winter; he also likes to help out seniors and veterans in the Boundary area by taking them boxes of finely cut kindling wood.

For the past 15 years, he's been involved in the Legion at Greenwood, serving as the President for five years. Currently, he is the first Vice-President. As well as going to the various schools each year to talk about the importance of Remembrance Day with the students, Paul organizes a service at the Cenotaph in Kettle Valley every November 11th.

Today, 81-year-old Paul, who likes to walk at least two miles each day, is happy he still lives on Rhone Road with a view of the old KVR. Best of all, he doesn't have to eat oats for breakfast or have barley soup for lunch!

Trans Canada Trail

The trans Canada Trail was once the historic Kettle Valley Railway, which ran through the town of Princeton as it made its way from Hope to Midway in the West Kootneys. The government of British Columbia took possession of the right-of-way of the entire Kettle Valley Railway line and local enthusiasts manage various sections. On September 9, 2000 this scenic, restored Trail was officially opened and is used for walking, cycling, horseback riding, cross-country skiing and snowmobiling.

Embark on your exploration of the Trans Canada Trail right in Princeton. To the West follow the Tulameen River through tunnels and over bridges to t he communities of Coalmont, Tulameen and Brookmere. To the East, the higher elevation takes you through grasslands, lakes and forests as you make your way to Osprey Lake. Enjoy the spectacular views with a 2% grade that makes for easy biking or hiking adventures. There are many historic and monumental sites available for you to discover along the way.

Subitted by the Princeton Chamber of Commerce

LOVE THEM QUAILS
Darcy Nybo

THERE IS AN INCREDIBLE BIRD that permeates the Okanagan; it is the quail. There are thirty-one species of quails, and they are the smallest of the 'game' birds. They are known by many names including California Quail, Catalina Quail, Crested Quail, San Lucas Quail, San Quentin Quail and Top Knot Quail. They are found in the dry, scrub areas, grasslands and orchards. The Okanagan Valley is the perfect habitat for them.

The concept of them being a game bird struck me as odd. Never have I seen a game bird that casually strolls across the street. Never have I seen a game bird that defies humans and seemingly goes out of its way to get IN the way! I wonder if 'our' quails know they are game birds. Maybe they are game birds, in a different sense. I wonder if they play the 'dodge the car' game on purpose?

I remember the first time I was the victim of one of their seemingly harmless little games. I believe the species I was dealing with were the San Quentin variety of quail, hardened descendants of the criminal birds from California. I was driving down a back alley by my parent's home, minding my own business. I should have known the alleys of Penticton weren't safe. I was so naive then, so ignorant to the marauding hordes that roamed the alleys and darkened scrub of the Valley.

As I said, I was driving along... and wham! There they were. They camouflaged themselves well in the brush beside the roadway and as soon as I came near the entire gang rushed my car. They came at me like a squad of deranged Lilliputians. I'll never forget their cry "We're crazy! We're crazy! We're crazy!"

I slammed on the brakes, fearful that I would crush one of these tiny beings. When I stopped, they slowed down. There I was, trapped by my inability to run over small, feathered creatures. They stopped, stared at me and then began walking in front of the car. I was snared in a net of quail.

The one I assumed to be the leader walked quickly ahead of the car, other males and females joined in and finally the children took their place in the macabre parade.

How had it come to this, I thought? Where were they taking me? They knew my prime directive was to do no harm and they were using it against me. Suddenly from out of nowhere rose the insane battle cry again. "We're crazy! We're crazy! We're crazy!"

As quickly as they had descended upon me, they were gone and I was left alone and trembling in the bright sunlight of an eerily strange day.

Years later, I moved to the Okanagan Valley and settled in the heart of quail country. I was afraid of another quail encounter, but the beautiful scenery and the fact that my family was nearby helped calm my frazzled nerves. It was then I realized that the quails of Okanagan Falls were probably of the 'Top Knot' variety, that being the knots on the tops of their heads are on too tight. These poor things rush frantically in front of cars, running madly until finally one of the gears in their tiny little brains stops slipping and they remember one very important thing.

They are BIRDS!

I hear their excited call of "I Can Fly! I Can Fly!" as they take flight upwards to all of six inches above the ground and then float to safety.

You've just got to love those quail!

PICKLES
Lois Robins

Pickles here, pickles there,
Pickles, pickles everywhere,
Pickles that I made myself
Are sitting on the kitchen shelf,
Hiding under basement beams,
Pickles even in my dreams,
Some are fat and some are small,
Jars are short, jars are tall,
Some from peppers, some from cukes,
Some from overgrown zucks.
Others come from veggie roots,
Even some from juicy fruits,
Made for grandma, made for kids,
Sealed with screw tops, sealed with lids,
Bread and Butter, Garlic Dilly,
Garden Beet and Piccalilli,
Mustard, Onion and the Gherkin,
All I've put a lot of work in,
What a pleasure, what a treat,
For each and everyone to eat
Standing back with joy and pride,
I hear the family come inside
And hit me with this gentle slam,
"Who eats pickles? Where's the jam?"

MAJESTIC MYRA
Randy Manuel

SHE HAS MORE CURVES than any woman I know, but majestic Myra has been taken into the hearts of all who know her.

Myra is the name given to the three-fingered canyon high in the lofty Okanagan Highlands above Kelowna. It is in this great canyon that Andrew McCulloch, chief engineer for the Kettle Valley Railway, mapped out the route that allowed him to hang the rails of the line on ledges, trestles and spidery steel bridges.

The story really begins in the late 1890s with the discovery of gold, silver and copper in the mountains and valleys of the Kootenay and Boundary country. To access this wealth, the Canadian Pacific Railway (CPR) built lines to service the mines and the smelters of the region. By 1898 the CPR's Columbia & Western had laid track as far west as Midway, serving the mining camps and towns of Greenwood, Deadwood, Eholt, Phoenix, Anaconda and Grand Forks.

It soon became apparent that a line needed to be extended westward to connect the Okanagan and Similkameen. The point was driven home into the hearts of the CPR and the governments of the day when the rival Great Northern Railway applied for and was granted a charter to build west from Midway into the Okanagan.

It was chartered as the Vancouver Victoria and Eastern. As their name implied, James J. Hill planned to capture all of the traffic between Midway and the coast by building a line that would go from Midway to Oroville, Keremeos, Princeton and Hope via the Coquihalla.

Upon the demands of the local population and others, the CPR also applied for and was granted a charter to build a competing line to the coast. Geography and politics dictated an all-Canadian route. In the far west the narrow confines of the mountains forced a compromise. In the canyons of the Tulameen and Coquihalla, the Great Northern had secured the only viable alignment, so the CPR swallowed its pride and together with the GN built and operated the railway on joint tracks westward from Princeton to Hope.

On getting the line over the hills into the Okanagan, McCulloch settled on a route around the north slope of Okanagan Mountain. His most challenging work was negotiating Myra Canyon. This great three-fingered gorge was named for Myra Newman, daughter of a track-laying foreman during the construction of the line in 1914.

The highest point in the canyon is 4127 feet at mile 86.6, where the grade enters one of two tunnels in the canyon. This is 3000 feet above the city of Kelowna.

The Railway measured distance on its Carmi subdivision from east to west with Midway being mile 0 and Penticton being mile 133.67. (All measurements in this story are in imperial as was, and still is the practice of the railways.) Myra station was located at mile 84.0 with the first of the trestles, tunnels and bridges starting at mile 84.9. The men of the KVR called the mile 85 section 'the continuous bridges.' At one point

Courage and sweat: building BC's railroads.

Photos courtesy of the Penticton Museum.

between mile 85.1 and 88.8 the tracks are only 3,800 feet apart, with the deep chasm of KLO creek separating them. This gives an indication of the distance McCulloch had to engineer just to move 'westward' that precious and costly three quarters of a mile.

Construction in the canyon occurred between 1912 and 1914. In the initial years of operation there were twenty trestles and two tunnels. One has to consider the technology of the day to truly appreciate the construction methods employed. Tunnels, bridges, trestles, and sharp curvature confronted the workers, who

had at their disposal only horses, mules, hand tools, hand drilling and black powder. Calculations of height, depth, and length of the trestles all were done by hand calculations. No convenient computers or desktop calculators here! The only assistance the workers had where steam shovels, and this only after basic rails were laid.

The shovels were used to fill gravel cars to provide ballast for the tracks. Thus it was easiest to build trestles first, then replace them or fill with earth at a later date. The canyon hummed with the sound of thousands of men working in the heat of summer, or in the high mountain's winter chill of -20 to -30 celcius.

No Chinese were ever employed during the construction of the Kettle Valley Railway, as the infamous Asian exclusion act was in full force, banning 'the yellow peril' from construction employment.

All of the bridges in the 5.4 miles of Myra canyon were built of local Douglas fir, framed and erected at the sites by skilled bridge and building crews. The first structures built used untreated timbers, giving a lifespan of approximately 15 years.

As related to me by Alex Price, engineering officer for the CPR on the KVR between 1956 and 1962, the first bridges began to be replaced by the start of the 1930s. Replacement trestles were built with only minor changes. Several of the large trestles were replaced by steel such as the one at mile 86.5 over KLO creek.

Two steel-through-plate-girder spans 45 feet long, two at 85 feet and one at 105 feet long gave the new bridge a length of 365 feet, as it soared 158 above the creek, curving from bank to bank on a 12-degree curve. This bridge was built up through the bents of the original trestle in 1931. As originally constructed, the trestle was 405 feet long. At mile 87.9, another massive trestle of some 750 feet long was replaced in 1932 with steel-girder spans. This bridge is 721 feet long, 182 feet high and is on a 12-degree curve.

As Alex Price relates:

> *Over the years as replacement trestles were built, only minor changes in the basic design were made. However, about 1956, changes became necessary. The main load carrying components in the structure - the stringers, caps and posts - were cut from select structural Douglas fir. These components were massive. Stringers, which span the 15-foot openings between the main vertical supports, are 10 inches wide, 20 inches deep and 30 feet long. Caps, which support the stringers on top of the vertical supports, are 12 inches wide, 18 inches deep and up to 20 feet long. Posts are 12 inches by12 inches and more than 20 feet long.*

> *Timber of these dimensions and grade were becoming extremely expensive and difficult to supply. Something had to be done. The result was a complete redesign of the structures. Dimensions were decreased, but the numbers of structural members were increased.*

> *For example, stringers were reduced to nine inches by 18 inches. Where six stringers were originally used to span a 15-foot opening, eight stringers were now used.*

> *The significant change was made from untreated timber to pressure-treated timber. The treating agent was creosote. The*

144

expected life for a treated framed trestle was now 30 years,
although there was no precedent for this figure.

The effort to rebuild the bridges and trestles was huge. The engineering staff of the KVR carried this out with the help of Peter Beulah and Gordon Brockhouse specifically. All of the work had to calculated to within a millimeter for each timber and drawn out in the framing yard, so that all of the predrilled bolt's holes would fit. This was compounded by the fact that most of the bridges had curves and banking angles together with ascending or descending grades. Each timber member was match marked to indicate its position on the plan in the trestle. All of this again without the aid of computers.

The canyon was not without its difficulties. The CPR never had 'accidents,' merely 'incidents.' For instance near mile 87.4 a derailment occurred on July 18, 1923, when an eastbound freight lost a car of dynamite over the bank and into the canyon. No explosion occurred.

The Kettle Valley Railway was one of the first of the CPR's operations to be completely switched over from steam engines to diesel locomotives. The Company bought new Canadian Locomotive Train Master units (H24-66). These had a different wheel arrangement than other 'breeds' of diesels that caused eastbound freight No.71 with unit No. 8909 to spread the rails and derail the 19-car train. This was not the first time this occurred; the sharp curves of the canyon, and the KVR in general, caused these engines to be banned from the Kettle Valley system.

The canyon holds another secret. In the 1920's the railroaders told tales of a small company of Chinese gentlemen, who would hitch a ride up from Penticton on a caboose. Near the big steel bridge at 86.5, the Chinese would ask to be let off. They would stand on the tracks until the train commenced its way eastward out of sight. The men always had tools of the mining trade in their packs. When asked about their prospecting efforts, the oriental gents would merely smile and remain silent. On one occasion, the curious railway crew let the miners off the back of the train and pulled the train forward in its usual fashion, but silently let the train come to a halt just as the caboose was about to enter a cut. This allowed the tail end crew to observe the miners descend into the east (upstream) side of the of the east fork of Canyon creek. They watched until the little group of men disappeared into the bushy bottom of the stream. To this day the location of the hidden Chinese mine has never been found.

The high mountain passes made it extremely dangerous for the crews working the trains. In the days before the installation of the Westinghouse air brakes, the trains' descent off the canyon and into the Okanagan had to be controlled by brakemen, who had to walk the top of the railway cars, stopping at the end of each car to turn the brake wheel. The job entailed leaping across the gap between the rocking railway cars often 12 to 14 feet above the ground.

On one occasion brakeman Reg Bean had just finished walking the length of the train and his last leap required landing on the back of the steam engine's water/coal tender. He successfully made the leap, but slipped on ice and fell off the tender landing spread eagled on the couplings between the tender and the boxcar. The engineer fortunately saw him fall, and brought the train to a halt. Reg said, "The engineer's face turned white when he saw me on the knuckle like that."

The tales go on but thus were the days of steaming the Kettle in Myra Canyon.

Sources: Altitudes in Canada, *James White; Interviews with Alex Price and Reg Bean.* Mile Boards on the Kettle Valley, *Joe Smuin. Okanagan Historical Society Report No. 12.*

MARGARET FALLS
Marilyn McAllister

Water surged through the jagged gorge
crashing to the floor below
over shelves of grey schist,
thrust upward
in some contorted portrait of a violent past
bearing witness to the collision of rock on rock
eons ...eons ago.
Now, moss hangs heavy over these rock walls
as sunlight eases through tilted cedars,
to rest on the dew-clad ferns.
Mighty trunks of fir
lift their branches to the sky above
and a tangle of fallen giants
anchor new life to this living floor.
Water leads through the narrow cut
to that chute of cascading foam
white, against the grey schist.
Cool mists rise to wet my cheek
and through the crystal spray
I see a sacred cave.

MANDY THE "HAUNTED" MUSEUM DOLL
Ruth Stubbs

ONCE YOU HAVE SEEN HER, you are never quite the same. She looks like a baby, but you know that it just isn't so, because of her vivid, cracked appearance, jaundiced eyes and the spooky way her eyes follow you wherever you go. Many stories surround this strange, but wonderful acquisition of 1991.

After her story appeared in the local newspaper, we were swamped with visitors from Quesnel. That was not to be the end. When the story about Mandy in the book, "*Supernatural Stories Around British Columbia*" was released, in late 1998, Mandy became a "household" word across Canada and the U.S. How did this all happen?

The Prince George Citizen printed an article; the Prince George radio station read it word for word and BCTV featured the story on the 6:00 news hour, which aired February 7, 1999. I was interviewed on CKNW, QR77, and received calls from CBC, CANADA AM and others from across Canada. Articles appeared in numerous newspapers, such as the National Post, Globe & Mail, Edmonton Journal etc. all the way to Alabama.

Our office phone rang off the hook. I wish I had recorded the number of calls. Now February is generally a quiet month, here at the Quesnel & District Museum and Archives, but not in 1999. We still had three feet of snow on the ground, but visitors from Alberta came especially to see Mandy, regardless of the time of year.

Montel Show and New York Trip

It's quite difficult to describe my experience in New York. I left on April 20 at 9:30 a.m. with the doll and the donor of the doll. I carried Mandy in a very new shawl made in colours of purple, with white snow-flakes, navy and blues. People at the Vancouver Airport looked very strangely at me because I wasn't carrying this "baby" in a normal way and the "baby" wasn't moving around. They finally got the nerve to ask what I was carrying and when I told them, they gave a loud whoop and promptly gathered for a good look at this doll.

New York was exciting and busy, with crazy taxi drivers (one who nearly ran over a man) and gigantic buildings.

We arrived at 11p.m. New York time. The Montel staff met us the next morning and put us in a taxi and told the driver where to take us. Five minutes later we were lost, as the driver had dropped us at the building called Addison Place, which turned out to be an apartment building. Another taxi later we were at the Montel Studio. Pre-taping, make-up and waiting were next on the agenda.

Finally I was ready. When it came to my turn, I was asked what was going on in our museum. I said that strange things *were* happening, but that I hadn't felt *weird* about the doll for many years. Sylvia Brown asked me what era the doll had come from. She also stated that because the doll is so life-like, it would have been scary when it was new. Mandy, she said, had originally belonged to a set of twins. They both died from polio. "We all need to be careful when obtaining antiques," she said. "Old things give off different kinds of energy."

Mandy has an energy implant. Sylvia said, "The energy of the doll is good, because she (referring to me) puts love into her work."

Much has happened since that New York trip. Avanti Pictures from Vancouver did a documentary on Mandy in a film called *Ghosts and Ghoulies*. This sparked yet another surge of visitors to our museum.

A lady from Surrey visited our museum the first week of November 1999 and stared at Mandy for a long time. When she got home, her house had been broken into and the only thing that was stolen was her porcelain doll.

The month of May 2000 brought something that baffles the staff to this day. The lamb, which is always in Mandy's case, was found under a rocking chair close by and no one knew how it got there.

During the summer of 2001 a visitor was trying to take a photo of Mandy (without permission I might add) when his camera jammed.

April 13, 2002 a visitor who knew nothing about Mandy was in the vicinity of the doll when she heard a baby cry. She looked around and noticed the booklet on Mandy. It then made sense to her.

The most recent episode happened just this summer. We had moved Mandy near the office. Oops. Not a good thing to do. At this particular time we were focussed on the history of Reid Street in Quesnel and the template we were working on went missing. Oh, yes, we found it, but weeks later. A month later, we moved Mandy to another room. Oops for the second time. A whole file on Reid Street went missing from the computer, never to be recovered.

Now you might ask, 'Do I believe that Mandy is "haunted?"' We've made peace, Mandy and I. She now smiles, very broadly when I hold her. How do I know? Well, someone took an image of Mandy and I with a digital camera and when viewed, Mandy was smiling from ear to ear. That photograph was discovered missing the following week. Oh dear, is this just another tale?

MAPPING THE GALAXY
Yasmin John-Thorpe

I'VE KNOWN LEWIS KNEE for over eight years. He is an astronomer, working at one branch of the Herzberg Institute Of Astrophysics (HIA) outside Penticton, British Columbia. The Dominion Radio Astrophysical Observatory (DRAO), on White Lake Road, is one of the two Federally-run Government observatories in British Columbia. Unlike DRAO, which uses radio telescopes the other, situated in Victoria, uses optical telescopes.

I asked Lewis to explain the function of a radio telescope.

"Unlike looking at the galaxy through an optical telescope, or taking an actual photo of the stars, a radio telescope sees what the sky looks like if your eyes could see radio waves," he stated, adding, "radio waves are out there but we can't see them with our human eyes."

The Observatory is nestled in an area known as the White Lake Basin, which is surrounded by hills and mountains. It was

Photos:
Yasmin John-
Thorpe.

purposely chosen for its natural 'bowl' formation, which helps to keep outside radio noise from disrupting the sensitive telescopes, listening for radio waves. At the site visitors can see acres of an old-design radio telescope (rows of telephone posts) still standing alongside the newer giant telescopes. Lewis explained that both British Columbia observatories are also used as educational resource centers for students studying astronomy and engineering.

"There are over 40 employees at DRAO and we have summer students working on their thesis," Lewis informed me. "We get both astronomy and engineering students.

Some return as employees after they graduate."

I wanted to know why it was important for scientists to know about radio waves.

"The Radio Telescopes collect data on the distribution and motion of interstellar gas clouds between the stars of our galaxy," Lewis stated. "This is important because planets and stars in our galaxy formed from these gases. What we see now are the leftovers and if we (scientists) are to understand how stars are formed, we need to study the raw material from which they are formed."

On rail tracks, close to the observatory's entrance, stand seven radio telescopes. They collect radio wave information, sending it to instruments housed in a small building near this track. The equipment then relays the data to computers in the main building. A metal mesh is incorporated into the outer walls and windows of the buildings at the site, to keep waves generated inside, by instrument and control system electronics and computers, from being detected by the telescopes outside.

"Although most of these gases have already formed stars," Lewis further explained, "this is an on going process here as there is very little of these gases left."

I asked what did we know now about these gases.

"These gases are made up mostly of hydrogen," Lewis explained. "And, remember radio telescopes can measure the speed of these gas clouds. We know these clouds move but because they are so far away, it may take millions of years to detect that movement."

On the site is a smaller telescope used to detect the sun's radio waves. Lewis explained the sun is close enough that its relatively weak radio emission can be easily detected with the smaller telescope. School children visiting the observatory can play a game of hopscotch in the yard. The solar system is set up along the boxes of the game, with each planet placed in their order of closeness to the sun.

In August of 2002, the Federal Government erected a new building at the observatory. Within the building is a new laboratory, where a highly sophisticated super computer for recording radio astronomy data is being constructed.

"If you recall the movie *Contact*," Lewis said, "the story was about the Very Large Array (VLA) radio telescopes in New Mexico. Well, that is where the super computer we are constructing at DRAO is going. It will be used by the Americans with the VLA."

After I left the observatory I had a much better understanding of the job of each instrument and on exactly what the scientists are working to discover.

Acknowledgements: My thanks to Lewis Knee for his assistance with this story.

MEMORIES OF FAYE'S BIRTHDAY PARTY
Beth Neville

August the twenty second was a special day
A time we decided to honour 'Dear Faye'
With a birthday party, an afternoon tea
To be hosted at Beth's place a quarter to three
There was some confusion
Friends had gathered to conspire
When Joanne announced "There is a fire
On Rolling Hills. I must take my leave now, for I fear
The danger of fire is far too near"
The power went out.
Our table was adorned for dining
No power, no coffee, we took to 'wining'
Wee sandwiches and Black Forest Cake we did taste
A cozy sojourn we had in haste.
The party was over
Then out on the street we could see
A menacing black cloud, to the east and far to the south.
With no power or telephone we felt gloom
Could this be our impending doom?
Then later
Neighbours had gathered in the square
Fear and anxiety filled the air.
When Henry in his wisdom decided,
That we were too hasty, we should abide it
And see where the wind will direct the flame
To trust in the Lord was the name of the game.
The Emergency Response team sprang into action
The Community Centre proved to their satisfaction
A place to prepare meals for firemen needed.
To fight an inferno which had to be heeded.
Before it reached those 'Rolling Hills' homes
The power came on.
The five p.m. news showed us the view
Of the fire that started at Lake Vaseaux
An osprey had nested on a power pole in spring
Which caused a 'short circuit' that did bring
A fire that gained 'Canadian National' acclaim
The army, firemen and Mars Martin Bombers came
To our village of Okanagan Falls.

MOM'S MEMORIES

(Taken from stories she told to her three daughters.)
Allene Halliday

James Island, B.C. 1919

MOM WAS EIGHTEEN YEARS old when she and her two sisters, Mil and Renee, left Victoria to live on James Island where they would work at Canadian Explosives Limited, otherwise know as the C.X.L.

It was January when Mom and her sisters took the train from Alpha Street Station to Saanichton where they disembarked with their suitcases. They walked down a long, dirt road to the wharf where the C.X.L. boat, 'The Monabel' was docked.

It was a short boat trip, but the sea was rough. The passengers were glad to step onto the James Island wharf. The girls picked up their luggage and walked along a boardwalk to the 'Green Boarding House' which was to be their home for more than a year while they worked on the island.

Mom (center), with Renee (left) and Mil (right).

Mom's dad, Bill Waters, had worked as a carpenter on James Island in 1918 while the plant was being constructed. He had lived in a tent during that period. The three sisters went to James Island for the first time to stay with their Dad for the summer. His tent was placed in a beautiful spot, right on a sandy beach — it was quite peaceful. They were lulled to sleep each night listening to the lapping of the waves on the shore. Mom grew to love James Island during that visit.

Their dad had helped to construct the 'Green Boarding House' which his daughters entered that January day in 1919. The matron met them in the spacious recreation room, where a fire blazed in a large stone fireplace. The sisters were assigned an upstairs room overlooking the water. Mom doesn't mention how large this room was that she and her sisters shared, but she and Aunt Mil chose the double bed while Aunt Renee took the single. Mom can't remember how Renee managed this since she was the youngest sister. However, based upon other stories Mom has told us about Aunt Renee, I'm convinced she was the canny one in the family!

There was only one bathroom upstairs. The dozen or more girls living on that floor would dash for it a 6:00 each morning because they had to be at work by 7:00.

Chinese cooks, who rang the bell at 6:30 a.m. to signal that everything was on the table, prepared breakfast. If anyone was tardy, breakfast consisted of bacon lying in solidified grease with cold fried eggs. UGH!

After breakfast the cook handed each girl a sack lunch, which had been packed the day before. When they opened the lunches at noon they found dry bread, curled up at the edges because there was no wax paper or Saran Wrap in those days to keep sandwiches fresh for hours. Mom would usually remove the meat or cheese filling and throw the dry bread to the crows, who certainly found it more appetizing than she did! Sometimes there would be a piece of dry cake along with some fruit, usually an orange or an apple. Mom claimed it made her detest the smell of either since everything in the sack lunch smelled of the fruit. The odour was so strong it was "enough to knock me over when I opened up the sack!"

Everyone worked long, hard hours – never less than nine. Everyone. There were no coffee or tea breaks. They worked straight through the day with only a half hour for lunch.

Mom was a 'caser', which meant she put the sticks of dynamite in the carton when the other girls had finished rolling them into their paper wrappings and crimping the ends. These girls earned thirty cents for each case they filled. There were fifty sticks to a carton and ten cartons made a case. Each carton of dynamite weighed five pounds; each case weighed fifty.

Mom collected the finished cartons and weighed each one to verify it was exactly five pounds. Sometimes the consistency of the powder would not be quite right. This would result in the dynamite being either too heavy or too light. When this occurred, Mom would have to remove those from the cartons and replace them with sticks of the correct weight. This process was nasty work, because the salt peter in the powder would eat into the cuticles of her fingers, causing them to bleed. There were no Band-aids then, nor were there any bandages near her work area. So she suffered.

The 'squirting house' was where the boys on the island worked. They were responsible for processing the bulk powder mixture in a 'sausage machine'. The machine earned this name because the powder came out looking like long strips of sausages, which poured into wooden trays on each side of their workbench. These trays were on wire slots. The boys used big brass knives that fit into these slots to cut the powder into the correct lengths. When five or more trays of powder were loaded onto a cart, one of the boys would wheel this heavy load to the powder rolling house where the girls made up the sticks of dynamite.

Sometimes the powder mixing building would rush too much powder though the 'squirting building'. If the boys tried to keep up with incoming loads, the machines would get too hot. When that happened, there would be a panic as the boys ran out of the 'squirting house' for fear the place would blow up! There were huge bunkers around each of these dangerous buildings to minimize the impact should one actually explode.

Mom's Uncle Herbert worked in the mixing house, which was the most dangerous place on the island. If anyone were to drop even a tiny bit of nitro-glycerine it would have "blown everyone to kingdom come!"

Mom used to worry about some of the girls crimping the paper on the sticks of powder. They would bang down hard on each end to be sure they were sealed. Not the kind of stuff anyone should be banging around!

The workers were forbidden to wear shoes with steel nails in them. They had brass nails instead because steel caused sparks which could set off an explosion. One day Mom found a girl about to slice a roll of powder with a steel penknife. Bad idea!

There was a narrow track outside a big sliding door adjacent to the scales Mom used to weigh the dynamite. A Chinese man drove his truck along these rails and loaded the finished powder cases onto it. These were taken up to the wax house to be dipped in hot wax which sealed them.

Entertainment was provided at 'the club' which had a recreation room, dance floor and a stage. Mom recalled a theatrical group coming up from Sidney to perform Gilbert and Sullivan's delightful *Pirates of Penzance*. Other times orchestras came over from Victoria to play for their dances. Mom loved to waltz with her partner up and down the length of the large hall on the beautiful hardwood floor.

There was a bar on one side of the room, but it was strictly for the men. Downstairs there were pool tables (also for the men).

Mom had hoped to return to James Island with her daughters, but was unable to do so. It would have been nice for us to have seen this place we've heard so much about.

MONTHS
Karen Miller

First a tribute to share some cheer
At the beginning of the year.

The following can be quite devine
If your lover asks 'will you be mine'?

Green is worn if you wish
To honour all of the Irish.

Eggs and rabbits made of chocolate
Hidden and eaten with relish.

Cards and letters mark these events
When presented to one's parents.

Hiking, boating, swimming a plenty
The warmth enjoyed by many.

On a very special date
Labour Day we celebrate.

This particular day to us bring
Memories to offer thanksgiving.

Ghosts and goblins enter the scene
Maybe someone will be a beauty queen.

Here our soldiers are thought of
With sorrow, reverence and love.

Finally, comes a time for us
To praise the birth of Baby Jesus.

MORE ELEGANT THAN JENNIFER
Shannon Reilly-Yael

(For all of you who've had Jennifers in your life)

WHEN YOU MOVED TO VICTORIA, you were a young seeker of refuge in trees. You grew up romanticizing the West Coast, thinking it was intrinsically hippy-happy nature on the seashore, where whales would come up and eat blackberries out of your hand and let you stroke their soft blubber noses above their smiling razor teeth. You anticipated ancient trees fat with the accumulated circumference of rings. You imagined deciduous trees kept their leaves all year. You may have even expected coconuts, or even bears that slept at night in gentle sea breezes.

You'd had a friend in school named Jennifer who was from Vancouver. She used to lament the unjust loss of her West Coast paradise whenever you slugged together through snow.

"The ocean, the ocean," she'd say.

You even nicknamed her that for a while, "Hey Ocean..." She loved it, naturally. It insinuated her beauty resembled those "blonde, aquamarine-eyed" heroine twins you read in the impressionable pre-pubescence, who taught you to value the phenotypically pubescence in women. And of course her being blonde and aquamarine-eyed was why you believed that the exotic and foreign West Coast must be so superior; you had brown hair and brown eyes and had never even seen an ocean.

You dyed your hair blonde but settled for your brown eyes, appeasing the reality of dominant genes and evolved chromosomes with the consolations of green eyeliner and the spectrum of catch-phrases such as "Summer Honey" and "Canola Field" applied as descriptions to the packages. With the packaging still fresh in the wastebasket, you hopped on a plane.

When you finally saw the ocean, you were like a Muslim at Mecca after a lifetime of poise for pilgrimage. You bowed down before it, crazed with the chaos of its rhythm, smiling and weeping and feeling like you were home. You were just eighteen, then. Looking back at this moment of communion, you realize it was then that you began resembling Jennifer. You were slowly attaining her. In Victoria, you could now more become her in your mind.

MOUNTAIN WILDFIRE
Janet Burkhart

The fire raged into the night,
This monster grew to show its might.
Fireballs racing down the mountain,
Sparks erupting like a fountain.

Shooting flames so very high
Into the dark and smoky sky.
Flames leaping tree to tree,
Miles of carnage for all to see.

Burning embers coming near,
Causing terror, panic, fear.
Firelights dancing; such a sight,
Families huddled close in fright.

Fire was started by a smoke,
Put your butt out not a joke.
Across the river grew this tower,
Showing us its monstrous power.

More fires burning down the road,
Firemen burdened by the load.
This new menace was the Master,
Premier called it a disaster.

One blazing week of sunny days,
Hard to see through all the haze.
Sleepless evenings in the smoke,
Causing us to wheeze and choke.

Looking skyward prayed for showers,
Needed rain for many hours.
Told the fire had receded,
Hope for some so sadly needed.

Now rebuilding soon would start,
Help these people from the heart.
Helping others is our plan,
Please pitch in, do what you can.

Printed in the Kamloops this Week, The Senior Connector, and the Barriere Star Journal in August and September Editions, 2003.

Mrs. Spraggs:
French Teacher And Lifelong Friend
Antoinette De Wit

In the early seventies, when I was just becoming a teenager, my family made the big move from a small British Columbia village to the mystery of life in a more urban setting in the Lower Mainland. I was going to be starting high school at Moscrop Junior Secondary in Burnaby.

I left our new house at 7:30 in the morning to be sure I would not be late on my first day. The school was about five blocks away and orientation was to be at ten. En route, there was nobody on the streets. When I arrived at the grounds, there were no cars in the parking lot. When I looked at the school, the blinds were drawn and all was dark. The main entry doors were locked.

I wandered around the school to look for the tetherball poles, hopscotch or square ball lines or even a place to play marbles. I could not even find a basketball hoop. This was my introduction to big city school life; this was my introduction to high school.

Around 8:15 the first cars started to arrive. I hid behind a wall because I did not want to be seen to be too eager to be at school, and perhaps be put to work before anyone else. I wanted to see what city teachers and students looked like, what they wore, how they walked; I wanted to hear their voices to find out if they talked the same. I wanted to see their faces to see if they smiled when arriving as school. I wanted to know if they looked friendly or evil and mean. Arriving early has its advantages.

Finally the schoolyard started to fill up with people of all shapes and sizes, wearing flashy new and interesting clothes, and carrying boom boxes and cigarette packages, school supplies and combination locks. They had more stuff that me. I brought a notebook and a pen and I wore an old blouse and shorts, with thongs on my feet. It was going to be a hot day and we were only to be at school for orientation, not classes. I started to worry and thought about running home to get more stuff, but there wasn't enough time. Were people looking at me, noticing my 'unpreparedness,' my fear, my anxiety, my confusion? I just wanted to go home.

The first bell rang and everyone headed for the doors and then into the hallway where notices were posted for all students to find out where their homerooms were located. Everyone starting Grade Eight had to head for the big gymnasium - that was easy enough - the gym doors were right in front of me. I took a seat in the front row and as others began to wander in, they all seemed to head towards the back, filling those chairs first. I did not understand, but I did not care since I did not know anybody anyway, and I was not even sure if I wanted to know them. They were weird.

I took note of a teacher on staff wearing old lady clothes and dark, horn-rimmed glasses. She looked very stern and very strict, as she stared straight ahead without even cracking a smile. She stood out because she did not seem like any of the others; she seemed alone in a crowd of adults, as I was alone in a crowd of overindulging Eighth-Graders. Who was she and would she be my friend?

Alas, her name was Mrs. Spraggs. She was a French teacher – my first French teacher and her room number was 124, down the hall on the first floor, on the right had side, next to a room with a sign saying *Girls' Lavatory.* Out of curiosity, I wandered in there one day, because I am a girl, and I walked out realizing my life had entered a whole new dimension. *Lavatory* is the city word for bathroom.

Mrs. Spraggs had a scary demeanour, but to me it was like someone wearing a Halloween costume – dark and gloomy, yet intriguing. I was sure she only dressed like that on working days. One day the costume would come off and there would be a wonderful, neat, interesting friendly, caring, warm and delightful person. I allowed her scariness to get to me and I paid attention more than in any other class.

Learning French was all very complicated and hard, and many students would spend a lot of time moaning and groaning, mocking and joking, talking and laughing, dozing or gazing. I on the other hand, felt determined to succeed.

The first test came back and it brought sadness to my heart. I got a C-. That minus sign really upset me – it was so negative and hurtful. I went home crying inside while other students who got minus signs and letter grades lower than a C, went home without an instance of worry or concern. They basically brushed the mark aside and declared they hated French. Somehow that made them feel better. Their behaviour and my dismay made me make a life altering decision: I would become a French teacher and Mrs. Spraggs would be my mentor, and one day when I would a French teacher, she and I would be friends.

I went to school the next day and looked forward to French class. I wrote a note on a small piece of paper and said: *"Because of that C- I've decided that I will become a French teacher.* I folded the note and put it into my textbook. I studied those 'er', 're', and 'ir' verbs every night. When we got into the past tense, I felt like MRS. VANDERTRAMP was my next door neighbour. I memorized; I recited; I asked questions; I answered questions; I scored high on those tests and never again saw another minus sign.

Mrs. Spraggs had faith in me and that sent my adrenalin to levels beyond previous recognition. She gave me extra stories to read and worksheets to complete. She introduced me to French music, children's stories and short plays. She gave me pictures and posters, and told me about bursary and scholarship programs I could strive for once graduated. As I walked on to the graduation stage at my senior high school, I remember saying to myself: *I am going to be a French teacher.*

A French teacher I am and Mrs. Spraggs has been with me all the way. We kept in touch throughout my university years. Today, she no longer teaches; she no longer wears the old lady clothes or the horn-rimmed glasses. She no longer looks scary, stern and strict. She smiles all the time. She is happy and enthusiastic, loving, kind, generous, warm and caring. She wears clothes that are light, bright and cheery, she has a huge and still growing family, lives in a beautiful home and soon will live in an even more beautiful home.

We get together many times a year to savour a speciality drink at a large Starbucks in Port Moody or to enjoy peanut butter sandwiches without crusts or to pick blackberries on her property in Coquitlam. As a teacher, she was an inspiration to me when I was a teenager and as a friend, she is still an inspiration to me now.

HYDRANGEAS—
A BOUQUET FOR ELOISE CHARET
David Herreshoff

Facing the judge, she stands to plead our cause.
She does not read, she has no need of script.
What she says is written on her heart
and flows in steady pulse into our hearts.
She tells the court why she stood on the road
and how she chose to sit in jail and fast.
Maternal instinct ruled, an impulse to
deal gently with the life that shares our Earth,
so that our children's children may live well.
Her daughter watches while she makes this plea,
learning from her mother how to live.
Recess. "All stand!" The judge departs. A large bouquet
is handed Eloise. Hydrangeas.
How perfectly appropriate are these flowers!
Consider what the translation is.
Hydrangea means vessel keeping water.
Now isn't that our Eloise herself,
a keeper trying to save a watershed,
herself a reservoir of hope and love?

161

MUSING:
A WOMAN REMEMBERS LIFE WHEN...

Cassandra McCroy

FOR THE FIRST DECADE OF MY LIFE, in the 1950s, I lived in Fort St. James with my father Slim, my mother Dora and my sister Karen. The memories of my happy childhood are rich and varied. We were blessed with a large but modest home with several acres on the shores of Stuart Lake.

At the time I was a child, the ruins of the old Fort were still present, overlooking the lake. From my recollections, the town had dirt roads and was populated, for the most part, by Carrier First Nation Peoples. At times, the Omineca people would visit.

We had no hospital or ambulance. The nearest hospital was in Vanderhoof. Women about to give birth would do well to stay in Vanderhoof several days before the due date of the baby. We had a post office, a theatre, several schools and, of course, the Hudson Bay Store. There was also a general store, a hotel and a corner store not far from where I lived. In the winter I remember watching Dad as he coached hockey on the outdoor rink close to the outskirts of town.

As free, happy children my sister and I had many adventures. We grew up with our cousins nearby and the native children next door. Our diet was very simple. We grew many vegetables. In the spring and summer we picked various berries for jam and ate wild moose, deer and grouse. We thrived and were healthy and strong, running in the fresh air. I can still recall the cup of Ovaltine and the teaspoon of Cod Liver to finish off each day.

My parents were very concerned about our education. We were students of Maria Goretti Catholic School and attended our Lady of the Snows Church, with its tall steeple. It is a beautiful historic church, built just up from the Lake. Pleasant memories flood back when I think of the Irish nuns who taught me and the parish priest, who often visited.

Mom and Dad entertained a lot. I can still see the ladies in their long gowns, sipping drinks by the fireplace, and the men dressed up, conversing with a relaxed air.

Dad was quite the storyteller and before bedtime I was favoured with stories about Skook Davidson, the famous Hudson Bay guide, and Rick Hobson the author and, of course, there was always stories about the war Dad had been in.

One hot summer day, while Dad was working at his sawmill and Mom was busy in the house, Karen and I were running after the chickens

162

who were penned near the garden, when I looked up to see a familiar sight - one which still leaves me now with a feeling of awe as it did then. I saw Chief Louis-Billie walking along the shore, coming for a visit. I adored him even though I'd never dared hug him or approach him too closely. After all, he was Chief to the native people and like their king to a small girl like me.

He was dressed in his fabulous regalia. He had on his headdress, with its leather-beaded cap, surrounded by eagle feathers. He wore the fringed buckskin jacket and pants appropriately beaded. His moccasins completed his costume. Karen and I quietly watched as he and mom shared tea outside on the lovely day. Chief Louis-Billie's visits were very comforting to me.

The general store, owned by the Dickinson family, was full of interesting articles. The licorice and penny candies were always a favourite. Many a day in the summers, Carrier and Omineca peoples would see me playing up on the road as they passed by. Calling me 'little lamb' in their language, alluring to my white-blonde hair, they would spirit me away to the nearby corner store for an ice cream cone. What a treat that was! We'd sit up on the round stools at the counter and choose our ice cream. Mom was a little perturbed, as I'd sometimes leave without telling her, which gave her cause for concern. Of course, she was concerned, as we lived on the lake and the drop-off was not too far out.

Several years earlier, my ten-year-old cousin was swimming and I was playing on the shore. Suddenly, I heard her screams for help. I was too young, being only six, so I ran up to the house for Mom, who was briefly tending to Karen. In the meantime a neighbouring teen had heard cousin Doreen's cries. She plunged into the water and rescued my cousin, much to the relief of my mother and the crowd of others who had gathered to help. The wonderful outcome of this was not only that Doreen was alive, but also the heroine, Mr. Russell's daughter, who had risked her own life, was also alive. This remarkable young girl was presented with a Gold Medal from the Governor General. You see, the rescuer was confined to a wheelchair, yet she courageously saved my cousin.

Left to right: Uncle John Rasmussen, Slim Powney (Dad) and Skook Davidson (Hudson Bay Guide).

Dad used to pack horses with my uncle John Rasmussen and Skook Davidson. He later ran a taxi business after the sawmill burned down. I can still remember him taking me out on a clear summer evening to watch the sawmill burn. There was nothing he could do to save it, but to my child's eyes it was a fantastic sight. Later, I would miss all the native workers who helped my dad, especially the ones working out on the booms.

My memories are vivid of the time one of these workers fell into the water and was brought up from the shore to the road, where my dad gave him artificial resuscitation and then sent him home.

Men to me back then were wild and rugged. So many crossed our threshold: healthy natives, burly loggers, packers, prospectors, bush pilots and guides. It is no wonder my mother felt the need to introduce us to music and dance, pretty dresses and rug-curled hair. She would wash my hair in rainwater or melted snow, which she heated on the big wood stove in the kitchen.

Thank the Lord we had indoor plumbing! There were still many who hadn't.

My idyllic childhood was about to undergo an abrupt change. My dad had shrapnel wounds in his legs and knees that were not healing properly. One day he returned from his check-up at Shaunessey's Veterans Hospital in Vancouver, and after a discussion with my mother, announced we would move to the Okanagan, where the drier climate would facilitate the healing of his wounds.

Oh, the memories of those early days of my childhood!

EVENING
Marlene Parsons

There is a stillness
in the waves upon the shore
a gentleness
in the playful dance of sun
a calmness
inviting me to walk
along a shimmering path of light.

As I move to the left or right
this path moves with me
ever beckoning me
to the glowing swell on the horizon
to the stillness
of One walking on the sea.

My Feelings Of The Penticton Ironman
Reg Gordon

I HAVE BEEN A VOLUNTEER for the past fifteen years for the Ironman race in Penticton. I get to see a lot of the emotions; the pain, surprise and heart break of the participants. Positioned at the end of the race, my team has the job of getting all athletes to return the 6" by 8" piece of cloth, held up by a band of elastic to the mid section of their body, which displays their individual number. As they finish, the video cameras of the announcing booths can tell who is that individual runner. With over 2000 crazy people willing to push their bodies to the maximum, this type of identification is effective.

Can you imagine asking your body to swim 2.4 miles? This year's winner did it in a time of 49 minutes and 37 seconds. Each of the two thousand participants tries to swim with speed and accuracy. Some literally swim over top of others with only one goal in mind: to finish with a better time than last year, or if it is your first attempt, finish within the allotted time.

Then they get on a bike and travel 112 miles. This year's winner did it in 4 hours and 50 minutes. Some of the travel includes an incline of over 12 degrees! Then they travel downward at speeds of over 80 km per hour on 1½" wide tires, hoping they do not have a flat tire or hit a pebble, which would make them lose control and end their attempt to become an Ironman. Once again a good time is the goal.

Now they descend from their bicycle seats. Some are bleeding because their seat has rubbed them raw. But they reach for the Vaseline, so they can finish the run portion of the race, some 26.2 miles. Legs cramp because they have been stationary on the bike for the past few hours. A superior time than last year is in each runner's mind. This year's winner did it in 2 hours and 52 minutes. Amazing!

To get a perspective on the event I talked to a few friends who have completed the course. No one could tell me why they ran the Ironman or could even put their reasons into words. The main thing was that it feels very gratifying to complete a feat like the Ironman. It's simply one of life's goals for a select few. Personally I feel there must be other gratifying events, which would not tax my body to its limits. Entering the Penticton Elvis Festival would tax only my voice for short periods of time.

I feel that this sport is probably the most selfish sport I know. It is all about, YOU, the Participant. Most of the participants are young and have growing families. This sport takes two to three hours or more per day of rigorous training and you must do this for a year or more. Some actually train for many years. I feel it is very selfish to steal this kind of quality family time away from your loved ones to abuse your body to the its very limits just to say 'I am an Ironman'.

The media is only interested in the top 10 to 20 athletes and all others are competing with themselves. There are many sports out there demanding each participant to be in some degree of shape. Most do not ask the body to endure the limits of pain and all of the pressure put on knees, ankles, hips and back, as well as muscles. The body often asks for relief by cramping itself. It hopes the person will stop and relax the injured area. There are many participants who do not even stop to relieve themselves. They simply relieve themselves while striding along, once more with hopes of getting a better time. To me this is not normal. But in my opinion, Ironman participants are not as normal or like an everyday Joe as they appear to be.

Some of the runners can tell when their bodies have no more to give. Whether they missed an aid station designed to nourish each Ironman with water, juice, fruit, power bars or any other type of lift the body requires, their bodies are just not able to ago any further. Not wanting to put their bodies in anymore danger, they simply quit. There is nothing wrong with that! There is no doubt that every participant wants to be an Ironman, but there must be a moment when you know it is time to stop and give your body a rest.

There wouldn't even be an Ironman Canada Triathlon if there were no background support such as the board of directors, management and the hundreds of volunteers needed to put on a race of this grandeur. The people of Penticton and around the globe would not get a chance to witness what the human body can and does endure when properly trained and called upon to execute.

The Ironman Canada Triathlon is a sport, which demands human traits such as dedication, determination, survivorship, perseverance, and that nerve that every athlete has, but must reach far down and hold on to, just to enter the race. Each must have the ability to display each trait when it is called upon.

In conclusion I feel I must take my hat off to everyone who enters, those who finish and those who do their best. Good for you. You took one of life's challenges and most of you won. With only one body per life, I do hope you treat your body with the respect it deserves.

MY HERO ELMER SALISBERRY
Wesley Nicholson

WHEN I WAS GROWING UP, my greatest hero was Elmer Salisberry, an old homesteader here in northern British Columbia. He made an impact on me and many others because of his concern for the future by protecting the environment before it was even cool to do so. He wanted to leave something for future generations, by showing people, like me, how to protect nature so everybody could enjoy it. He also gave me my first job, which was picking rocks and roots at the ripe old age of fifteen.

Elmer Salisberry

When I first saw old Elmer Salisberry with his deep tanned complexion and the callouses on his hands, I thought, "Boy, there's a man who has spent a lot of time in the great outdoors." How true that was. If he wasn't picking rocks or roots on the homestead, he was out hiking in the bush, enjoying nature and all that it had to offer.

But to me, he was more than on old homesteader. He talked and cared for the land and everything that was attached to it – the water, trees, animals and the soil itself.

Even though Elmer lived in the bush and hunted, the environment was very important to him. When he cleared land on the homestead, he made sure there was a strip of bush between each field for a windbreak or a watershed so all the topsoil wouldn't wash away during the spring runoff. He also kept the water in and around his homestead pollution free so the wildlife could still enjoy it. He only hunted when he needed meat. And he always took everything except the inside, which he left for the bears and birds to clean up.

Elmer also made sure the people he came in contact with knew about preserving the lakes, streams, forests and wildlife. He helped a lot of tenderfeet who were not too knowledgeable about nature, the wetlands and the wildlife in this region. He taught me, and many of my generation, about things we thought weren't important. Birds such as magpies, whisky-jacks and ravens help keep our forests clean by eating what humans leave behind. He also showed me how to track wild game through the bush and to leave the land the same way I found it. "Only leave footprints and not garbage," he would say.

Elmer is gone now, but not forgotten because of his gentle, good-natured ways and what he left for everybody here in Dawson Creek and the Peace River region to enjoy. I still remember the lessons he taught me about nature and the animals that make it their home. You wouldn't want somebody coming into your home and destroying it, so why should we do the same to the animals? They only have their instincts to go by. They have no way of knowing what will happen to this beautiful land if it's polluted and mismanaged.

Elmer's ideals are still practised by me, and the many people he came in contact with throughout his 83 years on this planet. Future generations will have much to enjoy. Thank you, Elmer.

GOODBYE TO FALL
Violet Smith

They fill the air, these dying leaves
That float on the freshening wind
Aimless in their direction.
Subject to the vagaries
Of a wind that scarcely knows,
Where to it is going itself.
A young winter wind, not yet sure
Of its own power,
Yet still nipping at the dying leaves
With a foretaste of power to be.
It hustles along the ground.
The fallen leaves, scurrying endlessly
To and fro, seeking a place to rest.
The sun, bereft of its summer heat
Gently touches the thinning boughs
Of the old trees,
So wise in Nature's ways,
Secure in the knowledge that already,
Their falling leaves will leave
A tender bud for them to nurture
Through the coming Winter,
For that is Nature's way.

NATURE'S ICONS
Esther McIlveen

WHEN WE LEFT the mountains in West Vancouver eighteen years ago, we wondered what could replace these plateaus. Living near and walking the dyke in Steveston has done it. Scotch Pond, Garry Point and the trail, along the dyke, have become the geography of my spirit.

I have discovered many icons there that bring layers of harmony and calm in a world that seems increasingly angry and discordant. One feels akin to dyke strollers, dog walkers and cyclists. Some enjoy greetings and others are content to remain in their private world.

Lighthouse at Garry Point.   *Photo by E. McIlveen, 2003.*

The snow geese, flitting playfully on the sky canvas with a mountain backdrop, remind me that as a child I wanted to fly and the closest thing to it was swinging as high as possible and getting dizzy looking down. When stress and worries hold me earthbound, the birds and kites speak of letting go and surrendering to the wind.

The lighthouse is a symbol of the creator who will guide and reveal any hidden snares that could ambush me. I need to keep short accounts with injustices, anger and negative thoughts. The sky beckons me to pray large prayers for our world that good will prevail over evil, for vulnerable children, turbulent youth and those who find their identity in the things they possess. Then I raise my arms to heaven in gratitude for health, for my home, for my family who know my imperfections and still love me. For friends and strangers, whose presence, bring a sense of well being.

The trees as lovely as a poem and nature's lungs, stretch out their arms and bid me breathe deeply their oxygen. No one will fell them here. I want these citadels to continue forever. Someone has said, nature never did betray the heart that loved her.

The water is both soothing and turbulent which reminds me that life is irregular with difficulties and hallowed moments.

The names on the benches have become acquaintances and are now inscribed in my tracks and I wonder what legacy will I leave behind. I am conscious of those who have adopted a trail to keep the landscape unpolluted and others who deface and toss away their rubbish.

Search & Rescue on the Fraser; Mythmaker, Dream Weaver, Gala Babe II, Golden Star. Photo by E. Mcilveen, 2003

The Search and Rescue on the Fraser and the boats - Mythmaker, Dream Weaver, Gala Babe II and the Golden Star suggest that we are all on an expedition. We may pass like ships in the night, or we can pause to befriend, act kindly and cheer each other on.

Holy, Holy, Holy, Lord God of Hosts, heaven and earth are full of your glory!

First published in the Richmond Review, December 2002

NARAMATA NOTIONS
Corlyn Cierman

THE EVENTS OF THIS STORY are true.

At the time of purchasing my present Naramata home I realized there was a ghost problem. Three of them.

As a ghost buster, who has worked to clear haunted houses, I saw no great difficulty in clearing them out.

The house was strange, chilly and oppressive. It seemed like a barracks, unloved, cold and very abused. The living room, where the sun shone through the windows brightly, was the only exception. After moving in, the fog inside caused by the ghosts began to clear up. I started to paint and clean out the negative forces. The three ghosts tried to block my progress. I experienced shuffling, voices, bangs, strange smells and missing items. I knew I was not alone. The kitchen was occupied by a female ghost in a house coat and slippers with dyed blond hair. She stood at attention at the kitchen sink and stared out the window. She revealed herself shortly after my arrival. One of the first changes I made was to replace the locks. One day the doors could not be locked, so I called the locksmith back.

He stood there, after inspecting the locks, and said, "There is nothing wrong with the locks!"

At that very moment the glasses in the far kitchen cupboard clinked together. When I opened the door, I could see no movement, BUT THE SOUND CONTINUED! With a little guiding help, my kitchen ghost went to the light.

The second ghost was a heavy breathing asthmatic man who resided in the basement. He was very disconcerting, but like all good husbands when my kitchen lady left he followed her.

Time went on. Finally the day to clear out the crawl space came. For some reason there was lots of old dirt. During the day, my ring disappeared to be exchanged for an arrowhead which I found on the basement floor. As I bent to retrieve it, impressions of 'don't touch' and 'don't handle' came forth.

I felt the former owner was responsible for this and the other manifestations. I was being watched!

I still had to deal with the third ghost. He roamed the perimeters of the house and property, staying close to the weeping willow tree. The pressure cooker feeling increased as he stalked about at night making disturbing strange sounds such as knocks and moans. He had straggly, dull coloured long-ish hair, wore a shirt and pants, and walked with a

171

stoop. I saw him clearly one evening going by the back window. His white spirit life force outlined him. A very dark colour shone just inside his life force. He looked at me with intense red, glowing eyes. He seemed to be a man on a mission! Was he trying to fence me in or out?

In the fall I began chopping wood. I could sense the ghost around me. When I came inside the house, he followed me. Very brave of him! He stood there, looking shocked. He said, "The way you chop wood, lady, I wouldn't f__k with you!"

He had reached his moment of truth. He asked to go home. I provided him with the way to the light, and he has never returned. My home was now clear of the spiritual, but the former owner still made his presence known. He had cast a pall of fear over the neighbours. He now had no guards or connections to the property, so he decided to bother me with other silly projects such as flooding my driveway and starting a fence around my property.

I was determined to rid the area of the useless anger and fear I felt he perpetuated. I succeeded. The day he stopped the fence project he announced, "I want to sell this property to someone else, so they can deal with you!"

He did sell the adjoining property and I have since been appointed caretaker. The neighbours get along and all is peaceful. Letting go can be priceless, be you human or ghost.

PRINCETON MUSEUM

THE GIFTING OF A WORLD-CLASS rock and fossil collection has resulted in a recent expansion of the Princeton Museum. The collection of fossils, petrified wood, minerals and rocks is one of the most extensive in the interior of British Columbia. Palaeontologists form B.C. and around the world are flocking to take a look at this incredible display of prehistoric artifacts. As well as the fossil and mineral collection the museum has many other historical displays including the 1905 Welby Stagecoach, a 1934 fire engine, old farm machinery, local Native artifacts, a butterfly collection, and various pioneer exhibits. Take a step back in time as you visit the Princeton Museum.

Subitted by the Princeton Chamber of Commerce

THE NIKKEI AND NISEI TRANSFORM KASLO

David Herreshoff

In the first year of the Pacific War,
crowded with involuntary passengers,
the sternwheeler Nasookin moored in Kaslo Bay.
The disembarking passengers were jeered
by some who gathered at the dock to watch.
The newcomers had come to be interned,
for reasons of security, it was claimed.
Their IDs called them "Enemy Aliens."
Given the chance, the town would have kept them out.
"Not in our backyard!" would have been the cry.
But then the town began to change its mind.
This is why: The Nikkei and the Nisei
brought new life to ghostly, dwindling Kaslo.
They taught, they worked, they cured, they ministered.
They showed convincing patriotism here,
continuing to love and build the land
where they were persecuted without cause.
The evidence is on the Langham's walls.
Ponder these relics, do not miss their meaning.
A site of racist phobia is a shameful place
but it becomes a shrine to unity
when hate is overpowered by love. At length
the Nikkei and the Nisei left our town.
Villagers sobbed and embraced them as they left,
seeing them no more as aliens
but cherished citizens, flesh of our flesh.
May things in this exhibit help us see
that change of heart and help us understand
that heritage is more than quaint nostalgia.
Painful wrongs are heritage too, tempting us
to falsify or to forget the past.
The Langham's exhibition counters that.

Note: The old Langham Hotel was the internment building. It had once been a miner's hotel, in the silver rush days. Now it is a beautifully restored heritage building, The Langham Cultural Centre. On the top floor of the old building is a recreation of the typical room allocated to a whole family sleeping eight to a room, during the years of the WWII Internment. Some of these people were born and raised in Canada; were Canadian citizens.

OKANAGAN WINE
Eric Linden

The weather channel on TV
Sparked Noah's recent comment'ry:

"Yeah, sure, you call for lots of rain
For 40 days and nights…
It's hardly rained AT ALL this year,
Why dontcha fly your kites!"

And Joan, his wife, without much fuss
Turned to her hubby, speaking thus:

"You know, my dear, ya can't be sure,
Sometimes they have been right.
Why dontcha caulk your leaky boat
And seal her good and tight!"

Then Joan, once more, filled Noah's glass
With Okanagan wine
And said, "I'll come and paint the deck
So she will simply shine."

They caulked and painted everywhere
Until the task was done,
Then marvelled at their handiwork
That glistened in the sun.

So proud was Joan, whose words were these:
"We'll call her *Noah's Art*,"
And Noah beamed with bursting pride –
Their boat looked truly smart.

A sign was ordered; when it came
The thing read *"Noah's Ark"!*
A small mistake – a major one
That somehow missed the mark

Next day it turned quite pluvious –
And rained for 40 days.
The nights, no better – they were rain…
The sun had pulled its rays.

Then off to cruise around the world
Went Noah with wife, Joan.
They took along some pets they had
So they'd not be alone.

Away they sailed – the Seven Seas –
Ah, what a grand old time.
Until they crashed on Ararat –
A floating "Ark" can't climb.

The skipper, he was drunk, you see,
On Okanagan wine.
The moral is: don't drink and sail
And you'll survive just fine.

UNUSUAL HOME
Elizabeth Wilson

FIVE YEARS AGO Elizabeth and Roy Wilson purchased a corner lot, one block off Main Street in Oliver, BC. The 1935 house and large lot resembled , more or less, the town dump. Today, hundreds of flowers and plants, fruit trees, and vegetables thrive in this wonderful habitat.

Elizabeth haunts local garage sales for the unusual. As a result, all year round , including Valentines, Easter, Hallowe'en and Christmas time, is an absolute delight to the eye, as the yard is beautifully decorated.

Seniors, physically and mentally challenged, tiny tots, teens and world travellers visit this unique garden. Everyone is welcomed.

Both physically handicapped, Elizabeth and Roy claim the activity and exercise involved is therapy in itself. The joy and pleasure brought to others enhances their lives.

The backyard chapel built in memory of 'mom' reminds us that this world, indeed, is God's Masterpiece.

ONE MAN'S VISION
Suzanne Buller

April 15, 1922
  Dear Diary:
  It has been ten years since my husband, Charles Hays, perished on the Titanic. Oh how I miss him.
  We were invited to return to North America on the Titanic by J. Bruce Ismay, chairman of White Star Line. We gladly accepted. This would allow us plenty of time, as we wanted to be near our daughter Louise during her difficult pregnancy. Charles also had to travel to Ottawa for the grand opening of the Chateau Laurier, which he had built.
  No official opening ever took place after his untimely death.
  I was approached to file a suit against the White Star Line but our family, unlike many others in first class, did not claim damages against White Star. When one is a guest, one does not sue one's host.
  We were returning home from England where Charles had found additional financial support for the plans he had for the Grand Trunk Railway. He was president of the G.T.P. when he took his ideas for the G.T.P. to Prime Minister Laurier. Laurier was very enthusiastic and supportive.
  Clara Hays

I have been very impressed with all that Mr. Charles Hays accomplished in his lifetime. He was awarded the Order of the Rising Sun in 1907 by Japan for his advice to the builders of the Imperial Government Railways. He was offered a knighthood in 1910 but declined the honour as he would have had to forfeit his American citizenship.

He had such grand plans for the G.T.P. and in particular for the northern coastal town of Prince Rupert. Prince Rupert was to be the northern terminus because it is closer to the Orient than Vancouver. Mr. Hays envisioned the Prince Rupert port surpassing Vancouver and promised a Trans-Pacific shipping company. Prince Rupert would also be the first city in Canada that was planned on paper before any major construction was started.

He had other grand plans for Prince Rupert: a new depot, freight yards, and new docks. Mr. Hays hired the famous architect Francis M. Rattenbury (designer of the BC Legislature, Empress Hotel and many of the most beautiful buildings in the province) to design a stately 450-room hotel. Just imagine what Prince Rupert would be like if Charles Hays were alive to fulfill his dreams. Oh, how grand that would have been!

ONE NIGHT IN THE AQUATIC
(Inspired by Don Burnett)
Jason Woodford

LOUIS ARMSTRONG: *ONE NIGHT in the Aquatic,* changed the hopes, ambitions and yes, the course of my life. I can still remember the heat of the spotlights. The sickly sweet feeling I had in the pit of my stomach as I watched the grand master on stage, while trying to forget the number of fries I had during the buildup. Man I couldn't get enough of those fries... unsurpassed in the Okanagan. I was on every high note, and hit the depths with every low – Louis led me through them all.

The old wooden boards heaved under the weight of the crowd. As people left that night, I sat on the grandstand looking out over the lake. The tunes still played in my ears. I prayed they'd stay with me beyond this night. I invited jazz into my soul. I knew listening to the melody of the breeze, I knew right then... I would some day join my idol in having one night at the Aquatic.

I just had to get puberty out of the way.

Kelowna – Summer, '69

"Daniel!" Mary-Beth Williams. The minx. "Now where do you get off standing me up last Saturday?"

Oh yeah, I guess I'd better come clean. "I was at practice. We got it Mary B. We're on our way to Van." She smiles that smile. Everything is going to be A-Okay.

"Well, you're just lucky you still got me superstar."

"How lucky?" Ouch. That look.

"I'll see you after," she calls as she leaves.

Under the stands, having their smokes as if waiting for some sultry dame to come on over and ask them to find her missing husband. They are so cool. If only someone would be cool enough to help me with my kit.

"Looking good Danny boy!" Hardy-har-har. See how good you look hauling a kick drum the size of Africa.

"Hey Dan, over here," called Amos. Friends like him are hard to find. Just pure luck he's also a fine guitar player. Together we set up the stage, a few of the other brothers showed up about ten minutes later... most of the work done naturally.

"Okay boys! You got your headline. Next stop after this the big city. It's going to be tough out there so enjoy this while you can!" said Barry,

our manager, never was short of performance inspiring rallying speeches. Of course we barely ever listened to him.

Amos looked over his black trim glasses. "Wow Dan, we made it – would you look at this setup?" The table had a luxurious cold buffet and in prime position was a 'good luck in going away' cake. Fortunately, they just put 'Congrats' on the icing.

"So, what's Mary-Beth make of it all?" Amos says wiggling his eyebrows.

"She's happy. She knows I'll come back for her."

"So you told her how long we'd be in Vancouver then?"

I'd gotten so caught up with the preparation. "Not exactly... no."

Damn. Wish I could be as expressive as Amos with my eyebrows.

Wow. It was like the whole valley was crammed in here. I'd been to great teen dances before, but this just took the cake. Of course this wasn't a bias statement at all. We headlined and we ruled the Aquatic. The dance floor was packed. I was stunned. I managed to spot Mary B. among the melee. She was such a great dancer. Every beat I played she matched with a swing of her hip. After all, as Louis had pointed out in my youth... it didn't mean a thing, if it ain't got that swing.

The night went by like a dream. Girls. Cars. Music. Summer magic. The parking lot was full as we finished our set. But the party had only just started.

"Okay boys, lets pack this stuff up..." Barry managed before being duly outvoted in favor of joining the party.

"I still can't believe it."

Amos tilted his head back before knocking back a bottle of beer. "What Dan, Jeez you've been jittery all night!"

"History man, the history! Think about it guys. Think about whose footsteps we've followed here, tonight... Louis Armstrong, Oscar Peterson... and now," ...in unison we raised our bottles, "The Strange Brothers Blues Band." Looking around at my fellow band-members, my fellow artists, my friends, I didn't want this night to end. Whatever happened in Vancouver, I knew that this night would be preserved as a fond memory, a fitting bookend to my childhood in what was probably our favorite playground.

"You know boys, we really ought to ..."

Amos raises his hand, "Peace Barry, peace. Let's keep this night at play."

With that he picked up his guitar and improvised the most original solo we never got around to recording...

Mary Beth fell asleep in my arms. Although I enjoyed the arrangement I knew it was time to move the party on. "I'll come back and help you fellahs in the morning. See ya later, alligator." On the second attempt I managed to lift Mary-Beth into my arms and wobbled to the exit. As I left, I heard a few plaintiff cries of "In a while, crocodile."

Ring. Ring.

Was that my head? No it was the damn phone! A slow painful "Hey" is all I managed.

"Dan? It's Amos."

"What time is it?"

"Ten-thirty. Dan, the Aquatic is on fire."

Chaos. A strange new reality. The mighty grandstand in flames. The heat rolled off the wooden frame on the lake like a scene from Dante's inferno. I looked around in desperation; a guy pushed past me. "What happened?"

The man gave me a foul look. "Damn kids." It would seem some kids had been smoking or something under the wooden structure. All I ever wanted was one night in the Aquatic. I had no idea it would be the last.

After talking with Don Burnett I was inspired to write this short story about the tragic loss of the Aquatic in City Park back in 1969.

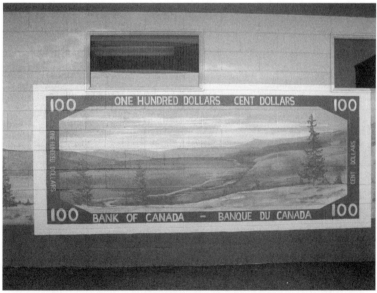

On the office building of Drs. Dickinson and Houston on Main Street, Penticton, this mural from Theme West Studios states, From 1954 to 1974 the Canadian $100.00 bill depicted the view from Campbell Mountain looking north over Okanagan Lake towards Naramata.

Photo by Yasmin John-Thorpe.

OUR SWISS CHALET RESTAURANT
Arthur Schmid

The following excerpt is taken from the book of my memoirs titled From The Swiss Alps To The Canadian Rockies.

IN 1987, MY WIFE RUTH and I opened 'The Swiss Chalet Restaurant' in White Lake, 16 miles north of Salmon Arm. The business became a popular spot featuring European specialties such as Wiener Schnitzel, Black Forest ham and red cabbage and veal sausages with hash browns. After only three weeks, we had 53 people for supper, and within a year and a half, we were serving 187 meals a day!

I would start around 5 a.m. making hamburgers, breaded veal cutlets, salmon steaks and preparing the vegetables for the day. The baking lady started at 7 a.m. I cooked all the breakfasts and served the tables myself. If I got bogged down I would ask our baker to assist for a few minutes, until I could manage alone again. For lunch we had a waitress who did a split shift from noon to 3 p.m. coming back in at 5 p.m. to 8 p.m.

Thursdays were my shopping day to Vernon. Hamburger and hot dog buns were ordered from the bakery. I also picked up soft drinks, grocery supplies, potato chips, frozen vegetables, cheese and butter etc. Ruth and I grew our lettuce, cucumbers, beans, cabbage, cauliflower and tomatoes in our greenhouse and garden at the farm. I would pick lettuce at

3 p.m. and make up salads in bowls, which I kept cool in the fridge to serve for dinners.

As soon as a customer was seated, we'd serve water, if they desired, along with a large basket of freshly baked, homemade buns with lots of butter. While they looked over the menu, we brought ordered drinks. Once they gave their order, soup or salad (with a choice of eight dressings) was served instantly, no waiting, something the customers really liked.

We played Swiss accordion and yodeling music on a tape deck, hidden inside a small wooden Swiss chalet. The customers not only enjoyed the pleasant atmosphere and good meal, but also the great view of the lake and surroundings seen through the many windows.

The restaurant was a huge success and I held on to it until September 1991, when I sold it. The new owners could not make a go of it and it was abandoned.

MORNING IN PENTICTON
Violet Smith

Through the mists of early morn,
the sun gleams its warmth
melting away the last of dewy dawn.
Bird songs, muted in the misty vale,
now fill the heavens
proclaiming a new day is born.
Eagles fly high with graceful abandon,
as free as the breeze
that bears them ever upwards.
From crag to crag, the mountain sheep
step daintily, light as thistledown,
foraging the lofty heights.
Tumbling down the mountainside
a stream murmers its endless song
and rushes to lose itself
in the lake below.
A lake that lies in quiet peace
lapping gently at the sandy shore.
Shines there, a city in the early sun,
the city of Pen - tic -ton.

OVER THE FENCE
Endrene Shepherd

i have no family here and so
this neighborhood is my family
i love it
i hate it
i watch it whenever i know
that it isn't watching me
i watch it so i can learn what it is i want to be
when i grow up
when i get as big as this neighborhood
when my alleyways have bicycles and sheds and old couches
moldering leaves and cigarette butts
old men looking for walnuts that have escaped from the neighbor's tree
crows screaming at cats that never come when i call kitty kitty
and
i wonder over the fences and i watch and retain
the voices of dogs
the voices of the children who call the dogs
the voice of the guitar that is played on the porch of the house on the corner
the taste of the air whipped into my face by a passing truck
grit
gravel
grass
broken bottles
slouching strangers
smiling seniors
strains of bohemian rhapsody gushing from the funny orange house
crab apples in the gutter
sunshine on the doorstep
this neighborhood sprawls and stretches and sings
i want to sing
just like that

OYEZ, OYEZ, OYEZ!
Penny Smith

SOMETIMES IT PAYS to have a loud voice. That was what Don Bowen discovered shortly after he arrived in Summerland in September of 1994. He was looking for some adventure and discovered it during the loud voice competition for a town crier. He won. Since then he has enjoyed his role immensely. In a town which embraces Tudor style architecture, Don, dressed in his costume, fits right in.

His attire is based on Captain Vancouver or Horatio Hornblower. It comprises a white lace dickey, green breeches, white stockings, black shoes with gold buckles, a gold waistcoat and from time to time, white gloves. The outfit is completed with a matching tri-corn hat with a feather and a large brass bell. This particular bell was used in an English school and weighs five pounds. The colours are gold and green, which represent the town.

His friend, Marje Jenkinson, who is dressed in a similar Dickens style costume complete with long dress, hoops and bonnet, often accompanies him on his town strolls. True to community spirit, Jean Lauer Costume Loft in Summerland produced the elaborate costumes.

Don carries a quill from time to time, with which he pens his numerous announcements. Like his ancient counterparts, Don opens stores, leads parades, announces the mayor is coming, as well as doing other jobs for the local chamber. He is available for anniversaries and birthdays, too, if you desire something unique.

Town criers have been around for centuries, originating in Greece. Royalty protected criers, hence the saying 'don't kill the messenger'. They evolved over the years and were picked from the upper levels of society, as they needed to be able to read and write. Town criers notified their illiterate neighbours of new laws, and news from other towns and cities.

There are a handful of town criers in Canada, but despite their numbers there are numerous competitions throughout the world. Don will be attending the Lord Mayor of Chester's Invitational World Town Crier Championship in Chester, England this June. We wish him much luck in his tenth year as town crier for beautiful Summerland.

PRINCETON
Gladys Archibald

The Similkameen and Tulameen
Are rivers of renown
And nestled in between the forks
Lies a quiet little town

Once known as Vermilion Forks
A pleasant sounding name
But when it was put on the map
Princeton it became.

I know I wasn't very old
When Grandpa drove us down
A narrow grade, across a bridge
and we were in the town.

I remember old log buildings
Pearly Russell in the store
I stayed so close to Grandpa
That I didn't see much more.

Nearly ninety years have vanished
I visit it again
There are no more log buildings
But the river is the same.

I often think about those days
And no matter where I roam
When I'm in the town of Princeton
I always feel at home.

PYRAMID OF THE NORTH
Darcy Nybo

BREATHTAKING VIEWS and remineralized soil. Peace in the park and a pyramid in a northern desert populated with clones. These may not seem related, however if you travel to the Okanagan Valley, you'll find out just how much these things have in common. They are all part of the Summerhill Pyramid Winery located in Kelowna, BC.

Summerhill Pyramid Winery is like no other winery in the valley. Its main focus is a pyramid that is a four story high, 3249 square feet, eight-percent replica of the Great Pyramid.

The Pyramid is used as a wine cellar and after fourteen years of testing every day, tasters chose the pyramid-aged wine almost unanimously as being smoother and having a better aroma, better than wines aged elsewhere!

The chamber appears to bring out the best of the best in liquids. It is well established that rather than rotting, milk turns to yoghurt within a properly constructed pyramid. Someone even patented the fact that razor blades become sharper in a pyramid. All this old technology is used in this modern day winery to produce some of the world's finest wines.

Summerhill's proprietor, Stephen Cipes, was a finalist for the prestigious Ernst and Young Entrepreneur of the Year Award. When Cipes first visited the Okanagan in 1986, the New York developer believed he'd found unique conditions to produce "intensely flavoured small grapes", the perfect base for sparkling wine.

Cipes brought grape clones from France and on his hands and knees, planted them. The winery follows organic growing practices. There are no herbicides or pesticides. Says Cipes, "This keeps the lake clean and our grapes don't taste of chemicals. These grapes are happy guys; they're flourishing. Our wines allow nature to speak for herself."

Summerhill wines are regularly honoured in international competitions. They won a gold medal in Champagne, France, against French Champagne. Even actress Drew Barrymore, while a guest at Summerhill, partook of their famous champagne in the cellar of the pyramid.

In May of 2003, the Enchanted Vines series of wines began shipping from Summerhill. The wines themselves were created by award winning winemaker, Bruce Ewert.

These three wines are very special. The Enchanted Vines Series are not only organically grown and pyramid aged; they are blessed with ancient ceremonial techniques to infuse the wine with intention. Chelsea Wise is the Medicine Woman and Shaman responsible for the blessing and enchantment of the Enchanted Vines Series. Every drop of each elixir contains the intention and possibility of deep peace, transformation and magic.

The first of the three, *Alchemy*, is infused with the power to awaken dreams and transform them into reality. The second wine, *Inspiration,* is the elixir for nurturing creativity. The final of the three is *Solus,* the sun united with the heart, sparks fire in our souls.

There is more to this amazing series of wines. Summerhill collaborated with Brian Froud to create three beautiful and unique labels for these wines. Froud is the genius behind the films *The Dark Crystal* and *Labyrinth,* and the best-selling books *Faeries, Goblins of the Labyrinth, Lady Cottington's Pressed Fairy Book,* and many others.

For every bottle sold of the Enchanted Vines Series, $1.00 US goes to benefit the non-profit organization Global Vision for Peace.

 If the positive attitudes, the view, the wines and the pyramid are not enough, there's still more to discover at Summerhill. The property is host to a restored Mallam heritage log home, which is next to the Kikuli first nations earth house. There is also landscaped Peace Park at the entrance to the winery, which encourages international understanding and world peace. It features a Peace Pole, which reads "May peace prevail on Earth" in 16 languages. There is a year round waterfall and a Koi pond with gardens and a satellite relief globe that overlooks beautiful Lake Okanagan and a view of the entire Okanagan Valley.

A visit to the Okanagan is not complete until you've seen the Pyramid of the North.

RANGE PATROL
Dawn Renaud

In 1967, J.W. (Bill) Pavle realized a life-long dream.

Bill was an aircraft mechanic in WWII. He returned from the airforce in 1944, creating Kelowna's first public bus line, the Siver Green. He helped his wife with her television show and participated in gymnastics with the eldest of this three daughters. He also enjoyed acting in little theatre, hunting, and fishing, but there was something else he really wanted to try his hand at: he wanted to be a rancher. In 1967 he bought Echo Lake Ranch, and set out to raise beef.

In the late 1960's, cattle rustling in the Lumby area had reached a point where ranchers knew something had to be done. Like most of the southern interior, there were miles of unpopulated range land, so it was easy pickings for anyone who wanted beef on the hoof. In 1970, a typical year, ranchers had reported nearly forty head missing and a more than a dozen more were found dead - some butchered, some simply shot and left. Like poachers, rustlers often operate under the cover of darkness, but in the area east of Vernon through to the foothills of the Monashee it was easy to kill an animal in broad daylight unseen, unquestioned, and unreported.

Ranchers were prepared to take things into their own hands. What could be done? In a meeting of the local cattlemen's association attended by local RCMP Cpl. Wes Knopp and Kamloops' Sgt. Ab Willms, the member in charge of stock investigations for the province, the ranchers agreed to form BC's first Range Patrol.

The idea was simple. The ranchers pitched in and rented a radio telephone, and drew up a schedule. Working in pairs, they would take turns with the radiophone and roam the range and ranch land in a well-marked pick-up truck, with no predictable pattern. They would show up night and day, anywhere they chose to go on public and logging access roads. They wrote down licence numbers of unfamiliar vehicles in unusual locations, and they stopped and talked to anyone they came across in remote areas. The radiophone allowed them to contact the RCMP if they saw anything particularly suspicious.

The intent of the range patrol was never really to catch the thieves in the act. Although the men were prepared to intervene directly if the need arose, they expected that it would not be necessary. And they were right. Because the range patrol was well advertised with roadsigns, bumper stickers, radio and newspaper coverage, rustlers were well advised to give up and stay home. Besides, now that the general public was more aware of the problems faced by the ranchers, they were more willing to call in anything unusual. So the end result was what the ranchers wanted: the number of missing and dead cattle dropped drastically over the first two years and stayed down. A side affect was an immediate reduction in poaching wild game. Who knew when or where the range patrol would turn up next?

Bill (middle).with Cpl.Wes Knopp and Len Hoffman.
Photo: Cattlemen Magazine, November 1972

The range patrol was an idea whose time had come. In November of 1972 Cattlemen Magazine ran a feature article on their success; by now range patrols were operating throughout the southern interior. In 1977 the CBC program This Land came to Lumby to interview the ranchers and RCMP who had been instrumental in developing BC's home-grown answer to an age-old problem.

Bill sold the ranch early in 1978, but not before he'd left his mark as a rancher.

THE RCSCC REVENGE: A RETROSPECTIVE
David Snyder

A CADET CORPS IS A MYSTERIOUS, sensitive, curious creation with all the strengths and weaknesses of discipline, leadership and emotional adolescence. A corps needs to be commanded with passion and craft; it does not cope well with change, confusion or inconsistency. Cadets want purposeful structure, which makes the world simple. If well led, it will thrive. For decades Sea Cadets not only thrived, they dominated the cadet world in Penticton.

To be a cadet can be a socially magical experience. Sea Cadets had a tradition which brought generations of Penticton boys' tribal comfort. Over the decades, thousands of Penticton boys wore a naval uniform. When a boy dressed in naval rig, he was a better, more mature, more confident young man. There was perfection in a mint white gun shirt, quality in a razor-ridged collar, and pride in a pair of mirrored-boots.

After the signaler barked, "Ten-seconds-to-sunset-Sir!" and the skilled bugler played, and the White Ensign descended toward the deck, oh... there was majesty!

Many a nostalgia-washed former cadet recalls, "It was part of who I was. Wednesday night at Nanaimo Street Armoury, the PO's Mess, starching lanyards, shining boots, ironing your pants in-side-out, selling holly, wearing the uniform to school, being a member of the guard, marching in the annual Peach Festival Parade, and sailing that old whaler on the choppy lake."

For decades RCSCC Revenge was the alpha-male of cadet corps in Penticton, offering boys 14-18 (and Navy League Cadets - boys aged 10-13) a naval tradition of seamanship, range, drill, communication and band. Formed in 1927 the corps paraded 60-70 boys weekly in the old prewar Armoury during the 1930's and 1940's, when our town was less than 8,000 people.

During the war years every high school boy was a cadet (girls did red cross work). Sea Cadets took a leadership role at school, and in the community. Their corps training they took most seriously. One hundred and ninety-seven Penticton Sea cadets joined the services. When a cadet joined the navy, and 90 did, the corps paraded at the train station to give that person a royal sendoff.

Cadet corps flourished because of dedicated knowledgeable officers, the challenging training program and cadets who were well led. Lt. Pete Loveridge (CO- 1927-42) and Lt. Wally Mattock (CO-1942-59) gave yeoman service to our community during the first three decades of the corps. In 1947, for his dedication, Wally Mattock was promoted Lieutenant-Commander.

After the war with a constant source of experienced RCNVR veterans, Revenge was a tour-de-force in the cadet world. Under Lt Don Colman's command, the corps was awarded the best corps in province in 1962. What an accomplishment in the golden era of cadets!

RCSCC Revenge Guard 1962

At Annual inspection 1972, Revenge paraded 100 cadets-30 Sea cadet males (age14-18), 20 Wrennettes (girls age 14-18) and 50 Navy League Cadets (boys age 10-13).

Many adults supported Penticton Sea Cadets in thought and deed: Don Coleman, Jack Kay, Jack Canrill, Bill Johnson, Roy Burt, Nels Stromgren, Gordon Hendrie, Dave Young and Ed Lansdell.

The corps folded in 1982 because of failed community support, and responsibility overload that crushed the inexperienced commanding officer, a recent high-school graduate, working his first job.

Over twenty years have passed since Sea Cadets paraded in Penticton. In 2004 two former cadets still serve; Lt. Colin Barton CD, is a sea cadet Officer on Vancouver Island, and Capt. Kurt Swanson CD is the CO of Penticton Army Cadets. Three distinguished retired Naval Officers first wore a naval uniform in Penticton: Cmdr. Bruce Melville CD, Commodore Ian Morrow CD and Admiral 'Dick' Leir CD.

Many Canadians credit cadets as being the vital transition to adulthood. As fundamental as picking cherries or apples, as swimming in the lake or climbing Munson Mountain, growing up in the South Okanagan was defined for generations of boys (and one generation of girls) by the customs, traditions and experience of Royal Canadian Sea Cadet Corps 'Revenge' in Penticton, British Columbia.

The last Sea Cadet Commanding Officer in BC to wear the old blue naval uniform was D.B.J. Snyder CO RCSCC Revenge 1972-75.

REMEMBERING CANADA'S GREAT POET
Esther McIlveen

But they had their place once,
And left a place to stand on

-Al Purdy

APRIL 21ST MARKED the second anniversary of the death of Al Purdy, our national poet. Some say he's the very definition of Canadian literature. Purdy was a two-time winner of Canada's Governor General's Award and was awarded the Order of Canada.

I was first introduced to Purdy's poetry at UBC. At the time I was seeking out Canadian writers. Margaret Avison was a personal friend and had worked with us in Toronto's Inner City. Like Purdy, she too had won the Governor General's Medal twice. Recently, she won the Griffin Poetry Prize in Toronto for her book, *Concrete and Wild Carrots*. It was a thrill to hear Margaret read 'Rising Dust' on the Internet at age 85. I wanted to lunge through the glass and give her a bear hug. However, most of her poetry was oblique and beyond me. Purdy's poetry was accessible.

The last time I saw him, he was in his 80's reading at Chapters in Richmond, British Columbia. He was wearing a brown suit, white high top running shoes with lanky legs sprawled out like roots of trees. Al was trying to find a poem and I called out the page number. He looked up and exclaimed, "My God, they take my poetry seriously!"

When he was dying, I sent a book my husband and I co-authored. *Would You Know My Name?* is about heaven, and I hoped to bring him some comfort.

Al Purdy was born in Wooler, Ontario in 1918 and was known as a 'poet of the people'. He rode the rails in his teens, dropped out of school in grade 10, was a wanderer and spent six years in the RCAF.

Purdy admitted he was a lousy poet in his beginnings. He was well into his mid-40's before he found his own voice. Al left a place for other writers to stand on, including Margaret Atwood.

In a strange way Purdy also extended permission to me. I have not owned my writing craft, as I should, I have dissipated my creative energies by investing disproportionately in the lives and dreams of others.

In a game we used to play, 'Simon, May I?' I have taken only baby steps in writing, rather than the giants steps Al's long legs took. I admire Purdy for his tenacity in perfecting his skill and for believing in himself.

"I just wrote," says Purdy. "I always just wrote. I couldn't live without it."

"Why should we all use our creative power? Because there is nothing that makes people so generous, joyful, lively, bold and compassionate, so indifferent to fighting and the accumulation of objects and money," writes Brenda Ueland.

Article first appeared in the Richmond Review, April 2001.

THE GARDEN OF ABBOTSFORD
Alvin G. Ens

Indelicately, with a fork, I squish my strawberries into ice cream
until red oozes like a massacre on winter's snow.
Now attack my prey,
savour for a moment the sweet tangy taste of conquest,
lose my head and attack again and again.
     My wife, genteel and refined,
slices berries onto a small glacial peak,
then gently hoists cach bleeding berry, cushioned in white,
like search and rescue some wounded skier on the slope,
and soothes with wash of coffee.
     My son hefts ice cream, berries, milk into blender
and whirring into creamy smoothness asks, "Where's the straws?"
And I quip, "Every berry has its straw; they're strawberries."
He sucks succulent sustenance slowly savouring sweetness
until slurp spells stop,
Then runs his finger round the rim to catch the last remnant.
     My daughter, the nibbler, loves berries – tempting, yielding,
savouring like stolen kisses – and plans each winter's date
with frozen memories of summer sweetness to lay them cold
upon the tongue to thaw waiting, yielding, indulging.
In pantry trophy case we store, jammed into jars for winter memories,
our summer conquests, carefully labelled Strawberry 03,
Strawberry & Rhubarb 03, Rasp. Jelly 03, and more
And await the next rich, ripe paradise in the Garden of Eat 'em.

Published in chapbook, Colours of Life *by MSA Poets Potpourri Society, June 2002.*

THE RESORT TOO GOOD TO KEEP A SECRET
Corinne Weisskopf

TEN-EE-AH LODGE IS THE ONLY property on beautiful Spout Lake in the heart of the Cariboo country, British Columbia. In Sushwap, a language still spoken today by the First Nations, "Ten-ee-ah" means big animal, or more specifically, the moose.

Buster Hamilton, a Sushwap Native, and his wife Milly, with Irish/Swiss roots, built Ten-ee-ah in 1942 as a hunting base camp and operated it until 1970. A wagon trail led from Lac La Hache to the camp. At the beginning Buster and his wife were the only ones to provide a guaranteed moose hunt. They employed two native guides. (Marc and Jimy's cabins are used today as staff cabins.)

With time the camp extended its offer to fishing, thus attracting many fishermen during the summer. In 1970 the place sold to Jean and Jeany Blitzan, who continued to operate it until 1980, when Stefan Witmer and his wife Regula, both Swiss, bought the place. Henry and Anny Weisskopf (a former Swissair Pilot and an Air Hostess) from Switzerland, took over the lodge in 1985, and promptly added new investments. The original main building was moved and enlarged. New cabins and a main house with a restaurant were added. The original hunting camp developed into a vacation resort. Werner and Rita Buser, friends of the Weisskopf's, became partners in 2001.

Ten-ee-ah Lodge today is one of the leading Wilderness Resorts in the Cariboo and has an excellent reputation. This remote place combines the attractions nature has to offer with gracious living. Guests can enjoy the cozy log cabins or campgrounds, the fine dining restaurant and a variety of activities such as horseback riding, motorboating, fishing, floatplanes flights, canoeing, mountain biking, hiking, dog-sledding, cross country skiing, snowmobiling or just relaxing. The list of activities has recently been expanded, with Ten-ee-ah Aviation, into sightseeing and charter flights. Under the responsibility of chief pilot, Henry Weisskopf, private pilots have the chance to achieve a floatplane or type rating. Aircrafts available are the De Havilland Beaver, Piper Super Cub or Lake Renegade. Spout Lake operates a seaplane base as well.

KELOWNA
Elizabeth Woodford

Peace and tranquil waters
Trees sway in the breeze
Who would have thought
That one stormy night
Could change the way we feel

The mountainside changed its look
From green to smoky gray
Mother nature's lightning strike
Took some of our lands away

We watch in horror as days go by
The fiery trees light up the sky
One week no one can comprehend
We all just want the pain to end

The firefighters fight each and every day
To save, to protect, to make a way
For the many fires, that they must quell
For all of them, a fiery hell

The thousands saved, the properties lost
The camaraderie, the unselfish care of others
Towards the People, the City, our Canada
Strong we stand together
Though crisis stays so strong,
But with help for one another
The days are not so long.

River Speaks
An Okanagan Story
Darcy Nybo

My name is Okanagan. I am a river. I am here to tell you a story about the way things came to be in a place now called Okanagan Falls.

A long, long time ago I was a grand, flowing river. There was a time when I flowed freely and became one with others until we joined with the sea. We still do, but it is not the same.

My story starts in a time when the people were new to this land and many powerful creatures roamed freely. The valley was peaceful then. Animals came to me in great numbers. They drank from me, taught their young on my banks, grew old and died by my side. The people; they respected me and sometimes they feared me.

We were happy then, the land and I. One day Whisper came and told me of a great creature. His name was Coyote or Senklip and he was to bring the king of all fish to my river. I told Wind the tale and he spread the word across the land. The people heard, but did not understand.

Sun bore down upon me and my water was given up in thanks for the warmth it gave my shores. Days later Sky gave it back again and the land grew lush and green.

With each new rain, new tales fell upon me. Tales of a shape changer who tricked women and coaxed his king fish to come up the streams and rivers of our valley.

I felt other stories too. There were stories of happiness and sorrow, forgiveness and anger, battles won and babies born. I tasted the salt of the sea and the fruit of exotic lands. I gained all this from the rains. Still, the one story that came loudest was the story of Senklip.

He was nearer now. The king of fish was coming and Senklip named them salmon. They would feed the animals and people of my banks. The animals gathered and drank this knowledge from me and waited for the great Senklip and the salmon he would bring.

With each passing day the tales became fiercer and angrier. Senklip wanted a bride and when he came upon a village and asked for their daughters, he was denied. Senklip would block the rivers and streams with great stone barriers so that no salmon would ever reach their shores. Time after time the tales came to us but we could not believe his anger could be so strong.

"He is lonely," whispered Wind.

"He is young," gleamed Sun.

I told them all, "We must warn those who dwell here. His anger shall arrive before him and we must be prepared."

195

Wind whipped around the villagers and pushed them away from me, but they would not leave. Sun shone so bright his reflection off my waters blinded them, and still they did not leave. Wind and I thrashed wildly together creating a terrible storm. Clouds moved in, Thunder and Lightening joined us and still, the people would not leave.

"We have done all we can," said Sun. "Now we wait and see how great this Coyote is against the will of these people."

The next day the earth shook as Senklip came to me. I felt him enter downstream and I waited. His anger was like a bitter root thrown into a pot of winter potatoes. I felt foul and tried to drown him, but I was no match. The salmon were with him.

Clouds moved in to chill the air but the people came to my banks to conduct their daily business. I watched as Senklip entered their midst.

"I am Senklip and I bring with me the king of all fish. With these fish in your river you will never go hungry. Let me join you at your fires." Senklip reached into the river with his great hand and scooped out two large salmon.

The villagers brought him to their fires and he showed them how to cook the salmon over an open fire so the salmon would be proud to give its life.

"I offer your village great foods and all I ask in return is one of your daughters as my wife." Senklip pointed to a group of young women gathered around an older man.

They giggled and whispered, then ran off to sit at their mother's side. After many agonizing moments the father spoke.

"We have little food and we must work hard for it. My daughters are worth more to us than easy work and a full belly. Leave us!"

Senklip was furious. He roared at the father. The father stood his ground. Senklip turned and rushed towards my banks.

"You will never again eat my salmon!" He howled at the villagers and dove into my depths. Within moments the surface boiled and exploded as tons of rock were forced upwards. Senklip bounded out of the water and stood on top of the rocks. "NEVER!" he screamed and dove back into the water.

My river bottom shifted, the rock shores collapsed into him, changing me, moving me, transforming me into something I was not. I rushed around him, trying to hold him down, to stop him from changing me even more.

A horrible grinding sound was heard as more rock was pushed upwards beside the first barrier. My grasp on him weakened as a part of me was transformed into a raging waterfall in a small space of eternity. I gazed up and saw Senklip climb to the top of the peak, shake himself and stride away from the village.

His anger had transformed me forever and the Okanagan Falls were born.

***

The rest of the story is not as spectacular. You will find most of life is that way too. Over the years Wind and I wore down the rocks until the Falls allowed the salmon to spawn. They were a beautiful sight. My banks still nurtured the animals and people of this valley.

Many years passed and more people came and made their home close to my shore. Each year Sun would melt Snow and we would overflow my banks with the joy of the coming spring.

The new people didn't like our celebration. They called it a flood and blasted my beautiful falls away. Wind said it was because people wanted to live closer to me. Sun said they should learn to swim.

HOME
Allen Reid

The Okanagan Valley
Is home to lots of us.
So far it's not too crowded,
We want to keep it thus.

So when you talk to strangers
Be careful what you say,
It's fine to have them visit,
But let's not have them stay.

Talk not of sunny weather
Or skies of palest blue,
Speak more of crowded highways
And what exhaust fumes do.

Talk not of sandy beaches
With bathing suit clad dolls,
Speak more of piercing cactus
And think if someone falls.

Tell them of the Scorpions' bite
Black Widows will bite too.
If that won't get them moving,
Then Rattlesnakes might do.

SALMON TOWN
Endrene Shepherd

here
fish are a way of life
salmon, halibut, eulachon

everywhere
the taste of fish is in the air
fish are in the blood of the people
see how they forge up second avenue in the rain?
see how their smiles are silver,
        their days are always deep and blue?
northwestern passions sparkle secret
thrumming and glimmering
  like midnight phosphorescence
   the spawn of the salmon
  the dreams of thousands of years
ocean upon ocean upon rock;
starfish and crab carapace
abalone and eagle
cedar and moss
here
fish speak the rhythm of time
they swim the song of seasons
beauty here is
always damp and deliberate
always silver and salt
always turning,
tuning in every driftwood heart
to the timeless cadence of tides.

SAVARY
Alan Longworth

Captain George Vancouver named this Isle,
He called it Savary Island,
The year was seventeen ninety-two.
A green and verdant island,
Was written in his log that day,
He chose to tarry here and stay.

The city's roar is far behind,
And tranquility prevails.
Ships and tugs and yachts with sails,
Pass Savary and pay no mind.
To this crescent isle of rock and trees,
Set amid a gentle sea.

An eagle casts his piercing gaze,
At a shallowing tidal pool.
An otter stalks the water's edge,
Offshore a harbour seal's at play,
Passing Orcas breath their spray.
It's just another Savary day.

The silence of the Savary morning,
Is pierced by raven's raucous cawing.
The gentle waters lap the shore,
As people wake from sleep once more.
To greet the island day,
And soak up all the ambience,
And children start their play.

The wind is rising, clouds scud by,
Rain approaches with the darkening sky.
Trees nod their heads to the rising surf,
Seagulls circle, squawk and cry.
Savary shows her other side,
The bleakness of a lonely isle,
Swept by winds and a powerful tide.

My week at Savary draws quickly to an end,
Here as a guest of a long time friend.
Memories of times long done,
Come rushing to the fore,
Of candles, wood stoves, horses,
Home cured bacon and more.
'Tis my hope that progress,
As it is known elsewhere
Does not come to Savary
And the people dwelling there.

*Savary is an island in the gulf of Georgia slightly north of Powell
River.*

GIANTS HEAD MOUNTAIN PARK
Sherrill Foster

ONE OF SUMMERLAND'S MOST familiar landmarks, Giant's Head Mountain can been seen from every location within the community. The Giant's Head is the remnant of a volcanic blast and is the core or the opening where the lava was emitted from this very ancient volcano. The whole area of Summerland was the site of a volcano over fifty million years ago. The Mountain's summit is 2,771 feet (845 metres) above sea level. By comparison, the elevation of Okanagan Lake is 1,122 feet (341 metres).

The rock's face, which looks southeast, resembles a man's profile and over the years the mountain has become a focal point for the town. It appears on the town's Coat of Arms accompanied by the motto "A Giant in Stature" and for Canada's Centennial in 1967, a community effort created Giant's Head Park, complete with winding road to the summit. A picnic area and washroom facility are below the summit and at the peak, a huge granite boulder is set in concrete and holds a time capsule to be re-opened in 2067. Along the peak's perimeter, a 360-degree panorama unfolds before you. Take a look at points of interest through various viewing tubes with information on each view. The Park was touted as "one of Canada's most imaginative Centennial projects". You can gain access to the park from Milne Road. Iron gates mark the entrance to the Park and you can park there or motorists can venture up the narrow road to a parking area, 1km from the summit. Two paths cut to the top; one steep path called Confederation Trail and one more winding and gradual, called Centennial Trail. Summerland Trail, which goes off to the north, overlooks the town. No matter which route you choose, you'll find the view spectacular!

SAVING AN AIRPORT
Manuel Erickson

WHAT WOULD YOU DO IF you were about to start a new job managing a small neighbourhood airport, and upon arrival you found the grass as high as a cornfield?

After cutting it, you discovered animals running freely and derelict vehicles scattered everywhere: pieces of aircraft, cars, even boats and trailers. Looking around, you noticed that the lack of fencing and nighttime security lighting had allowed all of the above to happen.

Worse still, the number of airport movements (taxiing, take-offs and landings) had dwindled to the point where the Department of Transport considered shutting down the air traffic control tower.

Most people would likely have given up after a while, but not George Miller. Under his confident guidance, and after applying the knowledge gained from years in the Air Force, he started making little Langley Airport vibrant once again.

A mild-mannered retired Colonel, George had served in Germany and Egypt, and as Base Commander at Moose Jaw, Saskatchewan (Canada's largest basic training base). During his distinguished career, he formed the Snowbirds in Moose Jaw (he was their first National Team Leader) and taught at Staff College in Kingston, Ontario.

In 1988, George retired after thirty-five years' service and chose to live in British Columbia so he could be among the snowy mountains that he said rejuvenated him. A good friend informed him the Langley Airport needed a manager and suggested he "throw his name in the hat."

George won the position over five other candidates.

Built as an emergency field for then Trans-Canada Air Lines in the 1930s, Langley Airport had a history to live up to; George saw that it did. To the job of Langley Airport manager, George brought the basic values he had learned in the Air Force: resolve, loyalty, leadership and steadfastness in the face of difficulty. He had a vision.

One of George's first conflicts occurred with some local pilots who loved to "fly willy-nilly," without rules or concern for other pilots or for nearby homeowners who didn't like engine noise on take-off. George excelled at turning these aircraft owners into allies. He showed them the improvements he proposed were for their own benefit, and without them, the airport would fail.

When George first arrived in 1990, there were only a few helicopter companies. Their machines made plenty of noise, disturbing adjacent homeowners, who complained to George, to the Township and to Transport Canada. George approached the companies' CEOs, proposing the establishment of a noise abatement program, "Fly Friendly", which had become successful in the United States. They willingly enforced the program on their pilots and noise complaints dwindled.

Today twenty-one helicopter companies — more than any other airport in Canada, including Toronto's Pearson, Montreal's Mirabel and Vancouver — call Langley Airport home. This success, coupled with the presence of airframe and radio repair facilities, resulted in other companies wanting to re-locate to Langley to take advantage of its attractiveness. George no longer needs to market to this niche; he has more applicants than available space.

Langley's international stature is strong. A group of touring South African students was surprised to learn one of their country's helicopters had been brought to the airport for repairs. Furthermore, two of the United Nations' helicopters used in Iraq were painted at Langley.

George Miller (right) with Canadian astronaut Chris Hadfield.
Photo copyright Michael Peare. Used by permission.

George improved the lighting system so that now there are security and runway lights, allowing night flying. George inaugurated the runway lighting system in 1994. His passenger was the Mayor. They taxied in the darkness to the end of runway, engine idling. George pressed a microphone button. The Mayor announced, "Let there be light!" The edge lights illuminated the runway and George took off. As he did, Langley Airport took off into the future.

A fence surrounds the airport, making it safe from wandering animals and people. Runways, taxiways and other areas are kept in repair. An internal fencing system keeps curious onlookers safely separate from

the area where aircrafts manoeuvre. A landscaping and mowing con-
tract has been let. Fuel, which had been dispensed by truck, at a great
cost, is now self-serve from two automatic pumps similar to those at
gas stations.

Each year, a growing number of citizens attend the two-day Canada
Day celebration at the airport. They enjoy the air show, rides, games,
demonstrations, and food. In 1995, when a religious organization ran the
celebration, almost five thousand people showed up.

George and Langley Airport took over Canada Day in 1996. They
expected perhaps eight thousand, but twenty-seven thousand came. In
2003, sixty thousand attended.

Now, over 100,000 movements a year take place. Back in 1990, there
were only 60,000. There are plans for a new east-west runway, which
will be built to supplement the existing grass one. New tenants will come,
among them a Royal Canadian Air Cadet squadron that will improve
business on the airport in the training of young pilots.

Today with the helicopter operations, two flight schools, over three
hundred private aircraft in older and newer hangars and NAVCanada's
extension of the control tower's hours, Langley Airport hums. It is at the
forefront of search-and-rescue, medical evacuation, fighting forest fires,
logging, student training and aircraft repair and overhaul.

It is "A Jewel in the Valley."

*Acknowledgements: With thanks to George Miller, Langley Airport
manager, my writers' group, the Rain Writers (notably Marlene
Barcos) and a special bow of gratitude to my Life Partner, my
wife, Martha Fraser: an editor* par excellence.

THE SEE YA LATER RANCH
Alan Longworth

HIGH ABOVE OKANAGAN FALLS, nestled under the shoulder of Hawthorne Mountain, long straight rows of grapevines look remarkably like the lines left by a rake in a golf course sand trap. Facing the northeast, Hawthorne Mountain Vineyards reach higher elevations than any other vineyard in the valley. This in itself is an oddity, but not nearly so odd as its history, and the history of its owners. The land was homesteaded in 1902, by the two Hawthorne brothers who eked out a meagre living on the slopes.

In 1919 the land was fenced off and sold to Major Hugh Fraser. The Major, born in 1885, had come out west at the invitation of Carroll Atkins, the playwright. He fell in love with the valley and stayed. The Major, as he preferred to be called, had graduated from McGill University and served his country overseas in W.W.I. He was taken prisoner in 1916 and remained a prisoner in a camp for officers until 1918 when he returned to his native Canada and Montreal. The Major was the son of a wealthy Eastern Canadian shipbuilding family. His mother is reputed to have started the Victorian Order of Nurses in Ottawa.

In 1919 he purchased the land from the Hawthorne brothers and contracted to have a stone built house on the property. The house still stands today, and has become the tasting, dining, and meeting rooms for the present Hawthorne Mountain Winery. The winery is easily reached by following Green Lake Road from the highway at the bridge entering Okanagan Falls.

There is a very unusual window in what used to be the living room in the Major's day. The glass is bent into the shape of a semicircle. This was built to accommodate a large circular birdcage in which he kept brightly coloured South American parrots. It is reputed that the birds could speak clearly and loud enough to call the outside help in for meals.

An employee at the S.Y.L. ranch at the time told me that one day a parrot escaped its cage and got outside. The colourful squawking bird spooked a team of horses and the bird got run over. This became a reason for one of the full-fledged funerals at the S.Y.L. ranch pet cemetery.

For many years everyone in the valley knew the property as the S.Y.L Ranch. Most believe the letters represent the words "See You Later" One story of these words is that the Major's wife left him a note in the frying pan simply saying. "See you later" and left the ranch never to return. This is by far the most popular belief among the residents of Okanagan Falls. Others believe the letters stand for "Sam You're Lucky," in reference to Sam Hawthorne, the previous owner and his sale of the ranch to the Major. Another popular belief is that the Major signed his correspondence with the words "See Ya Later." And the property became known among the locals as the See Ya Later Ranch.

The Major's wife remained at the ranch only three or four days after arriving from Montreal. It is said that after the bustling City of Montreal, she could not handle the isolation of the upland ranch and just walked away, apparently unwilling to stay with the Major in such lonely but beautiful surroundings.

The Major's personality in a way reflected the witnessing of wartime horror. He was very rarely seen laughing. He had a great love of his dogs and it is said he preferred them to people. At the demise of any of the dogs, they were wrapped in sheets, and all the staff and helpers were summoned to a proper funeral at the pet cemetery he had set aside at the south side of the house, complete with headstones that still adorn the property.

The Major is reputed to have mourned and wept for up to five days. This suggests to the writer that the death of the dogs may have set off memories, and deep emotional feelings of losses of his men on the European battlefields.

There is also a lighter side to the story of the dogs. The Major occasionally used to take his helpers into Okanagan Falls for dinner, and he would send Frank Bell, an employee, to go around the café and collect the bones from the other diner's plates for his dogs which had complete run of the house.

Frank Bell remembers The Major as a good employer. He stayed with him for three years at the height of the great depression. He also remembers the cleaning lady, who cared for the interior of the stone house, rode in the back of the truck to and from the Falls, while the dogs rode warm and dry with the Major in the cab. Frank recalls the Major used to get a great deal of mail. He asked an employee, Jim Sinclair, to get rid of it, most of it unopened. Jim asked if they might read some of it. Permission was granted, and the farmhands had a few guffaws as the letters were all from adoring women offering to be his bride.

Somehow a letter had got into the press from The Major's father, stating he would give him a million dollars if he would remarry. (Hearsay?)

It seems to be a fact the Major never mentioned his wife's name, for no one in the Falls has any clue what it was. He was a wealthy man; he owned a Lasalle car for the winter and an English M.G. sports car for the summer. In a way the S.Y.L. ranch was just a dude ranch.

The Major's regular income was derived from the trading of oil stocks. He had a full time cook at the house, and two full time helpers for outside work on the ranch, which consisted of a few cows and horses.

The Major was very generous within the community. He supplied all the stained glass windows for the United Church, also known within the community as the blasted church. He brought in, at his own expense, a group of educators to help the local young people achieve a better education, and he supported all community events.

Part of the S.Y.L. ranch contained the beautiful green, but alkaline lake a little higher up the road from the stone house. The major used it to skinny dip in the warm months.

The Bell family from northern Alberta bought forty acres across from the lake sight unseen. They were wrongly informed that the property had a house and barn. When the Major discovered a family with a bunch of daughters was to be moving to the property, he knew it would curtail his swimming activities, so he bought the land from them. The Bells took up residence in the Falls where the majority of them still reside.

The very first grapevines were planted near the house in 1961 and still produce quality grapes. The Major was very fond of parties and get togethers, and often held such events either at the S.Y.L. ranch house or at the community hall in Okanagan Falls. He would send out engraved invitations ending with the words "See Ya Later"

The Major had a highly educated young man from Okanagan Falls as his personal assistant and farm foreman. Bill Worth, the son of the Worth family running the O.K.Falls general store, helped the Major in his oil stock dealings and they became very close. Needing an heir to whom to leave his estate, Major Hugh Fraser took the unusual step of adopting Bill as his own son. At age twenty-one he became Bill Worth Fraser. Bill fell in love and married a Miss Debbie Strong; one of the teachers the Major had brought to the community.

In the interim years the Major purchased even more land on the east side of Skaha Lake. He built a house amid the orchard he planted, and Bill and Debbie Worth went to live there. In 1970 the legendary Major passed away, and Bill took over the ranch as sole heir. In 1980 the S.Y.L. was sold to an offshore investor, and in 1983 Albert and Dixie LeCompte purchased the ranch and by 1986 had opened a winery.

In 1995 the property was again sold to a group of investors led by Harry McWatters, and renamed Hawthorne Mountain Vineyards, later to be part of the Vincor family of wineries.

Eager to incorporate the history of both the Okanagan Falls area, and the Hawthorne Mountain property to the wine purchasing public via its product, the winery has embarked upon a new label for some of its 2003 vintage. The labels read, "SEE YA LATER RANCH" and have a picture of one of the Major's saintly dogs, with wings and a halo.

Acknowledgements: My sincere thanks to Ray & Lily Edmonds. Frank Bell ,George Thomas, and Dolly Duncan.

SUMMER OF THE BEAR
Dawn Renaud

THE SUMMER OF 1972, my brother Jeff and I spent a month with our father and stepmother on Babine Lake near Granisle, BC. Dad and Glenice were in the process of "building on," so we got to bunk on the livingroom floor. One night, we were just settling in to sleep when something thumpity thumped across the deck.

"What's that?" I asked.

"Just the cat," said Jeff. (Louis was the family pet, named after Grandpa because he was not fond of cats.)

Something else thumpity thumped across the deck. Whatever it was, it was a lot bigger than Louis. So big, it couldn't leap over the railing as Louis evidently had done.

I sat up in my sleeping bag and looked out into the dusk. "It's a bear!"

"Not likely," said Jeff. "Probably just a dog. Go to sleep."

I watched the dark shape saunter over to where the freezer sat under the dining room window. It stopped, turned, heaved itself up and put its paws on the lid. It peered in through the window at us.

Jeff was convinced. We stared back at the bear, then ran for the bedroom to tell Glenice. I don't know whether or not she believed we'd had a bear on the deck, but the next day our neighbour called to let her know we had ridden our bikes within an arm's length of a bear who was dining on saskatoon berries at the side of the road. I'm not sure what we would have done if we'd seen it.

Evidently it was content with the berries, because Louis eventually came back.

SHELLEY'S STORY
Richard Hunt

SHELLEY HAWN, FOUNDER, president and owner of Whole Foods Market, opened her first business in Summerland, BC in 1981. Housed in a tiny space just off Main Street, Summerland Whole Food Emporium was the first natural food store in the town.

By May 1983, Shelley opened a second store, Penticton Bulk Food Emporium, in the Penticton Plaza. Bulk foods had become a popular way of buying a wide range of foods. It seemed every town in the country had a new bulk food store, and Shelley was the first to open one in Penticton. It was an immediate success and everything looked very bright until, a legal dispute between the owners of Penticton Plaza and another tenant caused the termination of Penticton Bulk Food Emporium's lease shortly after opening. Fortunately, three months later, Shelley was able to move her store just two blocks away to a very high profile location in the 1500 block of Main Street.

After three weeks of renovations, the store re-opened in August 1983.

A much larger space, with better signage and Main Street exposure, was a real boon to the business. With no covenants restricting the type of items that could be sold, Shelley soon began to add new departments including fresh produce, frozen and refrigerated products, while pursuing her interest in natural and organic food.

By the end of the 1980s saw an addition of a whole section of vitamins and other supplements. At about the same time, a wide variety of packaged natural foods were added to the store selection. To better reflect the product mix, the store was renamed Penticton Whole Food Emporium.

Several years later, Shelley made the decision to have a new store built to accommodate the ever-increasing variety of incredible natural and organic foods being requested by her customers, as well as adding a natural foods café. In 1996, when the opportunity arose to move directly across the street, she took the plunge. The new store was opened in July 1996 with yet another new name to better reflect the new store image: Whole Foods Market.

From the outset, the new location was a success. Many people from across Canada claim that the Whole Foods Market is by far the best store of its type in the entire country!

In the late 1990's, Shelley began to develop a management team to handle many of the daily aspects of running the store, which was growing rapidly. With two new store managers, Shelley was able to focus on long-term plans. In July 1999, Shelley retired from daily participation in the running of the store so she could spend more time with her family and pursue her other interests. At the same time, she hired her husband, Richard Hunt, to perform her duties and develop new marketing plans.

Whole Foods Market has continued to expand its selection in all departments. An informative newsletter, website and Internet café were introduced, and other new developments are planned for the future. Over the years, the store has been fortunate to employ an exceptional team of dedicated and informed people. The current staff is simply outstanding, and they appreciate their significant contributions to Whole Foods Market. Most of all, Shelley continue to thank her customers for their incredible support for over 20 years in helping her to realize her dream of building a top-rated, made-from-scratch natural foods store in Penticton.

SHERIDAN FOX
Carol D. Loewen

ALTHOUGH THE CABIN OWNER warned us that Sheridan came often we were surprised when he appeared. We were assured the red head would likely drop by un-announced; even so we never expected to meet him as we did.

My husband, Fred, reserved a cabin on Sheridan Lake. We planned to stay for six days in August. Our holiday schedule: sleep in, share a late breakfast, canoe to our heart's content, walk the trails and read. We packed our necessities: food, clothes, books, paddles, and life jackets. Fred strapped the two-man canoe on top of the Volvo and we left Abbotsford. We stopped only for gas, lunch and ice cream.

Towards sundown, after six hours on the road, we arrived at our destination. Beside the driveway's entrance, attached to a tree, hung the "NEUFELD" sign. A comfortable cabin welcomed us, nestled in a cove under tall pine and poplar trees. A sturdy wooden deck faced the lake and was situated five steps above the sandy shore. It was furnished with a hand crafted, woodsy style bench, a white table and two lawn chairs. Fred added a footstool from inside for my feet.

The next morning passed lazily and breakfast was renamed brunch. With pleasure Fred put his craft into the clear water. During the following days we canoed the lake, paddling east along the shoreline, then west, and finally straight across. Traveling thus we inspected boats, cabins, coves and islands from our watery vantage point. Sometimes we put ashore and explored on foot. Arriving once more at the cozy cottage we walked the trails or sat outside and whiled away the time reading quietly until the evening meal.

One afternoon, the sun, slanting towards the west, cast a dappled shade over us as we read. Fred occupied one chair; I lounged in the other with the footstool under my feet. Because we were engrossed in our books, we did not notice a visitor approaching. Suddenly, to my right, I caught sight of something red moving close beside me off the deck. There he was, as foretold, trotting up without saying hello. Not a whisper of gravel underfoot gave away his presence. He passed the corner, walked to the stair post and sat down on the sand beside the steps.

It was Sheridan, slim and red headed as he had been described to us. There he rested and gazed out over the lake as though he were not intruding. As though we were non-existent. His proximity and handsome features thrilled me. Cautiously I moved to get a better view of our uninvited guest. I noted his pointed ears, delicate features and bushy red-brown tail.

I wiggled my toes without thought of consequences. Sheridan turned and stared at them. The light of lunch, dawned in his expressive eyes. He appeared to calculate the distance to his imagined mouthful. Had he moved? Was he crouching to spring? I have never been on the menu before. I must have blinked in surprise. As Mr. Fox looked up higher he seemed to recognize that I was too large for a quick snack. His eager anticipation faded into disappointment.

Now, with a shivery sense of having escaped by the skin of my toes, I was holding back the laughter. Again Sheridan revealed his feelings with a perturbed expression. A foxy question hung in the air. How did you contrive to fool me with those tempting toes? Warily, he got to his feet and began to steal away like a shadow drifting over the ground.

Once more he turned, his eyes accusing. You are laughing! And you have denied me dinner! I am disappointed and hungry. Then he slunk away into the woods, beaten at his own game by no skill of mine. A pleasure to meet you, Sheridan Fox; my thoughts followed him into the underbrush.

HISTORIC TROUT CREEK CANYON TRESTLE/BRIDGE
Jo Ann Reynolds

IT'S IMPRESSIVE IF YOU ARE on the canyon floor looking up through the steel girder tresses or standing on top of the span taking in the heart stopping view of the yawning Trout Creek Canyon below. The Trout Creek Trestle/Bridge on the Kettle Valley Railway line, was built in 1913, and remains as one of the most famous features on the railway. At 238 feet or 73 meters it was the highest structure on the KVR line and the third largest of its kind in North America. Engineer Andrew McCulloch would be pleased to see his engineering feat still the focus for transportation in the 21st century; albeit the pedestrian kind! In 2003 the community of Summerland raised enough money to deck and fence the historic structure to make it safe for the public and to create an incredible tourist destination for years to come. The Bridge is just off the Summerland portion of the Trans-Canada Trail and just a stone's throw from the Canyon View station stop of the Kettle Valley Steam Railway.

A SHOOTING STAR
Victor Gerard Temprano Jr.

Maybe today is already too ancient to be remembered
    Part of the unsolicited past
Little red girl, speaking pain into the dying light

                                  A

                          shooting star

Blasted might of all of the mighty hammers that once struck the lights
    away
bleeding like all of the dazed enemies under the earth
        hit away into the bathing night

                          An
                          apple
                          tree

      searched for in vain, in lustful wastefulness
pen-mark aging in a macro-universe
        ageless until some time squirms in

                          I

                  love
                  you

indeed, my life is long outlived
    the masterpiece that may have been is fallen into sorrow
the tales of beauty that may have kissed my ears, may
have eaten my tongue
                are lost

                      let me
                    go

A typical, clear night in the Valley, about thoughts and questions
*   posed while wondering in the company of the stars and the dark-*
*   ness.*

SKATING FOR GOLD
Lorraine Pattison

PENTICTON'S OWN STEPHANIE CAMERON captured silver at the 2003 Canada Winter Games for the novice ladies figure skating competition. Now aspirations for gold play on her mind with a renewed sense of confidence to be on Canada's Olympic team by age nineteen — just in time for the 2006 Winter Games in Torino, Italy.

Having met Stephanie, daughter of Don and Kathy Cameron, I was amazed how humbly she spoke about her young, illustrious skating career, pointing out her many ribbons, medals and trophies achieved at local, regional and national competitions. However, she overflowed with pride when she showed me the coveted silver medal taken from the Canada Winter Games.

Photo: BFP Studios

"Right from the start," exclaimed Kathy Cameron, "after I enrolled Stephanie at age five in the 'Learn to Skate' program at Glengarry Figure Skating School in Penticton, she stepped onto the ice and showed a natural talent for the sport, excelling to the intermediate level in just two months."

"I live on the ice, before and after school, and on weekends," explained Stephanie. "I train five times a week, concentrating on my balance and endurance levels because it takes a strong core body to take the friction of the jumps and spins, like the Triple Salchow and double Axel."

To keep her body supple and toned, Stephanie off-ice trains as well as practices ballet. For pre-competition warm-up, she jogs, stretches and uses visualization techniques. To relax, she listens to music.

I asked how she managed to keep up with her schoolwork?

"Stephanie is an honour roll student," her mother quickly responded. "Pen Hi School gives her study blocks and allows some assignments to be done on-line.

Having won many local and regional skating events, Stephanie entered more advanced levels of competition. But, in order to move from novice to junior level and then on to senior, it became necessary for her to leave the Okanagan for a club that offered higher-performance training under professional instruction.

The summer of 2002, Stephanie enrolled in a six-week course at the B.C. Figure Skating Centre of Excellence at Eight Rinks in Burnaby. Her new coach, Joanne McLeod, had the necessary credentials to accompany her to larger international skating meets.

Later in the fall, Stephanie competed at the BC/Yukon sectional skating championships, taking silver in the Novice Women's division. January

2003, at the BMO National Figure Skating Competition in Brampton, Ontario, she placed 9th in the short program and 10th in the free skate. Two months later, she accompanied the B.C. figure skating team to Campbellton, New Brunswick, for the Canada Winter Games. There, she captured silver.

Coach McLeod praised Stephanie saying, "She is passionate about the sport and this shows through her soul as she competes."

In June, after qualifying for 'Junior' level, she headlined with Canadian Champion Emanuel Sandhu during the "Rock the Ice Tribute," a song and skate to the Elvis Presley extravaganza held at Penticton's Memorial Arena. She found this to be an enjoyable experience as compared to the grueling pace of judged skating.

In July, she attended an eight-week summer school session at the Centre of Excellence. During an open competition there, she won another silver medal. Then, in August, she placed an amazing 4th as part of a team representing Canada at her first international event — the North American Novice Challenge.

That fall, she returned to the Centre of Excellence for four months extended training. Her grade twelve schooling submitted on-line.

In November, she competed in the Junior Ladies event at the BC/Yukon sectional Championships. Winning the William E. Lewis Trophy and gold medal, she became the top female skater in British Columbia. In December, she competed again, placing fourth at the BMO skate Canada Western Challenge Junior Ladies competition. This win advanced her into the 2004 Canadian Championships in Edmonton where she came in 13th overall out of 26 competitors.

Stephanie's diligence has paid off, making her one of the top Canadian contenders for the 2010 Olympic Winter Games. All the hard work required to place high in this sport has been as important to Stephanie as the destination itself. She not only focuses on the immediate goal but the process itself. This undying pursuit for excellence over the years is matched only by her family's commitment and belief in her talent and strength of character.

As Penticton's champion to represent Canada, the City of Penticton and the Senior Advisory Council presented her with the "Citizen of the Month" award for December 2003.

Stephanie's dream is singular, and that is to achieve greatness. With a tenacious will for competition and an unbridled eagerness to practice, she remains focused on gold. She truly has the mindset of a champion and I believe we'll find her standing on the podium to represent Canada at the Olympic Winter Games.

SMALL TOWN OKANAGAN
Alan Longworth

NESTLED BETWEEN HIGH ROCK WALLS and bounded at its north end by the shore of Skaha Lake, the village of Okanagan Falls sits placidly among the orchards and vineyards.

In its slow maturation the village has become home to heroes living in quiet obscurity and home to authors, painters, poets, musicians and actors in spasmodic retirement. There seems to be no logical explanation for this gathering of the heroic and talented in such a small community. Perhaps it is the ambiance; perhaps it is the internal need to escape big city life. Maybe it is pure chance, like fallen leaves finding each other on a still pond.

Almost directly across the street from me lives Bill Rupert. As he works in his garden wearing his Tilley hat, no one would suspect for a moment Bill's history.

Bill told an untruth about his age and joined the Canadian army just prior to World War Two. He served three years before he transferred to the Royal Canadian Air Force. He received a commission, then he was attached to R.A.F. 617 Squadron, a secret unit at that time, but at the end of the war it became known world wide as the Dam Busters Squadron. Bill flew 37 missions delivering the huge bombs, playing his part to destroy the massive German war machine. On his 38th mission his Lancaster Bomber was shot down and Bill baled out over occupied Holland. Eluding capture by the Germans, he was helped by the Dutch underground. They hid him for six and a half months. When Bill finally connected with the Allied forces he was suffering from malnutrition and all manner of parasites. After hospital recuperation, Bill wanted to return to flying missions, but because they felt he knew too much about the Dutch underground system, the military shipped him on a troopship back to Canada via New York.

Not far away in a house overlooking a lake, and surrounded my mementos of her years in Africa, retirement is just a word and not a state of being for Margaret Anne Hayes. Margaret went to agricultural college in Devon England to study poultry husbandry. It was there she met her first husband, an agriculturist and later she accompanied him to Kenya. Margaret gave birth to a baby soon after arriving at their final destination following a harrowing drive through the bush by Land Rover to an outpost some 350 miles form Nairobi.

After many adventures with wildlife, and the African people her husband was posted to Nairobi and Margaret began writing a woman's page for a newspaper. Later on Margaret married Charles Hayes, editing director of the Nation group of English language newspapers in Nairobi. She began freelance writing and photojournalism, meeting and entertaining a good number of African leaders. She eventually became the editor of Consumer's Magazine.

Margaret with her husband and family moved from Nairobi to Okanagan Falls and as a five-year project, started the South Okanagan Review. Fifteen years later they sold the paper to a Calgary editor, after having published a cookbook of Okanagan specialties and one on Kenya.

Margaret and Charles had published nine books between them before he passed away. Margaret's latest work has received rave reviews from a London Editor journalist. He states that Margaret has created a new literary genre he calls 'love letter as a biography'. The work is titled "I'M ONLY THE EDITOR" and is going to press as I write.

In a small house on the edge of town Vince Ford and his wife Rena find that their life's work continues on into retirement. Vince was born in England into a family of vaudeville entertainers. Encouraged by an uncle, Vince learned acting and ventriloquism. His family moved to Canada and at age seventeen he joined the Canadian Air Force. In their infinite wisdom, the military transferred Vince into the army. He continued his vaudeville acts, entertaining both officers and enlisted men. In his off duty hours he entertained at private functions. Over a thirty-four year span of service Vince wrote plays and acted and directed them. Often as an accomplished painter he painted the backdrop scenery for the plays. Vince retired from the military in 1987 as acting Major. (No pun intended.) He and Rena decided to settle in Okanagan Falls. He continued writing and producing plays and skits for the local seniors' centre and surrounding communities. Both Vince and Rena are accomplished musicians, competent in a variety of instruments. They add a dash of colour to the mosaic that is small town Okanagan Falls.

Just a block from my house, lives a man who survived eleven years in a Siberian gulag as a result of being in the wrong place at the wrong time. Directly behind me lives a person who makes a living writing and selling adventure stories. Another writes movie scripts and others write songs and poetry. I have but scratched the surface of the list of talented people who live and work in sleepy Okanagan Falls.

THE SPANISH MOUND
Eric Linden

The Spanish
Along forgotten, secret trails
Lie rocks that tell of olden tales –
Of men who came from distant lands
And crossed the vast, enormous stands
Of redwood trees and evergreens
Until they reached Similkameen's
Fair winds and fertile valley ground.
For several moons they stayed around.

With native slaves to pack their loads,
The Spaniards left their new abodes
And journeyed on, both north and east
To endless lakes – a water feast
That sparkled like a polished jewel.
Soon daily winds blew fresh and cool
As painted leaves fell from the trees
And frost came inching by degrees.

Winter
A steady moving fresher-brook
Flowed near a tepee town and took
Its gurgle past the Spaniards' lodge
Without the need to twist or dodge
Large boulders lying in the way
Before it spilled into the bay
And fed the hungry, waiting fish
With choicest bugs – their favourite dish.

Their lodge-pole longhouse by the shore
Had sod for roofing, sod for floor
To clock the north wind's icy whine
Which whistled thru the birch and pine
That flanked the rugged cliffs and beach
As far as one could see or reach.
The meadowlands turned snowy white
And time crept slowly day and night.

217

Their Mission
The Spaniards mission was to find
A treasure trove of any kind
Filled full of gems and precious things
Like diamonds set on golden rings
With topaz, ruby, garnet brace
Or emeralds, sapphires, silver lace
To thrill the King and Queen of Spain,
Who'd sent them sailing off again.

They tried with each new native tribe
To wheedle, barter, buy or bribe
That precious yellow metal sought,
Though not one ounce was seen or bought
Up in the northern wilderness.
Then, filled with great abjectness
They laid out plans for early spring
And wealthy finds that it could bring.

Spring
The geese returned as winter waned
And every day the sun remained
A little longer. Fields turned green,
The Spanish men grew restless, keen
To travel back the way they came
Where food was plenty, fish and game
Found deep in hills and mountain streams;
They'd dine quite well on such regimes.

A band of local native men
Was caught to carry packs again
Across the narrow winding paths
Where dangers lurk in Nature's wraths.
They reached the Valley of the Winds,
Made camp beneath the tamarinds,
Then roasted fresh killed venison…
Three winds blew cool in unison.

Valley of the Winds
The eastern sky was turning grey
With early dawn announcing day .
The Spaniards' camp became alive,
But then they saw they're missing five
Who slipped away sometime at night:
The slaves escaped – had taken flight
And left their masters where they slept …
The Spaniards snored, and off they crept.

The winds began quite gradually,
And seemingly prophetically –
Unlike so many countless days
They carried cawing of the jays
From nearby trees beside the bank
Of flowing waters. Wildlife drank
And wandered off into the woods –
The Spaniards packed their tents and goods.

The Spanish Mound
Along forgotten, secret trails
Lie rocks that tell of olden tales –
Of men who came to distant lands,
To kill and conquer, make demands
Unlike what local folks had seen,
Unlike the people who had been
The occupants throughout this land.
The native Okanagan band.

The Valley of the Winds would be
The final place those men would see.
Their bones lie in the Spanish Mound –
A secret spot that's still not found;
But pictographs on sacred rocks
Record the strange and ancient talks
Of wise old men, of chiefs and kings,
Of turquoise stones on silver rings.

A SPECIAL GUY
Johnny Eek

A cowboy's job is to work with cows
And find them better range.
He takes them high up the mountain
In fall, rounds them home again.

The wrangler keeps track of the horses
Packs water and rustles the camp wood.
Then the cook is an important fellow
He always makes food taste so good.

Now the cowboy keeps roping and riding
Treating sick cows and mending the fence.
Then he has to make sure cows have water
And salt is quite an expense.

A cowboy's work is on top of a horse
High in the saddle on his seat.
There isn't much work going to get done
On the ground, on his own two feet.

Now a cowboy is kind of a special guy
You can tell him by his clothes.
He always seems to charm the girls
When he goes to the rodeos.

I asked this cowboy about a friend of mine
And he asked, What did he do?
Well, he artificially bred some cows
And worked on the haying crew.

Now a cowboy is kind of a special guy
Like a knight in a shining armour.
He said, Don't think I knew that friend of yours
He must have been just a farmer.

STERNWHEELERS
Pamela & Martin Garrity

STERNWHEELERS ARE REALLY the unsung heroes of British Columbia. There seems to be little known of the work they did on the lakes and rivers of our Province. They were a common sight on the 572,000 square miles of our lakes and rivers.

They started out in the southern states of America as paddle wheelers. A sight that is common to most people who have been on a trip down the Mississippi river, or at least seen photographs of them majestically steaming their way, full of tourists enjoying the comfort and luxury of the trip.

In fact we seem to associate these boats with the United States but in fact there were some three hundred of them in Canada. Eventually they were here for a far longer time and did far more dangerous work.

The paddle wheelers were not built for luxury. They were built as the workhorses of the rivers, used to carry goods and materials for road and rail building. They were the cheapest and fastest form of transportation in their day.

They have been around since 1817, but they did not arrive in Canada until 1849. They looked the same then as sidewheelers with two large paddle wheels, one at each side. The paddle wheels were fashioned in such a way that with the force of the water, they were able to pull the weight of the boat through the water.

The first one to arrive was in the little town of Hope on the Fraser River in 1858. The boat was called 'The Surprise' and what a surprise it must have been. The folks seeing this large wide boat steaming in with its paddles slapping the water, whistles and boilers screaming, would not have had any idea just how popular these weird looking things would become.

It was not very long before it became obvious that the style of the paddlewheeler was not ideal for the narrow rivers of BC. Thus after a few different designs the sternwheeler came into being.

The principal was the same. There were still the engines and boilers, but instead of the two wheels one on each side, there was just one large wheel at the back. The boats were now much narrower and able to work more comfortably on the rivers so they were the perfect craft for the frontier waterways. These sturdy but basic and functional vessels were to serve bravely for a century.

The sternwheeler was a bluff-bowed vessel constructed entirely of wood with a completely flat bottom therefore needing very little water

221

to keep afloat, mostly as little as six inches. Due to the depth of their draft they were very buoyant and could go through canyons and rapids that would have destroyed other types of craft.

The engines had a single steam valve, which meant that all the steam came out at one time usually with an extremely loud screech. This was different from the steam train where the steam is let out slowly, making it much quieter.

In addition, the buckets on the stern wheel would slap the water, which sounded like a deep toned whistle. In essence the journey was very noisy. With the captain shouting his orders, the passengers and crew shouting at each other, the level of noise certainly meant that nobody slept on these 'cruises'.

Most sternwheelers could carry in excess of 100 tons of freight and often many passengers.

They had several attributes one of which was the ability to "grass-hopper" across sand bars and shoals. This was a most peculiar sight, the vessel had a block and tackle attached to the front of the boat so it could literally hoist itself up and move by steps across the sand until it reached enough water to re-float.

There were many incidents of boilers blowing up and some burning up completely on their maiden voyage. They were crushed by ice, swamped by gales, broken by rapids and burnt out by fires but many more served their masters for many years and became part of the everyday landscape.

Many a captain said, "They can do the impossible, and do it profitably". They carried passengers but not in any form of comfort. Passengers were expected to help run the boat. They would haul logs, help cook meals and sometimes even bale out. Often passengers would have to use their coats or blankets to block holes in the side of the vessel if the water was particularly rough. Of course they were still expected to pay their fare.

The sternwheeler soon arrived on the lakes of the province, where their jobs were a lot less strenuous and a lot more luxurious than their sisters on the rivers. The reports of boilers exploding and holes in the hull were almost non-existent. These sternwheelers were adapted more for passengers and smaller amounts of cargo.

During April of 1886, the first steam powered boat arrived on the Okanagan Lake only 32 feet long with a name just about as long. 'Mary Victoria Greenhow' was not a sternwheeler, but she was the thinking behind the Red Star that was launched two years later with the wheel at the back. She was to ply her way from Enderby to the railway of Sicamous. She was slow and leisurely but got the job done, just as long as nobody required any formal scheduling or punctuality.

It was late in 1892 that the proliferation of the sternwheeler started due to the CPR building one for the Okanagan Lake. This was to encourage settlers, in the area, to grow fruit. They needed to transport the produce out of the valley quickly, efficiently and on time.

So the first 'proper' sternwheeler on Okanagan Lake was launched May 3rd 1893. She was huge, compared any other boat previously seen. She could carry 200 tons of cargo. She had proper cabins, a dining room, and a deck for passengers. She had staterooms with white sheets on the beds. But best of all, she could travel the whole lake in one day. Now sternwheelers became the way to travel and to move cargo.

We still have the largest and most famous vessel moored in Penticton. The $180,000 Sicamous was launched in 1914. She had a steel hull and could carry a cargo and 500 passengers at an until then unheard-of speed: seventeen knots. Maybe she should also be remembered for her service in World War I, for carrying soldiers to war and the injured home, and for bearing news, good or bad.

She served the community well until 1931 when the road and rail started to put her out of business. By 1936 she was tied up for the last time.

It was the end of an era.

Sixteen years later she was towed to her present mooring for refurbishment, to become a living museum. The sad part is that she is one of the only two sternwheelers left in BC,

It would be safe to say that the sternwheeler played a major part in opening up the frontier for the gold miners, the road and railways workers, the farmers, the merchants, and the settlers. Though they were ordinary unassuming vessels, we should be very proud and thankful for their contribution to our history.

SAYING... TWO
Edwin Monson

as time unfolds,
the ways of these patterns,
leaves
many colours and sizes,
many shapes and textures,
what of these changes?

THE STOLEN CHURCH
Odell M. Bennett

ON A HILL, FACING LAKE WINDERMERE, in a small village of the same name, stands a little, nondescript church, surrounded by a picket fence. Both are in need of a coat of paint. A huge fir tree guards a stone monument commemorating the church's founder, one Father Henry Irwin, fondly known throughout the valley as "Father Pat".

The beauty of the church lies not in its appearance, but in its colourful history. In 1887, Father Pat arrived at Donald, British Columbia, a hundred miles from Windermere. Donald was the divisional headquarters for the newly built railway through the Selkirk Mountains. It was here that Father Pat erected the first church in this hitherto churchless wilderness. An English baroness generously donated a beautiful silver-toned bell weighing over a quarter of a ton. An ornately bound bible arrived from England's Theological College. St. Peter's Anglican Church was consecrated in 1889, causing much envy and jealousy from the neighbouring towns of Revelstoke and Golden.

A scant ten years later, commercial progress made Revelstoke the divisional centre. All that could be moved was to go to Revelstoke, including the coveted church.

Devout Anglican businessman, Rufus Kimpton and his wife were preparing to move to Windermere, where they owned the White House Lodge. Mrs. Kimpton was teary eyed as she contemplated leaving the beloved church to move to another churchless area. Mr. Kimpton watched his diminutive wife become sadder as they packed their belongings. As he went about his work, he came to a decision.

"Whither thou goest, my dear, so shall your church" he soothed his wife.

In the dark of night in the removal of Donald's business buildings, Rufus had the church dismantled, and loaded on a railway flat car. It would travel as far as Golden to await the following morning's departure of a barge which would carry it up the Columbia River to Windermere.

Unfortunately, during the overnight wait, thieves stole the bell. The loss was not discovered until the church was unloaded at Windermere. Many scathing letters, each one more belligerent that the preceding one, passed between the clergy of the three towns, containing much un-Christian like threats. Revelstoke demanded the church, Windermere the bell and Golden claimed, "Windermere had no right to the bell, since they stole the entire church in the first place."

224

The church was re-erected in its present location. Many born in the quaint little town were baptized, confirmed, married and eventually passed through its portals to eternity.

Rufus Kimpton passed away in 1934 and, fittingly, was buried from his beloved church.

Mrs. Kimpton, a bent, wizened little soul, invariably dressed in long, black attire, wandered the town for many more years, never missing a Sunday service. She passed through the church, one spring day, to join Rufus in their final resting place on another hill facing the lake.

More than a century has passed and though the silver toned bell calls all good Anglicans to worship in Golden, a replacement serves the good citizens of Windermere's stolen church.

TERRACE

TERRACE BC IS RICH with history. One of the longest and largest mutinies in Canadian history took place here; it was the cedar pole capital of the world, and rumour has it the infamous Al Capone and three of his henchmen hid out in the area in 1928.

The treasured Kermode bear has been adopted as our mascot. This beautiful white member of the black bear family is sometimes referred to as a Spirit Bear. Unique to our area, the Kermode is very elusive. If you're lucky enough to see one, count yourself among the fortunate few.

One of the most spectacular areas of BC lies slightly north of Terrace. The Nisga'a Memorial Lava Bed Park features Canada's youngest lava flow. Take a self-guided auto-tour or a guided hike to the cinder cone while you explore the culture, history and natural wonders of the Nass Valley.

If the snow and terrain found on Shames Mountain were anywhere else in the world, it would likely house a mega-resort. But in Terrace, a serene skiing experience awaits those who visit. Shames boasts a spectacular average snowfall of 1200cm yearly, making for a hard-to-beat experience!

Terrace is known worldwide as one of the best fishing spots anywhere, with world record catches. In 2001, an impressive 99-pound Chinook salmon was landed from the Skeena River. There are unlimited opportunities to catch the big one!

Submitted by the Terrace Chamber of Commerce

THE THUMB
Marilyn McAllister

We walked a razor's edge
that night at the thumb
and looked out over woolly hills of sage
that climbed in a blue phalanx
to the dark horizon
where the red globe of the sun
rested in an endless moment,
to bless the end of day.

Love clasped my hand
and held it tight
as we leaned against a hot, dry wind
that swept up a thousand feet of rock
to meet us at the edge of blue-grey dusk.
A wet wind,
heavy with the sweet scent of sage and pine
that cleansed our very souls
and promised a night of bliss.

Beneath the stars that night
we felt the living past
enclose us in its warm cocoon
of spiral dreams
that move the earth through time and space
to another day
and all along the Milky Way
a ghost-dance of new tomorrows
wait their turn
to move the empty hand of time

Could we have savoured more
the magic of that place
had we known the ash of a hundred fires
would rain down through a copper haze
to blanket the blackened earth?
Yet life renews
In blades of grass,
green on black,
that spiral up through smoke and ash
to find the sun, and greet the day
...and so the promise goes.

Union Bay

Marian Toews

One hundred years ago, Union Bay was a bustling coastal town
tracks laid along the beach brought trains
whose open boxes were piled high with coal
coke ovens let loose their fiery dragon's breath night and day,
searing the sky, creating a scene that was both hellish,
and eerily beautiful.

Today, Union Bay is a kind of museum piece, its narrow streets
haunted by yesterday's voices
along the beach and foreshore, tracks have been pulled up, the trains
made their last run half a century ago, their colossal voices
let loose one final organ peal, leaving behind a continuous echo
that faded into the surrounding forest until it was gone.

Jutting up from the sand still black with coal,
are the remains of a long pier, salted by the ocean tides and wind
swept spray,
the pilings march in snagglefile, their rooted beginnings
continue their secretive whispering begun a century ago,
remembering when they were trees standing among their kind.
Once they owned limbs to support birds and insects and indigenous
moss,
now they fall prey to these fickle creatures who join the salty sea
to eat them into oblivion.

Eagles soar overhead, a seal peeks over the surface that is its horizon,
keeping its body in its own familiar world, it gazes at the land
that might possibly be its idea of heaven;
a shore where its body will wash on the last day.

URSA
Sharon Ward

URSA WAS BORN during a snowy winter in a den somewhere above Twin Lakes in Kaleden BC.

She would have been perhaps ten ounces at birth, but grew rapidly so that by the time she left the den in April she would have been about a dozen pounds.

Little is known of her first years. She went unnoticed in the community of people below, but when she was of breeding age and began having cubs of her own, the people began to pay attention.

Ursa was often spotted gambolling on the hillside with her cub. One year she had twins and gave twice the entertainment.

Many residents and visitors alike spent warm summer days and evenings frolicking in the cool waters of Nipit Lake. What a joy to float along the lake and watch Ursa bring her newest baby down for a cooling plunge. (Black bears do not have sweat glands and lose much of their excess body heat by submerging in water in this warm climate.)

Ursa was a very vigilant and devoted mother. Her cub would be brought to the water's edge only if she deemed him to be far enough from the threats of people and dogs. In fact, when Ursa made her appearance, the cub was often left behind, hidden in the trees at first.

There was one day, just last summer, when Ursa came down to the water's edge with her cub. It was late morning and it was on the pond tucked in behind the lake, a place where humans are not usually encountered. But this time there was a human, hiding in the woods and watching as Ursa and her baby sank into the cool scummy water and proceeded to play. They rolled and splashed and wallowed for a full twenty minutes before Ursa gave the signal and they climbed the back to seclusion once again.

I often think it must be difficult being a bear in a world taken over by humans. Ursa and her kind must be always on the outlook for intruders in their territory. Usually these intruders know nothing of bears and their habits.

Ursa roamed the hills of Twin Lakes for over seven years as an adult mother bear. Not once in all of that time did she show herself or her offspring in the community. The closest she came was her frequent dips in the lake, always on the wilderness side of the shore. Never did she put her cub at risk. A better mother would be hard to find in any community.

This year was a difficult one for bears in this and many other areas. Still, Ursa was not one who dove into garbage.

The community around Nipit Lake is crisscrossed with natural bear trails. Bears go where the food is and in this diverse environment, the food is near the lake. The people are also near the lake and claim it as their own.

When hungry, I can be easily lead into a bakery. When not, I have much more willpower. When the chokeberries and Saskatoons are ripe, Ursa and her cub, with their fellow bears, follow their noses and chow down. Unfortunately, there are those in the human community who do not realize that *their* habits can lead bears' noses where they ought not to go.

Bears are largely nocturnal and roam far and wide searching out food. Of course their noses are one of the best resources they have for this search.

Ursa made a mistake. It was 2 a.m. and she was walking through a back yard. She was hungry and she was looking for food. Ursa could not have known that this particular backyard was a trap. She only wanted to feed herself and her cub.

This backyard had garbage. It also had people waiting; people with guns who sat and waited for her to come by and then shot her.

Ursa was a good bear; never aggressive; never seen in daylight. Ursa was a better neighbour than those who would bait and kill a mother and leave her baby to starve. Ursa is gone and the neighbourhood is saddened, empty and suffering a loss those foolish neighbours will never understand.

I still look for her on the hills.

SAYING... ONE
Edwin Monson

the crows and ravens came
of the deep cosmo sea,
these spirits of the shadows,
for the legacy
of what man, woman and
the child will be.

VOICES IN THE WILDERNESS
Susanne Haagsman

I LOOK OUT MY LIVING ROOM window at the picturesque view of Butler Ridge. There is nothing standing in my way to block the beautiful sight before me. Ahead of me lie miles of wide-open fields.

As I gaze into the distance I think about how close to nature I am. Memories of the last year flood my mind. It is springtime in rural northern BC. I get up early. Grabbing a steaming mug of coffee, I head outside to the sundeck. The morning air is clean, crisp and fresh. I breathe it in deeply, as I look over the vast farmland. I watch closely and silently while a doe mule deer cautiously approaches me. She paws at the ground with her hoof, looking for fresh, green grass. She pauses, sensing that I am there. She casually gazes up at me, and then continues about her business. She still has her warm winter coat and big, brown eyes.

There are many sounds in the early morning air. Swallows, sparrows and robins are chattering away as they busily prepare nests for their new families. Canadian geese honk a cheer as they fly over, heading north for the season.

This is my favorite time of year. There are so many signs of new beginnings – a fresh start and the end of a long winter.

At the same time spring is also when I have my guard up the highest. Bears are slowly rising from long winter hibernation. They are hungry and bringing their new cubs out into the world for the first time. They are very cute to look at, but are also one of the most respected animals. Getting trapped between a sow and her cubs could greatly inhibit ones life expectancy.

This is the busiest time of year for us on the ranch. My husband, James, is often away late into the night helping the cows with their calves. The calves desperately need their first drink of warm colostrum to give them a good start. This time of year, the temperature can still drop down to −15C.

Although the first signs of spring have begun to show, it is not uncommon to have it snow again. The calves need all the strength they can get to survive the cold. All are given lots of hay to keep warm. The smaller, weaker calves need to be moved into the barn the first few days.

One cold night the wolves came through. They stealthily, silently crept in among the cows in the early morning hours. There were probably four or five traveling in this pack. They selected three calves. They pounced on the first of their unsuspecting prey, tearing him from limb to limb, not paying attention to the calf as he cried in anguish. Slowly, painfully he finally succumbed to death. The wolves moved on to their next victim. This routine continued until they were full. The next morning the only sign of the events that had taken place was the bloody mess that they had left behind.

I watch my St. Bernard bark as he runs off into the bush. I see the hind end of a bear disappear over the creek bank.

"What's Clifford barking at, Mom?" The kids ask inquisitively.

"A bear," I tell them, "but don't worry. He ran away, he probably won't be back."

A lot of black bears travel through the yard, usually just passing through.

Clifford starts barking again. This time it's a fierce bark. Looking out the window, I see that the bear has returned. At one glance, I see it's a grizzly bear.

Grizzlies rule these parts of the world. They have no known predators, or fear. I worry over the safety of my dog but at the same time I need him to keep the bear from coming into my house.

Clifford's barks go unnoticed. The bear saunters up to the back deck. He stands up on his back legs, placing his huge, brown paws on the deck. We stare at each other, eye to eye. I yell at him, hoping to scare him. He finds this amusing. Since bears are supposed to be frightened by loud noises, I rush to the kitchen and grab pots and pans. I bang the pans together, hoping to chase off the massive animal. This amuses him even more. He drops back on all four paws and heads to the stairs. Bravely, Clifford risks his life and cuts him off.

The eight-hundred pound mammoth wants in the house. Dissatisfied, he heads to the front door. I watch him through the glass of the front window. Once again, eye contact is made. Again Clifford comes to the rescue but the bear is still not willing to leave. He plays cat and mouse with Clifford a while longer, until the dog can no longer run. He is exhausted. Finally, bored with the situation the bear leaves of his own free will. Luckily, no one was hurt.

During the summer, the wilderness is quiet. Deer bring their fawns out to graze in the lush, green grass. While Clifford naps a hungry coyote sneaks into the yard and eats one of my chickens, leaving only a pile of feathers behind.

Now it's haying time, the fields have had a chance to grow. We have to cut and bale thousands of acres to keep the cows fed and warm throughout the winter. As the haying is finishing, hunting season opens. I spend my early mornings and evenings looking for a bull moose. I am very much looking forward to the delicious taste of the fresh moose steak, served with new potatoes from the garden and homegrown salad.

The weather is still warm and the moose are still high up in the mountains where the weather is cooler. Halloween day comes and moose season closes. I have yet to see a bull. Oh well, better luck next year.

James has shot a big bull elk. It had a lot more meat than we originally expected. There should be plenty to get us through to spring.

The temperature has dropped down to –20C. The snow is falling hard and fast. Winter has arrived once again. The bitter cold bites my cheeks as I walk through the deep snow on a moonlit night; I listen to the coyotes as they howl toward the moon.

The next morning I watch in horror as the doe deer, which looked so beautiful in the spring, is now eating the pine trees that I ever so carefully planted last spring. Clifford is so used to her being there that he can't be bothered to bark at her anymore. All I can hope is that she will leave some of the trees for me. She is rapidly losing her beauty.

As I think of what a beautiful corner of the world I live in, my thoughts are ended by the sound of branches breaking in the cold. I look over just in time to see a big bull moose walking gracefully on the road ahead of me. This year he has won.

SUMMERLAND
Jo Ann Reynolds

PIONEER J.M. ROBINSON fondly described Summerland as "Heaven on earth with summer weather forever" and with bountiful sunshine, sandy beaches, fertile land and peaceful wilderness on the doorstep...well, you can almost believe it.

Summerland was one of the first communities in the Okanagan Valley to embrace the development of the commercial fruit industry. In the late 1800's a few stalwart ranchers and orchardists took up residence in "Riviere a' la Truite" (Trout Creek- Summerland district) after finding what was essential to good fruit production – a reliable source of water. Prior to settlement, the district had been a well-known stop on the Okanagan Fur Brigade Trail, a route used by the fur traders, gold miners and cattlemen from 1812 to 1885.

Summerland's original town site was nestled along the shores of Okanagan Lake a few miles north of Trout Creek. With J.M. Robinson's vision and CPR President Lord Thomas Shaughnessy's financial investment, they formed the Summerland Development Co. and began pre-emption of surrounding land for subdivision and sale to the pioneers, who were arriving daily aboard the great sternwheelers that plied Okanagan Lake. Incorporated in 1906, Summerland was a thriving lakeside community. However, lake transportation became less important with the coming of the railway in 1915 and that coupled with a series of tragic fires in 1922, which destroyed much of the business district along the lake, people began to migrate to the upper town site where the majority of commerce continues to be done to this day in a revitalized "Old English" style downtown.

WEEPING BIRCH
R.L. Diebolt

Summer fades and passes by
Colours change – time does fly
Shake loose your golden curls and laugh
For winds and play begin at last.

Berries, nuts and seeds all fall
With your leaves, you hide them all
I'll play the game of lost and found
And shuffle thru your heaps and mounds.

With gentle breeze, your trailing hair
Becomes a sight beyond compare
Tresses reach and sweep the ground
Like gauze and haze and fluff and down.

Tonight the snow comes – white and soft
Your arms outstretched to catch the lot
You bravely stand on quiet ground
While flakes fall quick without a sound.

And in the morn, sky pink and blue
Shines thru your hair – crystals too!
An angel here on earth we keep –
God gave you beauty while you weep.

The wind grows warm, your time has past
A veil of green is here at last.
With life renewed, and summer song
Breeze and you, dance along.

WHERE THE WILD THINGS GROW
Linda Steward

Ride them horses, now ride 'em hard;
Take them up those mountainsides.
Ride 'em thin then graze 'em fat
On mountain grass belly high.
And at night your campfire burns
A lonely light on darkened hill,
Hear the echo of the bells
As the horses eat their fill.

>And your freedom's in the wind song,
>Eagle's flight and the mountain pass.
>Up here the world can never touch you,
>You don't look down and you don't look back.

Climb them mountains, scale those peaks.
You can see forever from up here,
Get the lay of the land in the next valley,
Choose a way where the goin' looks clear.
Another night and you've made camp,
Your belly's full with a good hot meal.
You roll a smoke, tip back your hat,
And show that old guitar just how you feel.

>And your freedom is in the night air,
>The balsam smoke and the stars above.
>If you had your way you would spend your lifetime
>Just wandering the mountains that you love.

Pack them horses, now pack 'em tight;
Hit the trail by early morn.
See the mist rise in some lonesome valley,
Hear the raven's laughing scorn.
Frosty mornin', the bacon's fryin',
Your drinkin' coffee from an old tin cup
And the sky's the colour of roses cryin'
As the sun is coming up.

And your freedom's in this packing horses,
Ridin' trails and crossing streams,
And you wonder why it is that you still miss her.
Is it 'cause a man needs someone to share his dreams....

Ah... But she was just a woman
And her heart said she needed a home,
And you were just a gypsy cowboy
And in the mountains your were bound to roam.

So you ride them horses and you ride 'em hard.
You take them to the land where wild things grow,
Show the world that you can live a lifestyle
That died a hundred years ago.
And at night when the embers glow
And your whiskey is almost gone,
You feel the cold a little deeper
And know that winter's comin' on.

And your freedom is bound and quartered
By the season's swift sharp change.
Winter drives you to the valley
To live like a mortal man again,
...To wait for spring to come again.

And somewhere... she remembers riding;
The smell of balsam smoke on mountain air;
Remembers a gypsy cowboy
Whose life she could never share...

This was originally written as a song. It is in the key of G with a lot of A minors and has three distinct parts and a "bridge", as the structure of the words would suggest.

WINEMAKER OF THE YEAR
Yasmin John-Thorpe

BRUCE NICHOLSON OF PENTICTON, the winemaker at Vincor International Ltd., makers of Jackson-Triggs wines, has become the first Canadian ever to be nominated (in 2003) for the prestigious title "Wine Maker Of The Year" at the International Wine and Spirits Competition in London, England. Only six winemakers from four countries (Canada, Africa, Austria and Australia) were nominated.

Bruce did not win the title, but 17 of his wines under the Jackson-Triggs label were nominated and he did get to go up to the podium to receive the trophy for the Best Canadian Producer of the Year. In fact all 17 JT labels had already won awards.

"It felt like the Academy Awards," Bruce explained, adding, "I took Betty, my mother, to London with me, as my date. It was held, October 28th, at the historic Guild Hall with around 500 invited guests. During the banquet they served the winning wines."

Bruce joined the Chateau Gai Winery, which would later become Vincor International, in Niagara Falls in 1986 in Quality Control. He came to the partner winery, Casabello, as Cellar Master, in Penticton in May of 1987. In 1988, he became Winemaker, making his first Jackson-Triggs VQA (Vintner's Quality Alliance) wines in 1993.

"Vincor has been producing VQA for only 10 years," Bruce said, "and what is amazing, is that we've won 'Best Canadian Winery' three years in a row at the San Francisco International Wine Competition."

With continued world recognition came expansion at the Oliver plant. "We have a new facility with rotary fermentors," explained Bruce. "These rotate and automatically keep the pomace (skins of the red grapes) in contact with the juice. Red wine gets all its colour and a lot of its flavour components from the skins. This new machine," Bruce added, "looks like a cement mixer. There is also a new barrel room, which controls both the temperature and the humidity. At present it holds 3,500 barrels, but its capacity is for 5,000 barrels."

Bruce and his wife, Monique, have a young growing family. The eldest, a daughter, is named Julia. Their son is Cameron and the youngest is RuthAnne. When not working to perfect red and white wines at the Oliver plant, Bruce spends time at his Penticton home with his family.

As the industry continues to grow, so do the competitions and awards. In 1998, at the Okanagan Fall Wine Festival, Jackson-Triggs IceWine was the only wine that won a Gold Medal. In 2002 the magazine *Wine Access* awarded Red Wine Of The Year for the JT Shiraz. In 2003

Jackson-Triggs won numerous awards from the magazine, including the Best Riesling IceWine, Best Red Wine Of The Year for the Grand Reserve Red Meritage, a combination which helped JT to win Winery Of

The Year. Also in 2003, the Grand Reserve Red Meritage won the British Columbia Governor General's Award.

"My goal is to repeat what I'm doing," commented Bruce. "If we continue to have good summers, which produce top quality grapes, maybe someday we'll win that Winemaker of the Year Trophy."

Acknowledgements: My thanks to Bruce Nicholson for his assisstance with this story.

237

WISE WOMAN WEEKEND: NARAMATA

Samarpan Faasse

THE OKANAGAN IS RENOWNED for an abundance of sunshine and fruit. As autumn approaches with languid days, clear air and brilliant sunsets, we can slow down to enjoy the harvest of spring and summer's labours. This time of slowing down is a perfect opportunity to appreciate the changes that bring maturity to us on a personal level. In recognition of this, women of all ages gather in mid-September for the Wise Woman Weekend Retreat within the community of Naramata, to experience their beauty and potential.

Naramata is a unique and beautiful setting on the Eastern shores of Okanagan Lake near Penticton, where panoramic lake-views, the scent of sagebrush, and spectacular sunsets invite a restful, relaxed feeling.

The cycles of the seasons are reflected in each participant as we gather to honour and celebrate the aging process and the stages of womanhood. In this "company of women" our uniquely receptive and feminine energies expand to assist each woman's freedom and expression of 'Self'.

Since the inception of Wise Woman Weekend in 1997, a group of dedicated creators have brought women together in this event that is life changing for each participant. Women rediscover their creativity - their receptivity and, the joy as they dance, drum, sing, and share their stories together.

Workshops are given on subjects that empower each individual to take responsibility for personal wellness. Topics range from creative process to holistic health to sustainable living to the esoteric. There are opportunities to sample healing sessions in massage, Reiki, craniosacral work, reflexology and many other health alternatives.

There is a great network of friends old and new to support and challenge each woman to walk her own path with courage and wonder. After three days of learning and celebrating women return home rested, rejuvenated, feeling alive ... and planning their return for the next event.

SPEAKING MORNING
Victor Gerard Temprano Jr.

the blood-light is absorbed by the greedy clouds
> sucking all warmth from whatever we beings have left
a single Roman pillar of sunrise.

shadows seem to be so foggy,
  daylight reddens the town and the smoke of mankind snuggles the
  earth
the blackness is so long – the lights of Hell being behind them
> in the depth of the morning hopes do arise
fed by the ancient glory of day, of victory
> (of the sunrise winning out sunset)

  the clouds reach to steal the reflection of heaven
the dawn has come to pass, emptying today of all it's sorrow
sifting hate from lesser-hate, day from night

  a black thunderbolt steals across the sky
flat light, crossing over the mountains
flat light, entering today

a valley is dawn, is day, is dusk
> (each part being too beautiful to miss,
> and too saddening to see)

This poem is about a sunrise in the Okanagan Valley as viewed from my school bus and was submitted to show readers the beautiful dawns we have here.

WORKING THE RAILS
Ted Noakes

MILES OF GREEN SLOPES give way to dry plains as the train chugs along. I am fully enveloped as the steel tracks guide our locomotive travel deeper into the interior of British Columbia; into its forests, its canyons, its

valleys and its plains. Simultaneously, the journey delves deeper into the history of the province, its stories and its people. Every minute of the journey puts me in touch with the British Columbia of the present by way of its past. The train becomes more than a way of getting to the final destination in the Rockies. Rather, it is a

Photo: Yasmin John-Thorpe

way of touching experience and grasping why British Columbia is such a special place.

Over the last four years, I have had the distinct pleasure every summer of boarding the Rocky Mountaineer, once a week, as an onboard attendant. My job – *show the sights of British Columbia along the route the rails follow, while at the same time give the passenger an idea of what the people in the communities we pass are like, how they got there, and what drives the province and its people, both past and present.*

Over the two day trip, I weave the tales of those who panned for gold with those of the railway builders, the ranchers, the farmers, the politicians and all the while connecting these tales to the land, its river, mountains, trees, grasses and fields.

By nature, the job is that of a story teller, with every trip I tell a tale that will give an accurate impression of British Columbia, while giving those who have come to experience the journey from around the world the sense of why these places are more than just names on a map, more than places that are dear to my heart, that define me and make me proud to be from here.

When I was invited to contribute one of my favourite stories to this Anthology, I jumped at the chance. It was a storyteller's dream! The only problem was which one to tell. They came in all forms. It is easy to get lost in the histories of communities, some of the interesting characters such a William Van Horne, A.B Rodgers and the Maclean boys to name a few, who have woven colourful threads into the fabric of the legends that shape us and our province.

Even the passengers who come on board are stories within themselves! But when I sat down to think about it there was one that stood out for me, perhaps one of my favourites to tell and certainly one that stayed with guests. It was a story I learned during a car trip I made to Lytton in the winter of 2002. So here it is…

NAMED AFTER THE Secretary of State in B.C. during the gold rush, the town of Lytton has a "golden" history that stretches beyond that of the years between 1858 and 1870. It seems that the children of Lytton used to take their own gold pans down to the river (as late as the 1950's and possibly since then I was told) looking for gold themselves. Their findings were meager to say the least, but certainly were sufficient for what the children sought them for. They would then take whatever flakes they managed to find and go to the general store in town where the owner weighed them out and would then give them candy in return! A delicious bounty indeed.

Later, after the shopkeeper died his family was rooting around in the basement of the shop. What they found was a shock to say the least. He had kept the gold gathered over the years in quart jars. In the basement they discovered three quart jars full of gold that he had never converted into cash!

HOMELESS
Don Conway

Awake in the morning
Covered in frost
Enjoying the fireside
A dream I just lost

Gone is my breakfast
The crow had his fill
He sits and he stares
A smile on his bill

Down through the alley
Alongside the tracks
Inside the dumpster
All this for a snack?

Looking for pop cans
I spend most my time
The rewards are endless
Smokes and cheap wine

Laughed at by people
Works hard to get
Who's going to hire me?
I'm worthless don't forget

Back to my hollow
The sun leaves the sky
I wish I could end it
I'm too scared to die

The plight of those I see along the BC rail tracks has inspired me to write this poem.

WOODSMAN
OF THE OKANAGAN HIGHLAND
Joey Walker

FEW MOMENTS IN MY LIFE have given me such a strange sense of having lost centuries, as did the sight of Bill Riley in the golden light of a gracious afternoon, nearly thirty years ago. On that day, I met a great and brilliant being.

I was drinking coffee with a friend in an old miner's cabin along a forgotten gold creek, when past the window walked a man dressed in frontier buckskins, fringe drifting in the wind. In his left hand, was a homemade bow, over his shoulder a quiver of arrows, on his belt hung a hatchet and a knife sheath, and from his right hand dangled two willow grouse, feet up.

We invited him in for coffee, and he in turn invited me home for 'gopher stew'. 'Home' was a rustic camper hand-built on a six-wheel-drive army truck. The gopher stew was tasty. But the most compelling impression that lingered with me from that first meeting was that this human was profoundly contented with himself, and with his life. Bill had what some call 'nothing' and others call 'freedom'.

A couple of brittle animal hides lay beside a bucket of soapy water on his wood box.

"What's in the bucket?" I inquired.

"A deerskin," he replied. "I'm trying to make smoke-tan buckskin, but something usually goes wrong."

Within half an hour, I was hooked on figuring out his buckskin problem. Six years later, he had conquered buckskin, and I had become an adequate fur tanner. All those seasons of wild freedom had also allowed me to appreciate the kind wisdom of this unusual man.

Born among the pastoral hills of southern England, Bill couldn't remember a time when his nature didn't lure him into wild places. The son of a gypsy, his father had grown up in caravans drawn by horses along the back roads of England. In those days the 'Travelers', as they were known, were hunters and survivors. Whatever any one of them caught, pheasant, rabbit or pigeon, went into the soup pots. It was a hard, harried existence, which Bill's father, as a young man, chose to leave. He married a good-natured girl, and they came to own and operate two commercial orchards in the gentle countryside of Kent.

Young Bill was their only child, and he grew up working with them in the orchards. But his heart was never in such work. He forever wandered off, stalking rabbits along the hedgerows. He began to make bows and arrows before he was ten, and as time went on it became more and more difficult to keep him home. It ran deeper than his gypsy blood, for he wasn't drawn to groups of people or to the open road, but to following animal trails alone, to watching and listening to the forest, and to experimenting with wood, stone and steel. He was a born woodsman, and he walked an ancient path. Bill left England as the laws became too restrictive to allow him the freedom of his childhood years. He had long dreamt of the clean, cascading streams and uncivilized forests of the British Columbia mountains - where he roams to this day.

Photo copyright Joey Walker, 2004.

In 1990, I set about making my second video production around the skills of this talented craftsman. The first one was titled, 'Making Buckskin in Camp', and was sold to archers, hunters and mountain men, mostly by mail order. The second we called 'Living Wild' and it has been broadcast here and there all over the world. By great fortune during the production, millions of people have seen this documentary about a man in homemade buckskins, who left home one day with nothing - no knife, food, match, gun or axe – only his imagination and his love of the natural world.

Following him with a video camera through those remarkable months of his experiment, I was spellbound by the unique vision he held of survival. He adamantly refused to snare or trap an animal. These methods offended his sense of fairness.

"It doesn't feel good to catch some poor rabbit while I'm at home sleeping," he would protest. He held a reverent regard for frogs, fish and birds – in fact any creature that killed the flies and mosquitoes that made his existence miserable. He chose the long, responsible way to acquire his food, by eating plants and berries until he could build himself a bow and arrows. He learned to create weather-resistant shelters, fire with a bow-drill, rope, thread and soup from stinging nettles, cakes from cattail roots, and pots from tree bark. He fletched arrows with discarded raven feathers, made fur and buckskin with no tools, and smoke-dried enough meat to keep him going while he learned ever more.

Bill created things from his imagination that neither of us had seen or heard of before, one being a thick, warm blanket he wove from the black tree moss that hangs draped from interior evergreens like angel hair on a Christmas tree. Perhaps most intriguing of all, he found it no hardship, and genuinely enjoyed living wild.

The Canada Council supported the final edit of 'Living Wild' for broadcast, and the Knowledge Network aired it several times. Having won an educational media award for merit, many schools acquired the documentary for their libraries and classrooms. CHBC in Kelowna, even ORF in Austria, have aired this film.

It is somehow pleasing to know that, out there in the jungle of high-violence media assault, is a little story from the heart of a wise, noble and humble woodsman - from the Okanagan Highland.

THE AUTHORS

Kyle Anderson is an entertainer, musician and actor. He is proud of his small-town heritage and has spent his whole life raising his children, enjoying a diversified and fulfilling work career and being an active member in Penticton's arts and business community.

Odell Bennett is an artist and freelance writer born in Windermere, a small town in the East Kootenay's. She spent her first 65 years in the valley.She remembers Mrs. Kimpton very well.

Born a Blue-noser in 1947, in a fruit-growing valley in Nova Scotia, Vicki Bissillion grew up mostly in the Halifax area. A job transfer and a train led her to Bob, her husband of 35 years. Bob's job brought them to Kelowna in 1995, where they have since retired. Vicki took up writing in 2000 and Bob picked up a banjo. Their lives have never been the same.

Sonni Bone-Freeman is married and has three children. She has lived in Penticton since 1965. She has been a former editor, feature writer and columnist for the Penticton Herald. She has also been a talk show hostess on the Arts and on Herbs with Shaw Cable. Sonni taught creative writing at the Adult Education level. She co-authored the book, The World of Roses. *She is the immediate past president of the Penticton and District Community Arts Council. Sonni is now freelancing.*

Barb Bonthoux moved to Summerland, BC in November 1997. She had the privilege of joining a family strong in character with a well-defined history. Annette Bjorndal inspired her to write about the trials of making the decision to test for Huntington Disease (an incurable inherited disease). Annette's son tested positive in 2003.

Suzanne Buller resides in Prince Rupert and is a full time government worker, a part-time professional organizer and a part-time writer. She hopes that one day Charles Hays' vision for Prince Rupert will be fulfilled.

Janet Burkhart is a single parent, who only recently discovered a talent for writing poetry. She's had two poems printed in area newspapers. Two of her poems were accepted and published by the online Poetry.com. One titled "A Deeper Part Of Me" received the Editors Choice Award. The second "Emotions...Overflow From The Past" will appear in Poetry.com Best Poems And Poets Of 2003 *to be released in January 2004.*

Corilyn Cierman, was born in Vancouver and took her arts education in Vancouver and England. She is a psychic artist and healer. She also does silk scarves. Currently she writes a column for the Southern Exposure and conducts graveyard tours for the more hearty among us.

Don Conway is a 36-year-old BC Trainman, living in Chetwyn. He's been writing for about one year.

Darriel Dawne has lived in Kitsalano, a nice Vancouver neighbourhood, since 1999. She has traveled extensively across North America and East Africa. Currently, she is a freelance communication consultant.

Naomi DeLury is a registered professional biologist, who works as an insect ecology technician at Agriculture and Agri-Food Canada in Summerland, BC. Naomi conducted research on semiochemical communication of Ascogaster quadridentata *as part of her M.Sc. degree.*

Antoinette De Wit was born in the Netherlands and Came to Canada as an infant. Her passion for writing started at an early age. She has written a collection of short stories and poetry entitled Wrinkles and Rhymes *and a collection of short stories entitled* Ratz Tales.

R.L. Diebolt, a Canadian artist residing in Kelowna, gained much of her artistic education at Augustana University College in Alberta. With works in a variety of places, the artist remains true to self, using varied styles.

Home for Shirley Dobie has been the north, Dawson Creek, since 1952. She and her husband raised four children here. Earlier travels took them to the Yukon for two years, and later to Prince George for five years. Most of her poems, complete with pictures, go to her grandchildren in booklet form. This poem was published in the trade magazine Look North *in 2002.*

Johnny Eek is a Rock Creek semi-retired rancher, square dancer and cowboy poet. He sings to banjo or guitar and fiddles some foot-stomping tunes. Johnny is on the program at the Rock Creek Fall Faire and the Cowboy Campfire at the Canyon Creek Ranch. He has won several awards for his creations.

Alvin G. Ens is a retired teacher of high school English and now pursues his hobby of writing poetry and short stories. He is a member of Fraser Valley Christian Writers Group, Matsqui Sumas Abbotsford Poets Potpourri Society and Canadian Poetry Association.

Manuel Erickson has published short stories in Chicken Soup for the Canadian Soul *and in the on-line magazine,* Fireworks. *He is a pilot, has owned his own airplane and lives in Langley, B.C.*

Happily retired, Anita Ewart is a columnist with the RV Gazette, *Canada's premiere RV (recreational vehicle) magazine. Freelancing, short stories and novels are her current projects. When not traveling, she lives near Keremeos with her husband, Gordon.*

Samarpan Faasse attended, facilitated and coordinated retreats in New Zealand, India, Hawaii and Canada, where she's developed an understanding of meditation. She loves exploring creativity, celebrating everything, living fully in the moment and awakening these interests in others. Reach her at; samarpan1@shaw.ca

p.j. flaming (aka Pamela Irving) was the winner of Canada's first New Muse Award for poetry, resulting in the publication of her poetry book, voir dire. *She has three chapbooks in print, collaborations with other artists and publishers. She has been anthologized in the UK and Canada, and has appeared in literary journals* sub-terrain, Fiddlehead Review, Scottish Book Collector, *and* Hook & Ladder *(Ottawa). p.j. flaming has performed her work for both the Scottish and Canada Arts Council. She teaches creative writing, freelances for various media, and is writing a novel.*

April Fortin is a 13-year-old grade eight student at Glenrosa Middle School in Westbank, B.C. She has grown up in the Lakeside/Hillside community of Peachland, where she actively enjoys drama, singing, and creative writing. She can play the trumpet and drums. April and her family often take their sailboat "Catspaws" on extended Okanagan Lake cruises, but enjoy some of their most memorable family vacation moments in their own backyard.

Charlene Friesen likes to think the grass is greener on her side of the fence. When not ankle deep in her garden you can find her snacking in the kitchen, wishing it were spring.

Marguerite Fry lived in the Gulf Islands for many years. Each morning she looked out her window at an arbutus tree and the ocean. Such beauty inspired her to write poetry as a hobby. At 88 years old, she still writes the odd thing mostly about her family.

When Pamela and Martin Garrity came to Canada in 2000 from the United Kingdom, they settled in the Fraser Caynon. Finding the local history fascinating, they researched several aspects, settling on the Sternwheelers. They like to look at the history through different eyes.

Reg Gordon was born and raised in Penticton. He has volunteered for the Ironman since its inception. He wrote two books in high school and when he retires he hopes to return to both writing and painting. He lives here with his wife, Maryanne, children and grandchildren.

Gwendolyn Gregg is a retired Ontario Kindergarten Teacher who had lived in B.C. since 1985.

Susanne Haagsman lives on a cattle ranch near Hudson's Hope, BC with her husband and two children. She enjoys writing in her spare time. Her rural setting and her many encounters with different wildlife inspired this story.

Allene Halliday is a transplanted Californian who "discovered" the beautiful Okanagan several years ago. She now lives "south of the B.C. border" in Oroville, Washington.

Margaret Hayes has resided in Okanagan Falls since her arrival with her husband Charles in 1980. They came from Kenya, East Africa, where she had been a columnist for several newspapers and magazines both African and European.

Barbara Heaney has lived and worked in Westbank since 1995. She enjoys farming with the Paynter family in Westbank and is especially interested in herbal gardening. Any free time she has is spent writing and playing badminton. Barbara completed a B.A. in English Literature and Sociology in Saskatchewan and is presently working on a Horticulture Certificate through Okanagan University College.

David Herreshoff, is a retired English professor. He is the official Poet Laureate of Kaslo on Kootenay Lake, pop. 1000. Kaslo hoped to get into the Guiness Book of World Records as the smallest village to have its own Poet Laureate.

Richard Hunt has been involved in the natural and organic products industry for his entire business career. He started with a small dried fruit operation and by 1978 opened the first fruit leather factory in Penticton. He sold his interest in 1999 and joined the Whole Foods Market as general manager.

Tracey Jack resides on the Penticton Reserve with her husband and children. Her long-term goal is to produce a feature length documentary, which is currently in development. Her dream is to encourage aboriginal filmmakers to engage in modern story-telling filmmaking, which will be of the highest caliber and which will become the 'must see' films of the future.

Yasmin John-Thorpe is a co-founding member of Penticton Writers and Publishers. She has published Taking The Heat: Canadian Politicians In The Kitchen *and created and co-wrote short stories for:* Lovescape The Romantic Novella Magazine. *At present Yasmin takes Literary Literature courses at Penticton OUC Campus, as she'd like to write Children's books dedicated to her grandson, Eben.*

Over the years, Okanagan resident David Korinetz has been a machinist, an aircraft mechanic, an estimator and a computer programmer. He is now pursuing a career as a science fiction and fantasy novelist.

Katharine L. Kroeker is the author of Too Much For One Lifetime, *her autobiography. Her story is an amazing one of human triumph over incredible adversity. She is also the author of two episodes in a children's illustrated series that is based on her life.*

Ramon Kwok, was born in Vancouver's East End. He attended Strathcona School and Vancouver Tech. High School. He's worked as a labourer, a truck driver, a sawmill worker, a catskinner, an autobodyman and a real estate agent. He's lived all his life in sight of the ocean.

Ken Larson was a reporter in Moose Jaw and Vancouver, TV editor of CBC Vancouver, Managing Editor of 23 weekly newspapers in Edmonton and a national magazine, Canada Poultryman. *He owned a health food store before retiring in 2001 to Penticton.*

Eric Linden has made the Okanagan his home after living in a number of different places in B.C. He has always enjoyed writing and began composing verse after visiting Hong Kong. His works have become well know internationally via the Internet.

In 1993, Lorraine Lindy renewed her childhood interest in writing and began contributing to local newspapers, which she continues doing today. She is a member of the local writers' group in Rock Creek. She writes poetry, fiction and travel stories.

Carol D. Loewen is a freelance writer, who resides in Abbotsford, British Columbia with her husband. She is the mother of five children, two of whom are married and bring three granddaughters and one grandson for visits from Mission. Carol enjoys writing, sewing, gardening and drawing.

Alan Longworth was born in England. At age 8, praise from his teacher for one of his short stories piqued his interest in writing, but by age 14 his schooling ceased when he had to work on the family farm. By 21, he immigrated to Canada and began a multitude of physically demanding jobs, from driving big rigs to longshoreman. Still wishing to write Alan entered and has won a Canada wide limerick contest, 3 awards for posters seen in Canada and the U.S., and has published poetry and articles. He is an associate member of Penticton Writers and Publishers.

Randy Manuel was born and raised in Penticton. His family has been here since 1906. His grandfather, and father worked on the KVR, with his grandfather, Jack Beaton, being an engineer from 1915 to 1942. Randy has been the Director/Curator of the Penticton Museum and archives since 1986.

Marilyn McAllister has lived in the Shuswap - Blind Bay , that is - for the last ten years. The beautiful locale has inspired her to write poetry among other artistic pursuits.

Writing became a passion for Esther McIlveen while at the University of Alberta in 1970. Esther has been writing for newspapers for the past ten years. Currently, she writes a column, Grace Notes, with Richmond Review. She is co-founder of the Good Shepherd Drop-In Center, the President of The Father's Garden, Steveston, to save a hundred year old church, the author of a children's book, Cotton Candy Chatterbox, *co-author of* Time Echoes Softly, *and* Would You Know My Name?

Cassandra McCroy lives in the Okanagan, is the mother of five and grandmother of nine. As an adult student she continues to nourish her mind with learning. Her interest, at the moment, is Canadian History.

Sharron Middler has been an artist for thirty years, and a watercolorist for ten. She is currently applying her artistic talents to web development as well as her painting.

Karen Miller lives in Penticton and loves to write rhyming poems. She's had many of her tribute poems published in the local newspapers. She is compiling her favourite verses into a manuscript for future publication.

Edwin Monson writes brief poems, or "sayings" based on feelings from the culminations of the senses and experiences.

Dodi Morrison has written all her (long) life. She has written newspaper columns, magazine articles, and activist letters to MPs and MLAs. She has worked in several areas for CBC – children's books, seniors'comments and a daily children's program. Now she is working on a book.

Violet Nesdoly is a freelance writer from Surrey, B.C. She is a member of the Fraser Valley Christian Writers Group and has had some poems published in the past in Prairie Messenger, M. B. Herald, *utmostchristianwriters.com and poetsonline.com.*

Beth Neville comes from a nursing background. During her earlier years she also raised a family. This is where she gets her inspiration for her poems and prose. She enjoys this new hobby, as well as reading and doing volunteer work in her community.

Gayle Nicholson is a writer who hails from Scotland. David Kilmartin, the current director of the Penticton and District Arts Council, is an artist who grew up in New York. They lived on Hornby Island for a combined 21 years and were married in "The Round Room" of the Hornby Hall in 2001. They, along with their new son, Spencer Jack, now reside in Summerland.

Wesley Nicholson won Outdoor Canada *magazine's award for an article about an early environmentalist. He has been writing for many years, mostly about the locals and family. He enjoys his twin granddaughters and still uses a typewriter to create his many poems and tales.*

Born and raised in Kamloops, BC, Ted Noakes spent four years onboard the Rocky Mountaineer as a train attendant, sharing the rich history and beautiful sights with passengers from around the world. In September 2003, he began pursuing his Master's degree in Economics at the University of Victoria. Always looking forward to new opportunities Ted's next big challenge will be his marriage in May 2004.

Darcy Nybo is a multi award winning short story writer who lives in the Okanagan with her husband and daughter. She currently writes a monthly column for Inside OK Falls *and is at work on two novels. Her short story* Water Dragon *appears in* Tall Tales and Short Stories.

Marlene Parsons is a writer and researcher who resides in Richmond, BC. She and her family get away when they can to their little cottage on Mayne Island, where the pace of life is more in rhythm with the soul.

Lorraine Pattison was one of the original co-founding members of Penticton Writers and Publishers. She works as a screenwriter, researcher, editor, publisher, freelance writer and author of both non-fiction and fiction books. She's received diplomas, Certificates of Merit and a Community Service Award for her writing, as well as being included in Chatelaine's Who's Who Publication. Her writing, she feels, is now beginning to find its own path and voice.

Sharon Prafke is a resident of the Greenwood area and has lived in the South Okanagan for the past 35 years. She is an avid writer of historical romance novels and enjoys researching British Columbia history.

Maxine Rae, a 1961 Pen Hi Grad, came to Penticton from Saskatchewan in 1957. She began writing in 2000 after completing a course at Elder College in Chilliwack. 'The Spirit Called Her Back' to Penticton in 2001, where she now enjoys life writing and volunteering.

Shannon Reilly-Yael has a MA in Religion and Culture and a BA in Women's Studies and Religious Studies. She lives in Victoria with her three year old, where she sees the world through yellow glasses.

Born and raised in British Columbia, Allen Reid began writing poetry in 1997. He usually writes down whatever comes to mind, with his wife and son being good critics. He has written a 140 verse poem which he is currently turning into prose.

Dawn Renaud writes award-winning short fiction. Her CyberDimension Mystery *series for kids includes three novels, and she has far too much imagination to ever stop writing.*

Visually impaired for twenty-three years, Penticton author Lois Robins has self-published two books of poetry: The Other Side of Love *and* Dance to the Music. *An intro on one reads, "I think that I shall never see a poem I didn't like – by me!"*

Faye Rothlander was born and raised in Germany, where she trained and worked as a nurse. She met and married a merchant sailor, who wanted to settle down on land - in Canada. She is an enthusiastic reader, which woke the desire to write. She is presently writing her memories in short stories. Two of those stories have already been published, one in Toronto and one in Germany. Faye and her husband live in the small town of Okanagan Falls. She is an associate member of Penticton Writers and Publishers.

In 1999, Art Schmid and his new wife Claire bought a home in Penticton. They volunteer with the Gleaners Association. They dry fruit and vegetables that are donated to feed hungry people around the world.

Wolfgang Schmidt is a semi-retired rancher, journalist, author and businessman. He lives on his ranch in Rock Creek, BC.

Endrene Shepherd is a young artist and full-time Fine Arts student. She currently resides in Kelowna, and is looking forward to obtaining her degree and shooting across the world like a flaming star.

Penny Smith has been writing for over twenty years. She has several articles to her credit, one children's book, Ogopogo Dead or Alive, *and is co-founder of Penticton Writers and Publishers.*

Violet Smith was born in England and had her first poem published in England in 1988 at the age of 77. Her work has appeared in more than 10 publications in England and Alberta. She enjoys writing humourous, religious, and descriptive poems. Violet can look out the window and a poem can take form regardless of what kind of weather is outside. She is an associate member of Penticton Writers and Publishers.

David B .J. Snyder, CD A. de C., has been a resident of Penticton since 1970. He is a graduate of the University of Winnipeg 1968 and a former reserve soldier. David is a retired Penticton Secondary School teacher. He has four published works: A Drunken Dragoon (1981), Praying for Bastards (1998), From First Avenue (2000), and Revenge: A History of a Cadet Corps (2003).

Linda Steward was an outfitter and musician in the interior of British Columbia in the 1970s around Valemount, British Columbia. After a stint in Alberta, where she earned her degree in Psychology, Linda returned to her beloved mountains in 2002. She is currently an Employment Counselor, residing with her partner on the East Shore of Kootenay Lake.

Ruth Stubbs is the curator of the Quesnel Museum.

In 1960, with two dollars in his pocket, Klaus Sturze came to Canada from Europe, where he had trained as a hotel administrator. He made a fresh start and opened a retail business in Regina in 1967. He moved to Penticton, British Columbia in 1975 and was self-employed. He retired in 2003, turning to writing. He has self published a novel, several short stories and poems. At present Klaus is writing his memoirs.

Victor Gerard Temprano Jr. lives in Kelowna, B.C. He is a sixteen-year-old student who has become enamored with all forms of poetry. He likes emotions, he likes peace, and he likes change. He is part of a Student Activist Club.

Marian Toews is a Canadian writer living in Union Bay on Vancouver Island B.C. Her poetry, short stories and art have been published in several small literary magazines, as well as two anthologies put together by the Powell River Writer's Association.

Laurena Typusiak nags and nurtures her two sons and her hubby in the middle of an apple orchard in Oliver, British Columbia. Though she considers her family her full-time career, Laurena moonlights as a freelance writer.

Joey Walker is a range rider, living on a ranch in Bridesville, British Columbia.

Sharon Ward grew up in Delta and recently moved to the Okanagan. She is a retired Librarian. She has written all her life and is looking forward to continuing enjoying life with her many cats and dogs.

Corinne Weisskopf is the daughter of Anny and Henry. For almost twenty years her parents have been challenged with the development of Ten-ee-ah Lodge. It was their vision to own a cabin on a remote lake. Their hard work has turned their dream into a well-known resort.

Elizabeth Wilson and her husband recently moved to the Okanagan. She enjoys keeping her garden up for friends and strangers alike.

Jocelyn Wood is a sixteen-year-old student at Mount Douglas Secondary School in Victoria. She enjoys playing field hockey and likes to skimboard. She recently moved to Victoria from Penticton, and loves every minute of it.

Elizabeth Woodford is a resident of Lakeview Heights, Kelowna. She returned to her home country a couple of years ago with her family. The spectacular scenery of the Okanagan valley and the events since her return inspired this poem.

Jason Woodford is a new resident of Kelowna.

Helen Wyatt lives in Penticton and writes magazine articles. Her other writing projects range from children's stories to romantic fiction. She has completed a book on the 2003 Okanagan Mountain Fire.

Order Form

Great Gift Idea! Why not send your friends or relatives a copy of *To Hope and Beyond.*

Please send me: _____ copies of *To Hope and Beyond* at $15.95, plus $2.50 postage, per copy.

Enclosed is $_____._____

Name: _____

Street: _____

City: _____ Province: _____

Make cheques payable to:
Penticton Writers and Publishers
4011 Finnerty Road
Penticton, BC V2A 8W2

Order Form

Great Gift Idea! Why not send your friends or relatives a copy of *To Hope and Beyond.*

Please send me: _____ copies of *To Hope and Beyond* at $15.95, plus $2.50 postage, per copy.

Enclosed is $_____._____

Name: _____

Street: _____

City: _____ Province: _____

Make cheques payable to:
Penticton Writers and Publishers
4011 Finnerty Road
Penticton, BC V2A 8W2